The Agoraphobic Syndrome

The Agoraphobic Syndrome

Behavioural Approaches to Evaluation and Treatment

Geoffrey L. Thorpe
University of Maine

and

Laurence E. Burns
Rochdale Health Authority and University of Manchester

JOHN WILEY & SONS
Chichester · New York · Brisbane · Toronto · Singapore

Library of Congress Cataloging in Publication Data:

Thorpe, Geoffrey L.
The agoraphobic syndrome.

Includes index.
1. Agoraphobia. 2. Behavior therapy. I. Burns, Laurence E. II. Title. [DNLM: 1. Phobic disorders. 2. Behavior therapy. WM 178 T519a]
RC535.T47 1982 616.85′225 82-8562
ISBN 0 471 10495 7 AACR2

British Library Cataloguing in Publication Data:

Thorpe, Geoffrey L.
The agoraphobic syndrome.
1. Agoraphobia
I. Title II. Burns, Laurence E.
616.85′225 RC535

ISBN 0 471 10495 7

Typeset by Preface Ltd, Salisbury, Wilts.,
and printed in the United States of America.

To Our Parents
Barbara and Denis Thorpe,
and Helen E. Burns

Contents

Foreword xvii

1. The Agoraphobic Syndrome 1
Definitions and characteristics 1
Early accounts of agoraphobia 2
The validity of the agoraphobic syndrome 5
Epidemiology 6
Problems of under-inclusion and over-inclusion 8
Age of onset 8
Sex ratio 8
Marital status 9
Childhood problems 10
Intellectual and educational status 11
Occupational disablement 11
Features association with treatment 12
Clinical description 12
Fears of environmental situations 12
Fears of confinement 13
Panic 13
Physical symptoms 14
Cognitive aspects 14
Fluctuations 14
Associated symptomatology 15
Depersonalization and derealization 15
Depression 16
General anxiety 16
Fears and phobias 16
Obsessions and compulsions 16
Hypochondriasis 17
Personality deviance 17
Types of agoraphobia 17

2. National Survey of Agoraphobics 19
The sample 19
Sex ratio 20
Marital status 20
Religious preferences 20
Educational status 20
Occupation 20
Childhood of agoraphobics 21
Separation during childhood 21
Parental attitudes 21
Relationship with parents 21
Behavioural problems 21
Nervous disorder in the family 22
Consultations and treatment helpfulness 22
Marriage—background and relationships 22
Age of onset 23
Precipitating factors 23
Panic attacks 24
Fluctuations in agoraphobia 25
The effects of agoraphobia on the subjects' lives 26
Other aspects 28
Section 36 of the agoraphobic questionnaire 29
Normative data and sex differences 29
Marital status 30
Employment 30
Parental treatment for nervous disorders 30
Duration of illness by groups 30
Consultation with local doctors 31
Adequate help for the agoraphobia 31
Section 39 of the agoraphobic questionnaire 31
Normative data and sex differences 31
Marital status 31
Employment 31
Those wishing to work 32
Family nervous disorders 33
Duration of illness 33
Consultations with local doctors 33
Adequate help for the agoraphobic 33

3. Aetiological Factors: Physiological, Personality and Interpersonal Correlates of Agoraphobia 34
Background features 35
Physiological factors 35
Sex-correlated factors 36
Personality variables 38

The interpersonal context . . . 38
Family background . . . 39
Psychological gain . . . 39
Dependency . . . 40
Interpersonal conflict . . . 41
Assortative mating and pathogenic interaction . . . 42
Effects of agoraphobia treatment on interpersonal relationships 43
Summary . . . 46
Long-term follow-up after treatment of agoraphobia . . . 47
Direct influences . . . 49
Precipitating factors . . . 50
Conditioning events . . . 51
Interactive views of aetiology . . . 52
Conclusions . . . 55

4. Assessment of Agoraphobia . . . 56
Clinical and research issues in assessment . . . 56
General issues in clinical assessment . . . 57
Breadth of assessment . . . 57
The multimodal approach as an assessment framework . . . 59
Evaluation for therapeutic intervention . . . 60
Identifying agoraphobia . . . 60
Problem formulation . . . 61
The syndrome concept . . . 62
The clinical interview . . . 65
Questionnaire measures . . . 66
Marital adjustment . . . 66
Assertiveness and self-sufficiency . . . 67
Depression . . . 68
Inventories of agoraphobic behaviour . . . 68
Prognostic indicators . . . 69
Self-monitoring and behavioural observation . . . 69
Evaluation of therapeutic outcome . . . 70
What to measure . . . 70
Asynchrony among response measures . . . 71
Rating scales and self-report indices . . . 72
Phobic rating scales . . . 72
Self-efficacy scales . . . 73
Behavioural observation . . . 73
Limitations of behavioural tests: demand characteristics . . . 75
Reactivity . . . 76
Psychophysiological assessment . . . 77

5. Behavioural Treatment Research . . . 78
Definitions . . . 78

Systematic desensitization . . . 79
Early clinical and research reports . . . 79
Recent clinical research . . . 80
Graded practice . . . 81
Flooding . . . 82
Relevant versus irrelevant stimuli in flooding . . . 83
Brief versus prolonged flooding . . . 84
Imaginal versus *in vivo* flooding . . . 85
Individual treatment versus flooding in groups . . . 87
Patient-controlled versus therapist-guided exposure . . . 90
Comparative studies . . . 92
Flooding versus systematic desensitization . . . 92
Flooding versus cognitive-behavioural approaches . . . 95
Combined behavioural and pharmacological treatment . . . 98
Clinical management by means of medication . . . 98
Barbiturates and imaginal exposure . . . 99
Minor tranquillizers and flooding . . . 100
Antidepressants and behaviour therapy . . . 102
Summary . . . 103
Conclusions . . . 105

6. Additive Effects of Behavioural Techniques—A Controlled Trial . 107
Rationale for the present study . . . 107
Hypotheses . . . 109
Experiment I . . . 109
Experiment II . . . 109
Experiment I . . . 109
Definition of agoraphobia . . . 109
Subjects . . . 110
Source of referrals . . . 110
Selection criteria . . . 110
Drop outs from the project . . . 110
Characteristics of subjects . . . 111
Therapists . . . 111
Researchers . . . 111
Assessment . . . 111
Pre-treatment measures . . . 111
Continuous measures during treatment . . . 112
Mid-treatment measures . . . 113
Post-treatment measures . . . 113
Follow-up measures . . . 114
Treatment methods . . . 114
Interview . . . 114
Relaxation training . . . 114

Behavioural counselling (modified) 114
Systematic desensitization 116
Reinforced graded practice 116
Stress inoculation 117
Procedure 117
Experiment II 121
Results 122
Experiment I 122
Pre-treatment measures. 122
Continuous measures during treatment 123
Outcome measures 123
Independent measures 125
Analysis of therapists' effects 126
Experiment II 126
Pre-treatment measures 126
Outcome measures 127
Discussion 129
Experiment I 129
Comparability of groups 129
Representativeness of subjects 129
Expectancy 129
Outcome measures 130
Therapist effects 133
Experiment II 134
Comparability of groups 134
Characteristics of the groups 134
Representativeness of the subjects 135
Outcome measures 135
Prognostic variables 138
Hypotheses 140
Experiment I 140
Experiment II 140
Psychological assessment of therapeutic outcome 140
Demand characteristics 144
Further implications and developing trends 145
Appendices I to XIII 146

7. Behavioural Concepts of Aetiology and Treatment Effectiveness . . 166
Theories of the acquisition of phobias 167
Two-factor theory 167
The classical conditioning component 167
The instrument learning component 168
Criticisms of two-factor theory 169
Acceptability of the classical conditioning model 169

Adequacy of the escape/avoidance formulation 170
Counter-arguments in favour of two-factor theory 173
The preparedness hypothesis 173
The 'Garcia' effect 174
'Incubation' and classical conditioning 175
'Expectancy' and classical conditioning 176
Alternative aetiological concepts 177
Punishment 177
Conflict 177
Positive reinforcement 182
Expectancy learning 183
An integrated model. 183
Theories of treatment effectiveness 184
Habituation 185
A clinical paradigm 186
Self-efficacy 186
Multimodality 188
Non-specific factors 189
Expectancy of benefit 189
Reactivity of behavioural assessment 190
Concluding remarks 190

8. Clinical and Ethical Issues 192
Indications from the research literature 192
Systematic desensitization 192
Imaginal flooding 193
Graded practice and prolonged *in vivo* exposure 193
Cognitive-behaviour modification 194
The use of medication 194
Therapist characteristics 194
The clinical management of agoraphobia 195
Educating the patient and spouse 195
Presenting the rationale for behavioural treatment 196
Agreeing on a treatment plan 199
The role of the spouse or companion 200
Self-monitoring 201
Relaxation and cognitive techniques 201
Self-help groups 203
Ethical issues 203
Responsibilities of the therapist 203
Evaluation of progress 203
Comprehensiveness of treatment 203
Side effects of behavioural treatment 204
Conclusions 206

References 207

Author Index 225

Subject Index 231

Acknowledgements

Several colleagues and students at the Psychology Department at the University of Maine gave help, advice, and encouragement, and their contributions are gratefully acknowledged. Dr Roger Frey, Department Chairman, gave general encouragement and administrative support. Dr Stanley Pliskoff, Dr Alan Stubbs, and Greg Fetterman critically appraised early draughts of Chapter 7. Dr Gordon Kulberg, and graduate students Gary Barnes, Lorraine Cavallaro, Eric Freedman, Philip Smith, and Alan Zwerdling provided inspiration through stimulating discussions and enthusiastic case conferences.

Dr Christa-Maria Homann and Dr Roger Wilson of Bangor Mental Health Institute were kind enough to help in translating some medical terms into language understandable by psychologists. The friendship of the late Joseph Saxl, formerly Superintendent of Bangor Mental Health Institute, has been more valuable than he ever knew.

Ms Marian Perry, Ms Eva Benson, and Ms Anne Theriault graciously and competently accepted the burden of typing the bulk of the manuscript.

Carol Thorpe, and, in their own way, Beth and Timmy Thorpe, gave moral support and general encouragement, and were very pleased when the manuscript was finished.

GEOFFREY L. THORPE

I gratefully acknowledge the support of Katherine Fisher, President of the Phobics Society, Manchester; a former agoraphobic, her tireless work for agoraphobic sufferers everywhere is an inspiration to all of us. Similarly, my thanks are also due to Mona Woodford (The Open Door, Heswall, Merseyside) and Vanna Gothard (The Phobic Trust, Coulsdon, Surrey).

My appreciation is due to Mr R. Curtis who acted as an independent clinician, Mrs J. Hawrigg, our highly competent nurse therapist, Mrs B. Batty, who made the major contribution to the typing of the manuscript at the English end, together with support from Mrs P. Ingham, Mrs M. Rogerson, Mrs A. Day and Miss D. Plant, and to Mrs S. Sharp whose painstaking work in collating data from the National Survey of Agoraphobics and the controlled trial is nothing short of remarkable; H. Gwynne Jones, formerly Professor of Psychology at the University of Leeds, provided much help in the controlled trial.

Thanks are also due to Dr George Beaumont for his valuable support over many years, Mr J. Seldrup (assisted by Mr D. McCulley) for statistical help, and to Dr G. Cooper for additional support, all from Geigy Pharmaceuticals (UK) Ltd., Miss E. Beeney's help with statistical analysis is also appreciated.

I wish to thank the editor of Cambridge Medical Publications Ltd., Dr J. Eric Murphy, for permission to reproduce two tables (Tables 2.3 and 2.4) both of which were published in *The Journal of International Medical Research*; one in Vol. 5, Supplement 1, 1977, pp. 132–139 and the other in Vol. 5, Supplement 5, 1977, pp. 1–7. Similarly thanks are due to the editor of *The Nursing Times*, Ms A. Dunn, who allowed us to reproduce an extract from the paper written by nurse therapist Mrs J. J. Hawrigg, which appeared in *The Nursing Times*, **71**, 33, 1975, pp. 1280–1282.

Finally my appreciation is due to all those subjects who took part in the National Survey and the controlled trial; their help has provided greater understanding of the agoraphobic syndrome.

LAURENCE E. BURNS

Foreword

The agoraphobic syndrome is the commonest and most distressing phobic problem which presents for treatment. Its clinical picture has remained impressively similar since its first comprehensive description by Westphal 111 years ago, though the latter referred to men while most patients today are women, which may reflect a change in referral patterns rather than in true incidence. The aetiology of the disorder is as obscure today as it was at the time of Westphal's classic paper. Just before Westphal, Benedikt called the condition 'platzschwindel' in drawing attention to its vertigo-like features. Since then many have searched for organic factors. Recent attention has focussed on potential disturbances of lactate metabolism and on mitral-valve prolapse, but as yet these have not been established as particularly central aspects of the syndrome. Organic factors seem more important in that rarity known as space phobia or pseudoagoraphobia, which is a different condition, and the precise nature of the deficits in space phobia remains to be unravelled.

Agoraphobia is especially interesting as it is clearly a phobic avoidance disorder, yet it also has many features in common with mood disorders like anxiety states and, in a certain proportion of sufferers, with minor depression. Why there should be this intimate relationship is puzzling, especially as a wide variety of other specific phobias seem not to be so closely connected with mood disorders though they share with agoraphobia the phobic features of involuntary avoidance of situations which most would regard as innocuous, and the evocation of anxiety when such avoidance is not possible. The connection of agoraphobia with obsessive-compulsive disorders is evident in that both are avoidance syndromes and are often complicated by mood disorders, though spontaneous panics are far commoner in agoraphobia.

A big change in this field has been the development in the last 15 years of effective treatment for the avoidance syndromes of phobic and obsessive-compulsive disorders. Agoraphobia is now eminently treatable by the behavioural treatment of exposure, though there seems to be a lingering myth that exposure is suitable only for specific phobias rather than for more diffuse phobias like agoraphobia. Total cure of all symptoms is exceptional, but relief of most of the handicapping avoidance is usually possible. In several countries studies have demonstrated that agoraphobics retain their gains for up to 7 years after exposure treatments. Therapy may involve no more than 4 hours of a therapist's time. Moreover, treatment is often possible by self-help alone, and many sufferers have treated themselves without a therapist merely by using a suitable self-help manual. This indicates that the essential practical aspects of the therapy have now been defined, even though the theoretical mechanisms at work remain to be elucidated.

There is now a huge literature on the subject which is difficult for the outsider to digest. The authors have rendered a service to scholars by diligently putting it together in this volume and by indicating their own extensive work.

Institute of Psychiatry, London PROFESSOR I. M. MARKS

CHAPTER 1

The Agoraphobic Syndrome

DEFINITIONS AND CHARACTERISTICS

According to ancient legend Phobos was a Greek god who could frighten his enemies; his resemblance was painted on masks and protective armour for this purpose. Thus, phobos or phobia came to mean 'fear', 'terror', 'panic' and/or 'flight'. Psychopathologists concur that phobias are special kinds of fears that, to a greater or lesser extent, interfere with the everyday functioning of the individual. In addition, the fears should be the predominant symptom; other definable psychiatric illness, such as obsessive-compulsive neurosis, should be absent, (Mavissakalian and Barlow, 1981).

It is generally accepted that phobic states, especially those of an intricate nature, consist of a number of important characteristics. Burns (1982a) has indicated that these states usually involve:

1. Strong responses affecting three systems:
   (a) The cognitive system: the sufferer experiences feelings of apprehension and fear. Patterns of thought are frequently unproductive, irrational and anxiety-generating; they appear to be often related to an inability to cope with the feared situation and the psychophysiological arousal evoked by it. Thoughts about the need to escape from the situation may become prominent; if such escape occurs the sufferer may engage in ruminative self-defeating thinking involving poor self-esteem, a sense of failure and of being demoralized.
   (b) The psychophysiological system: a high level of arousal of this system may involve greatly increased muscular tension, rapid heart rate, hyperventilation, feelings of faintness, heightened blood pressure, etc.
   (c) The behavioural system: the intense distress may result in a withdrawal from the fear-provoking situation; if contact is maintained with the situation impaired performance may be witnessed. Alternatively, if the fear produced by the anticipation of entering the phobic situation becomes overwhelming, avoidance behaviour may take place;

this is likely to be followed by a rapid decrease in the fear and the psychophysiological arousal.

2. Strong responses which are beyond voluntary control. Attempts on the part of the sufferer to manage the fear and psychophysiological arousal usually end in failure.
3. Strong responses which are excessive and quite out of proportion bearing in mind the demands of the situation.
4. Strong responses which have a tendency to persist, despite fluctuations in intensity, over a lengthy period of time.
5. Strong responses which are not allied to the stage of development of the individual nor are age specific.
6. Strong responses which may be thought of as maladaptive.
7. Strong responses which involve good insight on the part of the sufferer who recognizes that such responses are unreasonable and that most people do not manifest such reactions in similar situations.
8. Strong responses which frequently involve social components; thus the sufferer may try to conceal the problem because of embarrassment.

The above characteristics form prominent features of the agoraphobic syndrome, the most crippling of all phobic disorders encountered in everyday clinical practice.

EARLY ACCOUNTS OF AGORAPHOBIA

The term agoraphobia was coined by Westphal, a German psychiatrist, who, in 1871, published a monograph *Die Agoraphobie*. The term derives from the Greek word 'agora' meaning a market place, an assembly, or the place of assembly. However, in recent years several authors (Eysenck *et al*., 1972; Rycroft, 1968; Wolman, 1973) have defined agoraphobia as an intense fear of open spaces. Used in this way the term is both semantically and clinically incorrect. The Greek root chosen by Westphal does not denote open spaces *per se* and does, indeed, fit the clinical facts in that the sufferer is afraid of public places, which may or may not include open spaces; there is a strong tendency for the fears to become much worse as the distance from familiar surroundings increases (Slater and Roth, 1969).

Although the term agoraphobia was coined just over a century ago, the syndrome has almost certainly existed for thousands of years. Hippocrates, the father of modern medicine, who lived between the fifth and fourth centuries BC reports on an individual who 'through bashfulness, suspicion and timourousness will not be seen abroad, loves darkness as life . . . he dare not come in company for fear . . .'. Burton (1621) a keen observer of morbid fears, in his monumental work, *Anatomy of Melancholy*, wrote: 'Montanus speaks of one that durst not walk alone from home for fear he would swoon or die . . . or, if he be in a throng, middle of a church, multitude, where he may not well get out, though he sit at ease, he is so misaffected.' Sauvages (1770) described the dizziness of phobic anxious patients and reported on a woman with such a problem when she entered a public building. A century later Benedikt (1870) used the term *Platzschwindel* which translated literally means 'dizziness in public places'. Benedikt considered the central feature of the agoraphobic syndrome to be dizziness rather than fear. Interestingly enough, most agoraphobic sufferers place emphasis on the autonomic and somatic accompaniments of the symptoms rather than the psychological or cognitive experiences. Snaith (1968) speculates that, had the term survived, there might have been increased investigation of those processes by which emotion is converted into the somatic sphere of experience.

It is worth recording that, over the years, other terms have been used to describe the agoraphobic syndrome. Examples include anxiety hysteria (Freud, 1919); locomotor anxiety (Abraham, 1913); street fear (Miller, 1953); phobic-anxiety-depersonalization syndrome (Roth, 1959); anxiety syndrome or phobic anxious states (Klein, 1964) and non-specific insecurity fears (Snaith, 1968).

However, the term agoraphobia is now in universal use. The French terms 'peur des espaces' and 'horreur du vide' and the German term 'Platzangst' have the similar literal meaning as agoraphobia. These terms have influenced both psycho-analytic as well as behaviour therapists in the formulation of their theories. Fear is seen as the primary element in the psychopathology and that it becomes attached to certain locations; additionally, there is no fundamental difference between this experience and the other states subsumed under the term 'phobia'.

Westphal (1871), in his monograph, gave an excellent and detailed description of three male agoraphobic sufferers who found it impossible to walk through certain streets or squares or who were able to do so with much anxiety. Some localities were more difficult of access than others, the sufferers walking far in order not to traverse them. The use of alcohol assisted the sufferers to pass through a feared locality with comparative comfort. Westphal pointed out that there was no loss of consciousness, hallucinations or delusions to cause the fear. The agoraphobics experienced great comfort from the companionship of men or even inanimate objects such as a cane or vehicle. One even sought, without immoral motives, the companionship of a prostitute as far as his own door.

Westphal noted that the fears were worse when there was no boundary to a large open visual field; they diminished when a boundary was imposed. For example, one of the sufferers, a clergyman, felt dizzy as soon as he went into the open; relief was obtained by creeping around hedges and trees or by putting up his umbrella.

Westphal described a large number of anxiety-type symptoms: palpitations, trembling, apprehension of impending insanity or death, blushing, various social and anticipatory anxieties, etc. He identified two sufferers who had experienced epilepsy earlier in their lives and discussed at length the possible relationship between the problem and anxiety and other neurotic symptoms.

Subsequently other research workers (Harper and Roth, 1962) have shown an interest in agoraphobics, some 40 per cent of whom have features reminiscent of temporal lobe dysfunction.

Another early account of agoraphobics is provided by Cordes (1871). Although describing similar symptomatology to that recorded by Westphal there is a difference in two respects. Cordes placed emphasis on cognitive processes—that anxiety can be evoked by the cognition of the patient and not in an automatic way in response to environmental stimuli. This view is very much in line with current thinking. Emphasis was also placed on the role that crowded places could have in the generation of anxiety, an observation apparently not recorded by Westphal.

A further early account of agoraphobia is provided by Legrand du Saule (1885). The clinical description involves a female patient which the writer considered to be unusual as the disorder was more frequently observed in men. There is little doubt that today, at least in Europe and North America, the great majority of sufferers are female although this could be a reflection of changing social roles and other factors which will be discussed later.

There are a number of other accounts of agoraphobia written at the end of the last century or at the beginning of the present century (Clevenger, 1890; Freud, 1894; Kraepelin, 1906; Prince and Putnum, 1912). Biographies and autobiographies of agoraphobic sufferers are comparatively rare, presumably for fear of friends or relatives learning about their disability. Two early autobiographical accounts serve to illustrate the acute problems encountered by the sufferer. 'Vincent' (1919) described the gradual onset of the agoraphobic symptoms following a traumatic incident in which a boy in the village was murdered; fears developed of high hills and of fields in which the grass was cropped short like the grass on a well-kept lawn. Fears of crowds of people arose and, later, of wide streets and parks. Ugly architecture greatly intensified the fear. Less anxiety was experienced during darkness or during a snow storm, probably because the view was restricted. At times the phobias were much more pronounced than at other times but the problem was always present.

Leonard (1928) identified a spasmodic increase in agoraphobia at the age of 30 years subsequent to several years of intermittent anxiety unconnected with particular situations. Initially, brief visits to a city filled him with a surging sense of the impossible. Later, following his wife's suicide, intense panics developed. 'I start a little walk down the street about a hundred feet from the house. I am compelled to rush back in horror of being so far away, a hundred feet away, from home and security. I have never walked or ridden, alone or with others, as a normal man since that day.' Leonard described the intensity of his emotional state as ranging from vague anxiety to an intense fear of impending death. Despite his attempt to overcome his panic by self re-education ('try and try again'), the net result was the opposite to that intended; he merely succeeded in making his condition worse.

'Vincent', who retained his anonymity, revealed in his paper that he was a person of leadership in his town and a public speaker of some ability. No one, apparently, knew of his disability; he never sought treatment for his fears. Leonard was a professor of English at the University of Wisconsin; few people apart from the closest of relatives knew of his problem.

Other accounts of agoraphobic sufferers are provided by Raymond (1946), Lazell (1973), and Law (1975).

THE VALIDITY OF THE AGORAPHOBIC SYNDROME

In view of the variation of symptomatology of which the agoraphobic sufferer complains it can be argued that it may not be valid to recognize the syndrome as a distinct clinical entity; rather, agoraphobic fears should be looked at as occurring in a variety of clinical contexts such as depression or generalized anxiety. Evidence supporting the view that the symptoms typical of agoraphobia are closely related to one another comes from factor analytic studies. Dixon *et al.*, (1957b) investigating the fears of 300 psychiatric out-patients, found a factor loading with agoraphobic symptoms. In a study of 274 subjects Roth *et al.*, (1965) measured a number of characteristics and a loading on an agoraphobic factor was found (fears of going out, depersonalization, panic, etc.). Marks (1967), in a study of seventy-two phobic subjects, found a similar loading. Snaith (1968) in factor analysing the responses of twenty-seven agoraphobics and twenty-seven specific phobics on the Fear Survey Schedule, demonstrated an agoraphobic cluster of fears. Further evidence of similar loading is provided from investigations by Marks and Herst (1970); Schapira *et al.* (1970); Hallam and Hafner (1978).

Another line of enquiry supporting the validity of the agoraphobic syndrome relates to the evidence that there seems to be little continuity between fears in non-phobic populations and fears in agoraphobic populations. Snaith (1968) investigated three populations—agoraphobics, specific phobics and normals. The cluster of agoraphobic fears were found to occur very rarely in the normal population, unlike the cluster of specific fears which occurred very frequently. Thus, although there was some continuity between the fears of the specific phobics and the normal population, no such continuity appeared to exist with the agoraphobic fears. Further support for this finding is provided by Hersen (1973). Accordingly there seems little doubt that there is a constellation of agoraphobic symptoms which are related to one another which supports the view of Marks (1969) that the core symptoms of the disorder appear so constantly together as to require unitary consideration.

There is some evidence concerning the relationship between agoraphobia and depression and anxiety. According to Roth, Garside, and Kerr (1972) minor agoraphobic symptoms may be observed in depression and anxiety. On the other hand, depressive episodes are often seen among agoraphobics (Bowen and Kohout, 1979; Marks, 1969). In a clinical review of the concept of agoraphobia Hallam (1978) argued that labelling a reluctance or refusal to leave home or other place of security as phobic avoidance has given the misleading impression that the syndrome, of which this behaviour is a part, has an underlying unity and coherence based on a fear of public places. Hallam contends that insufficient attention has been paid to differentiating the syndrome from anxiety neurosis; agoraphobia, he argues, might not be a central core feature of a phobic syndrome but a variable feature of patients whose neurotic anxieties have a multitude of different sources. This view has little support when the results of long-term follow-up studies are considered (Munby and Johnson, 1980); patients diagnosed as agoraphobic are not diagnosed as generalized anxiety or depressive states in subsequent years; the agoraphobic state remains the same state.

Arrindell (1980) has made an important contribution to the discussion in his study. The responses of 703 non-institutionalized phobics to the Fear Survey Schedule (FSS–III), were factorial analysed utilizing a principal components procedure. The results clearly point to the specificity of agoraphobia and that agoraphobia is not reducible to a different subset of fears or to a general trait of fearfulness. Higher-order factor analysis demonstrated both phobia and agoraphobia to be independent of neuroticism (anxiety or general emotionality); in addition, the agoraphobia dimension was shown to be independent of the phobia factor.

Arrindell points out that, in studies quoted by Hallam (1978), only depressive states had been compared with anxiety neurotics while the employed diagnostic criteria were rather vague; it would have been preferable to examine closely whether a group of agoraphobics differ and, if so, in which ways, from anxiety neurotics, depressive neurotics and other clinical typologies.

EPIDEMIOLOGY

There is a dearth of empirically based information concerning the distribution and prevalence of fears and phobias in the general adult community (Burns and Thorpe, 1977b). However, a major survey of fears and phobias in the general population is being undertaken and preliminary results have been reported (Burns, 1980a,b); the survey involves analysing the responses of a 10 per cent stratified, random, age-related sample of adults, aged 15–55 years, taken from the practices of seventeen general practitioners. Unfortunately, few of the early epidemiological studies differentiated phobic states from the other neuroses although exceptions were two American studies by Lemkau, Tietza, and Cooper (1942) and Hollingshead and Redlich (1958), both of which reported a prevalence rate of 0.5 cases per 1000 of the population. A later study, by Langner and Michael (1963), indicated a prevalence of 260 cases per 1000 for phobia; this almost certainly represents an overestimate; few of those designated as phobic appeared to have their everyday functioning disrupted to any significant degree.

Fear survey schedules have been used to assess fears in normal populations, (Greer, 1965; Grossberg and Wilson, 1965; Manosevitz and Lanyon, 1965; Scherer and Nakamura, 1968). Most studies have used college students, a significant percentage of whom have fears with strong social components. Unfortunately, these studies do not provide much information about the incidence of phobic disorder in the general community.

One of the most important contributions to our knowledge on the epidemiology of phobias in the general community was made by Agras *et al*., (1969). Data were collected by interviews of a probability sample of the household population of Greater Burlington (Vermont); a 1 : 193 sampling fraction was used and a total of 325 persons were interviewed. Agras and his co-workers developed an interview schedule which listed forty commonly feared situations; data was also collected on the intensity and duration of the fear, avoidance behaviour and treatment. A separate questionnaire of twenty-one items was used for children below the age of 14 years. The questionnaire responses were examined by a psychiatrist in order to identify all phobic or possible phobic subjects. Each of these subjects were then interviewed by another psychiatrist to determine the diagnosis, the history, treatment of the disorder and the degree of disability. The total prevalence of phobia was estimated at 76.9 per 1000 of the population. Of these, 74.7 per 1000 were considered to be mildly disabling; the remainder were considered to be severely disabled, severe disability being defined as the absence from work for an employed person and an inability to manage the common household tasks for a housewife. Of the phobic population there were 6 cases of agoraphobia per 1000, that is 8 per cent. Of the phobic patients being treated, (2.2 per 1000), 50 per cent were suffering from agoraphobia.

These findings are supported by Marks (1969) who reported that 60 per cent of the phobics treated at the Maudsley Hospital, London, were suffering from agoraphobia. Although clinical samples may be taken as unrepresentative of the distribution of phobias in the general population, agoraphobia being over-represented in view of the severity of the disorder, it is interesting to note that, in a self-selected sample (N = 463) of readers of the British weekly magazine *Woman*, over 95 per cent of whom were females, Burns and Thorpe (1977a) reported that 49.68 per cent appeared to be suffering from agoraphobia.

A number of studies (Terhune, 1949; Errera and Coleman, 1963; Hare, 1965; Frazier and Carr, 1967), suggest an incidence of 2.5–3.0 per cent of phobic patients among psychiatric patients. Judging from the description of these phobias the majority of them are agoraphobias. Only Clapman, Freeman, and Sclare (1956) report a higher incidence; the study indicated that approximately 8 per cent of their sample had predominantly phobic illnesses. Errera and Coleman (1963) suggested that as many as 20 per cent of psychiatric patients have significant phobic symptoms. This figure is confirmed by the Hollingshead and Redlich (1958) study.

PROBLEMS OF UNDER-INCLUSION AND OVER-INCLUSION

Problems of under-inclusion and over-inclusion need to be referred to briefly (Marks, 1970).

Although the term agoraphobia is used to describe fears of going out into public places, patients may present with a wide range of clinical features. A patient may present with not only agoraphobia but a miscellany of other phobic disorders and a wide range of non-phobic symptoms such as depersonalization, derealization, hypochondriacal symptoms, depression and obsessional symptoms, etc; in these patients the use of the term would be under-inclusive as it describes but a part of their total clinical picture.

Alternatively, in some patients, some travel phobias or claustrophobias or fears of crowds may occur as isolated symptoms; in such cases the use of the term would be misleading as it is over-inclusive.

AGE OF ONSET

Agoraphobia normally begins in young adult life (18–35 years). The age of onset appears to be similar to that of anxiety states and social phobias (Lader and Marks, 1971). Marks (1970) and Bowen and Kohout (1979) report two peak ages of onset, at about 20 years and at about 30–35 years. Table 1.1 shows the mean age of onset for various studies.

Table 1.1. Mean age of onset of agoraphobia

Researcher(s)	Year	Population	Mean age of onset
Marks and Gelder	1966	Out-patients	24.0
Marks and Herst	1970	Open door sample	29.0
Berg *et al.*	1974	Open door sample	26.0
Solyom *et al.*	1974	Out-patients	19.6
Shafar	1976	Out-patients	32.0
Buglass *et al.*	1977	Out-patient married housewives	31.0
McDonald *et al.*	1979	Out-patients	28.0
Bland and Hallem	1981	Out-patients	31.0

Rutter *et al.*, (1968) claim that agoraphobia is rare in childhood while Marks (1969) believes that the condition infrequently starts at age 40 years onwards.

SEX RATIO

Most studies indicate that two-thirds or more of agoraphobics are female. Table 1.2 shows the number of sufferers and the percentage who are female

Table 1.2. Studies showing percentage of female agoraphobics

Researcher(s)	Year	Number of subjects	Percentage female
Tucker	1956	100	89
Roth	1959	135	70
Warburton	1963	53	89
Klein	1964	32	81
Marks and Gelder	1965/6	84	89
Snaith	1968	27	63
Solyom *et al.*	1974	43	90
Shafar	1976	68	87
Chambless	1978	27	78
McPherson *et al.*	1980	56	66

in published reports on agoraphobia where the sample contained at least twenty-five subjects. These findings are similar to those obtained in anxiety states, (Kedwood and Cooper, 1966; Wheeler, White *et al.*, 1950; Wood, 1941), and other phobic states (Frazier and Carr, 1967; Kolb, 1973).

There are many reasons which may account for the large preponderance of female sufferers. Social and cultural factors may play an important role. The pattern of parental reinforcement, childhood learning and socialization experience may be of some significance (Fodor, 1974). Traditionally the woman has been tied to the home and may have been less motivated to obtain work. Thus, despite changing social roles, it is more acceptable for women to remain at home and husbands may reinforce dependent behaviour in certain cases. As women may have a narrower range of interests the focus of anxiety is more limited. Another aspect is that women are more likely to report fears than men (Wilson, 1967). A further explanation arises from the work of Asso and Beech (1975). Their research indicates that, during periods of high arousability (e.g. a few days before the onset of menstruation), women may be particularly vulnerable to acquire aversive responses. Further research is needed to confirm their findings. Some women aged 53–56 report that long-established agoraphobia has disappeared overnight; hormonal changes occurring during the climacteric may be important. George (1982) has been investigating biochemical correlates in agoraphobics.

The syndrome is essentially the same for those men who become agoraphobic (Chambless and Goldstein, 1980); however, their disability may be less severe perhaps because familial and societal pressures militate against men becoming incapacitated in this way.

MARITAL STATUS

There is no evidence that agoraphobics are unusual with regard to their marital status. Most studies show them to be married to spouses of average age (Buglass *et al.*, 1977; Marks and Gelder, 1965; Webster, 1953).

CHILDHOOD PROBLEMS

Marks and Gelder (1965) make comment on the fact that there are several reports which indicate that, during the childhood of agoraphobics, there was an incidence of enuresis, fear and night terrors of up to 50 per cent.

Harper and Roth's (1962) research showed that their phobics had a significantly commoner history of childhood phobias (60 per cent) than their controls.

In the study by Shafar (1976) 36.75 per cent of the agoraphobics were judged to have had a very unhappy or disrupted childhood; bereavement was seen to have played a part in about a third of the cases.

Berg, Marks, McGuire, and Lipsedge (1974) surveyed by questionnaire 786 women of an agoraphobic correspondence club on the incidence of past school phobia; 22 per cent admitted to school phobic tendencies, a proportion similar to that found in fifty-seven non-phobic neurotic controls. Although past school phobia predicted an earlier onset of subsequent agoraphobia and a more severe psychiatric state as far as symptoms not specifically agoraphobic are concerned, Berg and his colleagues believed that school phobia leads to agoraphobia in only a small proportion of cases and that both conditions reflect a lasting tendency to neurotic illness. In a later paper on the same sample Berg (1976) concluded that school phobia occurred in the children of agoraphobics to a greater extent than would be expected; the average incidence for children aged 7–15 years was 7 per cent (5 per cent for boys and 9 per cent for girls). However, the average incidence in children aged 11–15 years was 14 per cent. Women with school phobic children reported having had school phobia themselves to an undue extent.

Unfortunately, most of the data on childhood problems is of a retrospective nature. A well-controlled study of Buglass *et al*. (1977) investigated concurrently psychiatric symptoms in the children of both the agoraphobic group and matched normals. The children were divided into two groups—those up to and including the age of 15 years and those 16 years of age and older. Using check-lists and ratings the authors concluded that there was no evidence of greater morbidity in the children of agoraphobics or in controls in either the younger or older age groups. Interestingly a somewhat higher, but non-significant, proportion of control children were found to be psychiatrically disturbed.

As an alternative method of comparing the groups Buglass and her co-authors totalled the number of phobic and control families with disturbed children. Seven families in each group contained one or more disturbed child. A total of seven children (all ages) of phobics and ten children of controls were rated. There was no evidence that the presence of agoraphobia was conducive to psychiatric disorder in the offspring. Examining the distribution of individual symptoms in the children of the two groups indicated a similar prevalence in each; in particular, there was no excess of childhood phobias in the offspring of agoraphobics; 18 per cent of the phobics' children and 25 per cent of the controls were rated as phobic. The authors point out that nearly all of these were specific phobias of animals or insects and were of a type and severity expected to be fairly common among children. An important finding was that none of the phobics' children were agoraphobic or showed school refusal. It can be concluded, therefore, that there is no convincing evidence for any major detrimental effect of the agoraphobia on the offspring.

INTELLECTUAL AND EDUCATIONAL STATUS

There is no convincing evidence that agoraphobics are in any way unusual with regard to intelligence or education (Gelder *et al.*, 1967; Gillan and Rachman, 1974; Marks, 1969).

In a study of forty agoraphobic sufferers carried out by the authors and to be reported later in this book, the mean IQ of the group, as assessed by the Standard Progressive Matrices (Raven, 1960), was approximately 99. The mean Verbal IQ was approximately 92 (Mill Hill Vocabulary Scale, Form 1, Senior) (Raven, 1965).

OCCUPATIONAL DISABLEMENT

The employment opportunities for agoraphobics are clearly reduced by the condition. In the study by Marks and Herst (1970) only 23 per cent of the agoraphobics went out to work, a figure which is significantly lower than the comparable national average. The severity of the agoraphobia and other problems did not differ between those who worked and those who were housewives. Although there is some suggestion that working agoraphobics may have gone to work to avoid being on their own at home, their chief characteristics related to an independent outgoing personality in the past and present and a range of socio-cultural variables which included being young, being of higher education, having few children, etc.

In the study 60 per cent of responders who were housewives stated that they wanted employment outside the home. However, most of the evidence suggested that these responders were more severely ill than those agoraphobics who did not wish to work. They had more severe phobias and other psychiatric symptoms (depression, etc.); their everyday functioning was affected more; they had more fears of being alone and were at their worst then. Many would probably have been unable to cope with a job and they may have been expressing a desire to escape from their problems rather than a genuine wish to work in its own right.

Personality and socio-cultural factors were also operative in those who wished to work. They rated themselves as having been more sociable and independent in the past. Not surprisingly, they had a lower income; they had been of higher occupational status in the past. Clearly the frustration caused by the disability is an important factor in wishing to work in addition to the increased severity of the illness.

FEATURES ASSOCIATED WITH TREATMENT

Most research reports indicate that agoraphobics seek treatment in their thirties. The mean age for treatment at the Maudsley Hospital, London, is 34 years (Marks, 1969). This figure is not unlike that obtained for other neurotic-type problems. In a study on sixty-eight patients Shafar (1976) reports a mean age of treatment of 39 years. According to Marks (1969), the average time to elapse before the patient was handicapped was 15 months. On average 2 months later help was sought from General Practitioners. However, 34 months elapsed from the onset of the phobia before help was obtained from a psychiatrist and 57 months from spiritual or religious healers.

Nearly all agoraphobics seek the advice of their General Practitioners. In a study by Marks and Herst (1970) 95 per cent of the sufferers contacted their General Practitioner; 67 per cent had seen a psychiatrist. It appears that a lack of treatment was associated more with personality, than with illness, variables; untreated phobics were judged to confide less in intimates and strangers; to score high on social timidity and social anxiety and were less comforted by the presence of other people.

Psychiatric treatment was a function mainly of illness rather than social or personality variables. Not surprisingly, post-psychiatric treatment was associated with increased severity both of phobias and of related symptoms while in-patient treatment correlated with the greatest severity and handicap of all.

Ramsay (1975) reported data on the treatment-seeking behaviour of Dutch agoraphobics. Low-cost treatment was advertised by the Phobics Society; only 56 per cent of members availed themselves of the offer. Ramsay concluded that this poor percentage may be taken to reflect a low level of motivation for change. However, as the delivery of the health services in Holland is very different to that in Britain, it is difficult to draw firm conclusions from the figures without further research.

CLINICAL DESCRIPTION

The clinical picture presented by agoraphobics remains relatively unchanged from the clinical and autobiographical accounts since Westphal's (1871) description. The syndrome involves the principal features shown below.

Fears of environmental situations

Situational fears which are important include going into public places—streets, shops, crowds; enclosed spaces such as theatres, churches or lifts; travel on public transport—trains, tubes, buses or planes (but not usually in private cars or ambulances); travelling over bridges or into tunnels and remaining at home alone. Fears of these situations usually exist in various combinations.

Fears of confinement

Situations involving confinement or restriction of movement can evoke intense feelings of anxiety or panic in the agoraphobic. Examples include sitting in a barber's or dentist's chair; queueing in a shop; sitting in a bus or talking to a neighbour. In these and similar situations the agoraphobic feels trapped with no appropriate line of escape available. Many agoraphobics appear to plan out escape routes in advance. Open spaces, like wide streets and parks, have difficult escape routes as there are few places to which to run.

Panic

Acute panic is one of the most distressing aspects of agoraphobia. A vivid description of panic experienced by one sufferer is given by Hawkrigg (1975):

> I was inside a very busy shopping precinct and all of a sudden it happened: in a matter of seconds I was like a mad woman. It was like a nightmare, only I was awake; everything went black and sweat poured out of me—my body, my hands and even my hair got wet through. All the blood seemed to drain out of me; I went as white as a ghost. I felt as if I were going to collapse; it was as if I had no control over my limbs; my back and legs were very weak and I felt as though it were impossible to move. It was as if I had been taken over by some stronger force. I saw all the people looking at me—just faces, no bodies, all merged into one. My heart started pounding in my head and in my ears; I thought my heart was going to stop. I could see black and yellow lights. I could hear the voices of the people but from a long way off. I could not think of anything except the way I was feeling and that now I had to get out and run quickly or I would die. I must escape and get into the fresh air. Outside it subsided a little but I felt limp and weak; my legs were like jelly as though I had run a race and lost; I had a lump in my throat like a golf ball. The incident seemed to me to have lasted hours. I was absolutely drained when I got home and I just broke down and cried; it took me until the next day to feel normal again. It leaves you with a hopeless feeling, because you know it will happen again and again.

Many agoraphobics fear fainting or dying during a panic attack. During the attack, which may last for a few seconds or up to an hour, it is difficult for the patient to retain a rational pattern of thinking. Clinical experience indicates that weeks of successful therapy can be undone by a few minutes of acute panic. As Leonard (1928) pointed out, panic attacks left him even more prone to further attacks for weeks or months afterwards and placed further restrictions on what mobility he had managed to gain. Once a panic attack is over it may be several months before the patient returns to the scene of the attack.

Physical symptoms

The physical symptoms are similar to those seen in other anxiety states and include dry mouth, sweating (frequently of the palms, of the hands and armpits), acute tension around the stomach region and at the back of the neck, increased heart rate, dizziness or light-headedness frequently accompanied by a feeling of being about to faint, increased respiration rate, trembling and a feeling of weak legs.

Cognitive aspects

Leonard (1928) wrote about his fear of fear, especially after panic attacks; this alludes to the anticipation of the anxiety, physical symptoms, etc. The agoraphobic is much more likely to be able to undertake a short excursion if she is motivated to do it on the spot rather than if she is asked to do the same trip in an hour or a week later.

The pressure of having to attend a daughter's wedding or a parent's funeral, and the fear of letting others down, can quickly assume significant proportions (Vose, 1981).

Cognitions associated with the anticipatory anxiety include thoughts about losing control or becoming confused; losing one's memory; having heart attacks or other physical illnesses; being unable to get home or to other places of safety; fainting in public and being surrounded by onlookers devoid of any understanding.

Fluctuations

There is little doubt that the agoraphobia can fluctuate on a day-to-day basis; thus, on some days, the agoraphobic can do much more than other days. Changes in the environment can assist or hinder. As recorded earlier, Westphal (1871) recognized the influence which human companionship, or even inanimate objects, could have. Agoraphobics generally feel better in the presence of a reliable companion, be this animal or human. Even being accompanied by an infant or a small child, who could offer little assistance, can be of great help. However, a minority of patients find it easier to travel alone.

Agoraphobics adopt a number of stratagems to manage their disability; for example, a route may be planned to pass the homes of friends, the doctor's or even the police station. In our experience the patients rarely need to make use of such arrangements; the possibility of such assistance is sufficient to help them to deal effectively with their anticipatory anxiety. Other factors which Marks (1969) reports as being useful to agoraphobics include having a walking stick, shopping basket on wheels, wearing dark glasses, sucking sweets, having a bicycle to push rather than ride, darkness in the cinema, sitting near an exit, etc. Legrand du Saule (1895) wrote about an army officer who felt anxious about crossing a square while he was dressed in civilian clothing but not at all when he wore his uniform with his sabre at his side!

Any stressful event might make the agoraphobic worse; however, events which heighten motivation (rage or anger, for example), can enable the patient to extend activities usually on a temporary basis.

ASSOCIATED SYMPTOMATOLOGY

As Hawkrigg (1975) pointed out, many non-phobic and other phobic symptoms are commonly present in the agoraphobic syndrome.

Depersonalization and derealization

The term depersonalization was first used by Dugas and Moutier (1911). Both depersonalization and derealization are strange, complex and essentially private experiences which the individual has difficulty in communicating (Davidson, 1966; Roth, 1959). A prominent feature is a feeling of change involving either or both the inner (depersonalization) and outer (derealization) worlds and carrying with it a vague but uncomfortable sense of unfamiliarity. Thus, the subject may complain of feeling temporarily strange, unreal, dreamlike or cut off or far away from the environment. Depersonalization and derealization may be of any duration from a few seconds to months.

These symptoms occur at times in many agoraphobics. Roth (1959) reported a phobic anxiety-depersonalization syndrome which usually followed a sudden change in the patient's life situation. Roth and his colleagues indicated that agoraphobic patients who report depersonalization make up a distinct group and that there are certain similarities between this group and temporal lobe epilepsy (Harper and Roth, 1962). It is true that depersonalization can occur in such temporal lobe disturbances but there is no evidence that agoraphobics with depersonalization have any form of temporal lobe dysfunction.

In the study by Harper and Roth (1962) 37 per cent of sufferers reported these symptoms. In the Buglass *et al.* (1977) research, significantly more agoraphobic patients (37 per cent) reported current depersonalization experiences than controls (13 per cent) and it tended to be more severe. However, the two groups did not differ significantly in past history of depersonalization. In considering these figures it should be borne in mind that transient depersonalization may occur in as many as 50 per cent of a normal population without any significant difference between women and men (Nemiah, 1975). Although transient attacks of depersonalization and derealization may occur in isolation there seems little doubt that the onset is more likely to follow extreme anxiety or panic, frequently accompanied by hyperventilation. Marks (1970) speculates that the processes may be a cut-off mechanism which is triggered when anxiety reaches a certain level.

Depression

Bearing in mind the nature of the disability it is, perhaps, not surprising that agoraphobics react by becoming depressed. There is little doubt that they suffer from repeated episodes of depression in that they complain of depressive mood, feelings of hopelessness, crying spells, irritability, lack of interest in everyday activities and difficulty in falling asleep (Bowen and Kohout, 1979; Marks, 1969). Whereas mild retardation and suicidal ideas may occur, severe retardation, nihilism and bizarre delusions are not features of the syndrome. If the depression increases, the agoraphobia tends to get worse; panic attacks may become more frequent thus resensitizing the subject and motivation to cope may decrease. Conversely, the agoraphobia will improve as the depression lifts.

In the study by Buglass *et al*. (1977) depression was clearly demonstrated in 30 per cent of their sample; it was present to a minimal degree in a further 17 per cent of sufferers. It needs to be borne in mind, however, that there may be an element of self-selection since sufferers without depression may simply seek less help.

General anxiety

Many authors have commented on the link between general anxiety and agoraphobia. Buglass *et al*. (1977) have demonstrated that anxiety is the most common symptom in agoraphobia; it was clearly present in 80 per cent of their sample. The sufferer typically experiences free floating anxiety regardless of the situation she is in; it forms a pervasive background of tension which may be constant or may fluctuate for no apparent reason. The anxiety often merges into the acute phasic disturbance of panic attacks.

Fears and phobias

There is conclusive evidence that many agoraphobic sufferers have a range of fears and phobias. Of the sample studied by Buglass *et al*. (1977) 93 per cent were found to be suffering from a variety of fears and phobias apart from the agoraphobia. Fears of heights and of enclosed spaces were the most common; in some instances the severity was such as to disrupt the everyday functioning of the individual. A severe to moderate fear of developing a panic reaction was reported by 63 per cent of the subjects.

Obsessions and compulsions

Although many agoraphobics complain of having irrational thoughts (Hawrigg, 1975), there is little evidence to suggest that obsessions play anything but a minor role in agoraphobia.

The same is true for compulsions, the commonest of which involves checking. Gelder *et al*. (1967) found that subjects who responded badly to desensitization and psychotherapy treatment had more severe obsessional symptoms.

Hypochondriasis

Buglass *et al*. (1977) looked in their sample for evidence of fears about bodily health in non-phobic contexts. Of the sample 53 per cent were classified as hypochondriacal; these subjects differed significantly from controls. Most agoraphobics with hypochondriasis had reasonable insight, recognizing their symptoms to be irrational but three were convinced that they had some physical disturbance. Of these with the hypochondriasis 37.5 per cent expressed concern about having a fatal illness.

Personality deviance

According to Shafar (1976), 75 per cent of her sample of sixty-eight agoraphobics exhibited personality deviation (defined as the presence of permanent personality traits which were harmful to the subject's social, including marital, adjustment). Personality deviance was exhibited by a similar proportion of social phobics. Shafar found that 20 per cent of agoraphobics were anankasts, a significantly smaller proportion than that seen in the social phobics. Hysterical personalities were noted in 28 per cent of agoraphobics (the proportion being similar to that of the social phobics); the author found that the 'non-responders' group to treatment (systematic desensitization, *in vivo* training and supportive psychotherapy) contained a significant excess of hysterical personalities.

TYPES OF AGORAPHOBIA

Goldstein and Chambless (1978) identify two types of agoraphobia; complex and simple.

The majority of agoraphobics fall into the former category which is characterized by:

1. Low levels of self-sufficiency due either to high levels of anxiety or lack of appropriate skills. These sufferers are seen as highly dependent, unassertive people with acute social anxieties.
2. Onset under conditions of conflict, generally of an interpersonal nature. The agoraphobics may find themselves in an unhappy, seemingly irresolvable relationship, under the domination of a spouse or parent. Because of their inadequacies they feel trapped in the conflict, unable to move.
3. A tendency to misunderstand the casual antecedents to emotional distress. Agoraphobics are seen to have a repressive response style; they show an inability to label feelings such as anger; they experience such feelings as diffuse autonomic arousal which is then labelled as inexplicable anxiety.

Alternatively, they may briefly experience anger but quickly suppress it and deny it, only to become anxious instead.

4. Fear of fear as the central phobic element. Panic is the hallmark of agoraphobia. Anticipatory anxiety can elicit an attack of panic. Such fears increase dependency; the sufferers cannot afford to alienate those on whom they rely.

In the view of Chambless and Goldstein (1980) neglect of any of these elements of complex agoraphobia will lead to eventual relapse.

Simple agoraphobia is the term attached to those agoraphobics who do not show the personality characteristics or the conflictual environment of complex agoraphobics. Fear of fear is basic to this group as well but the agoraphobics first experience panic attacks as a result of physical conditions such as hypoglycaemia or endocrine imbalance. Once these underlying problems have been resolved, the fear of panic attacks and avoidance will yield readily to treatment. Although an interesting attempt at the categorization of agoraphobics has been made, little empirical evidence is presented by the authors to indicate that the assumed characteristics are valid or to suggest why the anxiety should be experienced in public places rather than at home where, presumably, exposure to conflicting relationships is likely to be increased or to support their contention that, if the presumed elements are not treated, then relapse is the inevitable outcome.

CHAPTER 2

National Survey of Agoraphobics

From the early to the mid 1970s the authors started to collect data from a large sample of agoraphobic sufferers in the United Kingdom. The purpose of the survey was not only to confirm previous findings but also to systematically investigate clinical and other aspects of the syndrome. Although there had been many descriptions of the syndrome and there appeared to be good agreement about many of the clinical features, much of the information was based on single case or small group studies, with the exception of the study by Marks and Herst (1970); this study, however, sought information on somewhat different aspects of the syndrome. Some preliminary findings from the National Survey of Agoraphobics have already been reported, Burns and Thorpe (1977a, b).

THE SAMPLE

The sample of subjects was obtained by means of publicity in the mass media—local and national television, radio and newspapers; agoraphobic sufferers were invited to write for a copy of a detailed seventeen-page questionnaire. In addition, help was enlisted from the main phobic organizations—The Phobics Society (Manchester), The Open Door (London), The Phobics Trust (Surrey) and Merseyside and Yorkshire phobic groups; in this instance the agoraphobia questionnaire was sent out to members of the organizations as part of regular mailings. It was, of course, appreciated that members of these organizations might have phobic problems other than agoraphobia. In a random sample of 569 members of The Phobics Society (Manchester), Burns and Thorpe (1977a) reported that 80.66 per cent appeared to be suffering from agoraphobia.

A total of 1528 questionnaires were distributed. Approximately, 74 per cent of these were returned; of the questionnaries returned approximately 12 per cent of the respondents reported that a diagnosis of agoraphobia had either not been made by a medical practitioner or that the individual was not presently suffering from the condition. This left a sample of 963 subjects. (It should be noted that the data presented below may refer to a somewhat smaller number of subjects where data is missing.) There was provision for subjects to include their names and addresses separately from the questionnaire; in our judgement there was a good geographical distribution of subjects covering the United Kingdom. The mean age of the sample was 43.6 years (standard deviation 11.0 years).

SEX RATIO

The percentage of females is 88.16%; the male : female ratio is 1:7.45. Thus, our findings confirm previous findings (Marks and Gelder, 1965, 1966, and others).

MARITAL STATUS

The marital status of agoraphobic sufferers is: single: 10.80%; engaged: 0.52%; married: 71.03%; remarried: 6.13%; separated: 2.39%; widowed: 6.33%; divorced: 2.80%. These percentages appear to be in keeping with the appropriate Registrar General's figures (1973). The mean age of marriage was 22.6 years (standard deviation 4.3 years).

RELIGIOUS PREFERENCES

Church of England: 62.4%; Roman Catholic: 11.4%; Methodist: 5.2%; other preferences: 10.8%; none: 10.2%. We understand that these percentages are within the expected range of religious preferences within the United Kingdom.

EDUCATIONAL STATUS

After leaving school 11.9 per cent of the sample had further educational opportunities at college; 0.7 per cent went to University.

OCCUPATION

Of the sample 28.67 per cent had a job outside their homes. This is a somewhat higher figure than that reported by Marks (1970). Those who were working were classified according to the Registrar General's Classification: Class I, 2.2%; Class II, 13.7%; Class IIIa, 45.9%; Class IIIb, 11.1%; Class IV, 12.6%; Class V, 14.4%. Significantly more male agoraphobics had a job outside the home ($P < 0.001$). The great majority of working agoraphobics (76.4 per cent) felt that the condition hindered their ability to work sometimes or often; 48.1 per cent of the respondents felt they would change their job if it were not for the agoraphobia; often they felt trapped and unable to apply for new jobs. Of those not having a job outside of their home 83.2 per cent would take such work if it were not for the agoraphobia; there was a significant sex difference ($P < 0.01$) with more men expressing the wish to have a job outside of home. Full- or part-time paid work at home was undertaken by 15.9 per cent of the sample. The mean number of hours worked was 20.7 h (standard deviation 13.9 h).

CHILDHOOD OF AGORAPHOBICS

Separation during childhood

During the first 5 years of life 93 per cent of the sample were brought up by their parents; for age 6 years onwards 87 per cent were brought up by their parents. Of those brought up during their childhood by their natural parents a rather high percentage (37.6 per cent) appear to have been separated from their parents for a variety of reasons (illness, divorce, military service, etc.), for at least one period of 3 months or longer.

Parental attitudes

In an examination of parental attitudes a high percentage of the sample regarded their fathers as being strict (42.1 per cent) and their mothers as being over-anxious (43 per cent). Significantly more females regarded their fathers as being underaffective ($P < 0.05$) and their mothers as being overprotective ($P < 0.05$). The signficance of these results warrant further investigation.

Relationship with parents

There were no significant sex differences regarding the closeness of the relationship with the mother. However, significantly more male agoraphobics ($P = 0.004$) considered that they have a distant relationship with their father.

Behavioural problems

As we have seen in Chapter 1 there have been several reports (Marks and Gelder, 1965, and others) which indicate that the incidence of behavioural problems of agoraphobia during childhood is high. The following problems were reported in the Survey: nightmares 30.7%; bedwetting 13.7%; sleep walking 11.6%; stammering 3.6%; nail biting 29.5%; thumb sucking 6.7%; trouble with police 2.1%; slow in making friends 28.6%; fears about going to school 32.4%; feeling too easily hurt 69.7%; fears of the dark 45.8%; fears of animals 13.1%; other fears 46.8%. It is interesting to note that there is a striking similarity on a number of problems (nightmares, bedwetting, nail biting, thumb sucking, and stammering), between the percentages obtained by Lapouse and Monk, 1959) in a study of 482 normal children and the percentages of agoraphobics reporting the same problems. Thus, a tentative conclusion must be that there is little evidence that agoraphobics during their childhood experienced more behavioural problems than normal children. A number of problems (stammering, slow in making friends and trouble with the police), occurred significantly more frequently (all at $P < 0.001$) in boys than in girls.

NERVOUS DISORDER IN THE FAMILY

A number of studies report on the incidence of nervous disorders in the family of agoraphobics. The figures range from 21 to 40 per cent (Roth, 1959; Roberts, 1964). Harper and Roth (1962) indicated that there was an incidence of 33 per cent of neurosis in the families of phobics. In the Survey 28.1 per cent of the mothers of agoraphobics had treatment for some nervous disorder; the figures for fathers are 13.1 per cent and siblings 34.9 per cent.

CONSULTATIONS AND TREATMENT HELPFULNESS

Of the sample 95.8% had consulted their local doctor about the agoraphobia; 76.6% had also seen a psychiatrist; 16.4% had consulted a religious or spiritual healer about their problem; 9.2% had received treatment from a non-medical hypnotherapist; 3.5% had consulted a psychologist. A range of treatment had been received: 95.81% had received tablets; 28.9% relaxation training; 28.3% psychotherapy/psychoanalysis and 13.5% religious/faith healing; 15 to 18% of the sample found these treatments very helpful. However, of those who received behaviour therapy (10.7%), 31.4% found this form of treatment very helpful. Hypnotherapy was received by 14.9% of the sample; 23.1% found it very helpful. However, one disturbing result to emerge was that approximately 74 per cent of the respondents felt they had not received adequate help for their agoraphobia.

MARRIAGE—BACKGROUND AND RELATIONSHIPS

The mean age of the spouses of the respondents in the Survey was 44.8 years (standard deviation 11.2 years). The jobs of the spouses were classified according to the Registrar General's classification: Class I, 4.3%; Class II, 23.4%; Class IIa, 16.2%; Class IIIb, 37.8%; Class IV, 13.7%; Class V, 4.3%.

According to Marks (1969) the marriages of agoraphobics tend to be stable. However, Goldstein (1970) suggests that 'agoraphobic symptons develop concurrently with feelings of wanting to break the marriage or violate the strictures of the marriage contract'. Wolpe (1970) talks about 'the agoraphobias of unhappily married women low in self sufficiency in whom, apparently, the fear evoked in physical isolation is related to a persistent but unrealisable fantasy of liberation from the marriage—unrealisable because it is fearfully seen as leading to a social abyss'.

In the Survey, when married agoraphobics were asked to rate to a four-point scale the effect the condition was having on the marriage, 21.5 per cent felt it was putting a considerable strain on the marital relationship. As will be seen later, when subjects were asked to rank the most important ways in which the agoraphobia was affecting their lives, 13.1 per cent of the sample gave an impaired marital relationship as the *main* effect; there was a sex difference in that 14.18 per cent of the female subjects felt that marital disharmony was the main effect whilst this was reported by only 8.93 per cent of the male agoraphobics ($P < 0.025$).

AGE ON ONSET

In the Survey the mean age of onset was 28.02 years (standard deviation 10.35 years). This finding confirms findings reported in Chapter 1. A statistically significant ($P < 0.001$) sex difference was established; the mean age of onset for men was 24.25 years (standard deviation 10.00 years) and for women was 28.51 years (standard deviation 10.30 years).

Although Rutter *et al*. (1968) reported that agoraphobia occurred infrequently in childhood 9.3 per cent of the sample claimed that the agoraphobia developed below the age of 16 years. Additionally, although it has been argued (Marks, 1969) that the condition rarely develops from age 40 years onwards, 13.2 per cent of the sample reported that they developed the condition at the age of 40 years or more.

PRECIPITATING FACTORS

Roth (1959) indicates that as many as 83 per cent of agoraphobics report a precipitating event; Friedman (1966) on the other hand reports a figure of only 10 per cent. Clearly the frequency of precipitating factors varies widely according to what should be regarded as a precipitant. Everyday clinical experience suggests that, in many cases, the condition may begin after some alteration in the life style of the individual; events such as serious illness in the subject, bereavement, pregnancy, traumatic events 'down town', etc., have been reported. An event reported by the sufferer need not necessarily have triggered off the agoraphobia; such events may have occurred previously without any aversive consequences. However, it may be that the event occurs at a time when the individual is particularly vulnerable to stress (Asso and Beech, 1975).

In the Survey 70.3 per cent of the sample reported a precipitating event, with significantly more females reporting an event than males ($P < 0.01$). A second event was reported by 26 per cent of the sample. Table 2.1 lists the precipitating events.

Thus it will be observed that the most frequently reported category is the fifth—subject directly exposed to some traumatic event whilst out. (Examples: 'A car mounted the pavement and nearly knocked me down'; 'I felt faint and nearly collapsed while queuing in the supermarket'; 'I was accosted in the street by a group of thugs and injured'.) The next more important event was the death of a relative or friend. In 13.1 per cent of cases the agoraphobia is reported to have developed following an illness; in 7.83 per cent the birth of a child and in 1.81 per cent a miscarriage (25 per cent of the female sufferers reported at least one miscarriage). Vicarious learning experiences may play a role in some cases; 5.87 per cent report witnessing traumatic events while out. (Examples: 'I saw a lady trapped under a bus'; 'The lady in front of me in the supermarket collapsed'; 'When down town I saw a friend have a bad epileptic fit'). The only significant ($P < 0.05$) sex difference was that more men reported that they were subject to direct traumatic experiences than women.

Table 2.1. National Agoraphobia Survey—precipitating events reported by agoraphobic sufferers

	First event (%)	Second event (%)
Death of a relative or friend	23.04	24.28
Illness in relative or friend	4.37	9.83
Illness in subject	13.10	6.36
Strained marital relationship	3.77	6.36
Strained family relationship	2.71	5.20
Subject directly exposed to traumatic event (out of home)	32.23	28.32
Subject witnesses traumatic experience in others (out of home)	5.87	5.20
Birth	7.83	6.36
Miscarriage	1.81	1.73
Other	5.27	6.36

PANIC ATTACKS

As we have seen in Chapter 1 the panic attack experienced by the agoraphobic is the most distressing aspect of the condition. Data was collected in the Survey on the symptoms agoraphobics experience during a panic attack (see Table 2.2). Data was also collected on the worst thing which the sufferers feared might happen during a panic attack. A first fear was reported by 98.4 per cent and a second by 35.4 per cent. Table 2.3 lists the fears.

It will be observed that the fear of greatest concern is the fear of fainting or collapsing; it is our experience that agoraphobics do not faint during a panic attack. Fears of having a heart attack, a brain haemorrhage or palpitations are also prominent. These findings support the views of Buglass *et al*. (1977) that the most commonly cited fear of agoraphobics was the fear of becoming physically ill.

Table 2.2. National Agoraphobia Survey (random sample of 100)—percentages of agoraphobic sufferers experiencing various symptoms during a panic attack

	Percentage
Feeling nervous and tense	93
Feeling dizzy or faint	83
Feeling agitated	80
Palpitations	74
Weak legs	73
Trembling/shaking	72
Feeling totally unable to cope	66
Stomach churning	65
Sweating/perspiring	65
Shortness of breath	59
Feeling confused	58
Feeling things are not quite real	57
Feelings of losing control	52
Feelings of tightness/pressure in the head	43
Difficulty with eyes (blurred vision, etc.)	36
Feeling of becoming paralysed	19

Table 2.3. National Agoraphobia Survey—agoraphobics' worst fears of what could happen during a panic attack

	First fear (%)	Second fear (%)
Death	13.2	19.7
Fainting/collapsing	37.9	15.8
Heart attack	4.1	4.0
Losing memory	0.3	0.9
Becoming mentally ill	5.8	7.0
Causing a scene	6.2	25.8
Inability to get home/to place of safety	5.9	8.5
Losing control (e.g. becoming hysterical)	7.4	6.7
Other personal illness	10.4	9.7
Other	8.6	2.1

FLUCTUATIONS IN AGORAPHOBIA

Clinical experience indicates that agoraphobic sufferers show marked fluctuations in their condition on a day-to-day basis due, apparently, to a variety of factors. Westphal (1871) in his monograph gave due consideration to these factors. They include the presence of a trusted companion (human or animal), deserted streets, being confined (at dentists or hairdressers), queuing, closeness to a place of safety, pre-planned visits, etc. Marks (1969) provides a comprehensive review of factors which may affect the behaviour of agoraphobics.

The Survey attempted to assess these factors. Of 963 sufferers 89.5 per cent reported that the agoraphobia fluctuated on a day-to-day basis. There was a statistically significant sex difference with fewer male sufferers reporting fluctuations ($P < 0.001$). The results indicate that the five most fearful factors for agoraphobics, in order of importance, are: being in a trapped situation (at the hairdressers, etc.); having to queue in a shop, etc.; increase of distance away from home; having a definite appointment; domestic arguments and stress. Factors which make the agoraphobic feel better, in order of importance, include: when out, having a way open for a quick return home; being accompanied by husband/wife; sitting near a door in a restaurant/hall, etc.; talking the problems over with a friend; focussing the mind on something else; talking the problems over with the sufferer's doctor; being accompanied by a friend; talking 'sense' to oneself (e.g. providing reassurance).

THE EFFECTS OF AGORAPHOBIA ON THE SUBJECTS' LIVES

The agoraphobic condition might be expected to interfere with the everyday functioning of the family; as the restrictions increase the sufferer may require an escort to and from work; social activities may become severely curtailed; husbands and children may have to do the shopping; the agoraphobic provides an inappropriate model for her children and an inability to interact with the children in the natural environment outside the home may deprive the children of valuable learning experiences which could affect their development. In severe cases the subject may demonstrate acute anxiety when alone at home—thus the husband may be forced to take time off work and economic resources may come under strain.

In the Survey subjects were asked to list the main ways in which the agoraphobia was affecting their everyday life and to rank these in order of importance. The results are shown in Table 2.4. As will be seen 27.8 per cent

Table 2.4. National Agoraphobia Survey—effects of agoraphobia on subjects' lives

	Choice						
	1st (%)	2nd (%)	3rd (%)	4th (%)	5th (%)	6th (%)	Not listed (%)
Guilt feeling re children	5.3	7.1	7.2	2.3	0.6	0.1	77.5
Travel restrictions	9.9	8.3	6.9	3.6	1.5	0.1	69.6
Lack of social contacts	27.8	26.7	14.7	5.1	0.5	—	25.1
Marital relationships	13.1	14.1	11.2	5.3	0.8	—	55.5
Unable to work	16.9	12.3	8.4	4.5	1.3	—	56.6
Personal psychological effect	20.5	15.9	18.3	11.8	2.7	—	30.8
Other	3.1	4.5	4.5	5.7	4.0	0.3	77.9

Table 2.5. National Agoraphobia Survey—effects of agoraphobia on subjects' lives

Rank order of first choice					
Rank	Male (N = 112)		Rank	Female (N = 818)	
1	Unable to work	(41.96%)	1	Social restrictions	(28.85%)
2	Lack of social contacts	(28.57%)	2	Personal psychological effect	(22.62%)
3	Personal psychological effect	(10.72%)	3.5	Marital dysharmony	(14.18%)
4	Marital dysharmony	(8.93%)	3.5	Unable to work	(14.18%)
5	Travel restrictions	(4.46%)	5	Travel restrictions	(11.00%)
6	Other	(3.58%)	6	Guilt feelings re children	(5.99%)
7	Guilt feelings re children	(1.78%)	7	Other	(3.18%)

Table 2.6. National Agoraphobia Survey—effects of agoraphobia on subjects' lives

	Total number of responses—sex differences (ignoring rankings)					
	Males (N = 111)		Females (N = 818)			
	N	%	N	%	χ^2	P
Guilt feelings re children	16	14	201	24	5.82	<0.025
Travel restrictions	26	23	267	32	4.05	<0.05
Lack of social contacts	97	87	624	76	6.02	<0.025
Marital relationships	40	36	389	47	5.63	<0.025
Unable to work	81	72	337	41	38.56	<0.001
Personal psychological effect	83	74	583	71	0.38	NS.
Other	32	28	181	22	2.31	NS.

of those responding listed social restrictions as a first choice as being the way that the agoraphobia was interfering with their life. Next in order of importance was the personal psychological effect (examples: feelings of inferiority, lack of self-confidence, etc.). However, if, instead of looking at the overall results of the first choices, the differences between male and female responses on this choice are examined (Table 2.5), it becomes apparent that the most important factor for men is an inability to work (41.96 per cent) whereas only 14.8 per cent of the females considered this to be the most crucial factor; this result is statistically significant ($P < 0.001$). More women than men reported adverse personal psychological effects ($P < 0.001$). More women also complained about travel restrictions ($P < 0.05$). If the order of response is ignored and consideration given solely to the total number of responses, several sex differences are observed (see Table 2.6). On this basis both sexes now regard the lack of social contacts as the most important way the agoraphobia is affecting their lives although significantly more men report this than women ($P < 0.025$).

OTHER ASPECTS

It was reported by 57.1 per cent of the agoraphobics that the condition came on gradually over a period of 3 months or more. Most felt that during an emergency (such as a sudden illness of their husband, etc.) they could do more than they could normally do, presumably because there would be little time for the anticipatory anxiety to build up. Most of the respondents saw their husband/wife as providing the most sympathy and understanding of their fears. Next in line were daughters, psychologists and social workers. The most unsympathetic were neighbours followed by relatives and doctors.

A significant number (66.1 per cent) of the agoraphobics despaired nearly always or often about getting better; this is perhaps not surprising when it is considered that high percentages had received treatment and felt that they had been inadequately helped.

Many of the agoraphobics are aware of the relationship between self-defeating or anxiety-generating cognitions and the onset of panic. It was believed by 45 per cent of sufferers that merely thinking about one's problems would almost always or often trigger off a panic. Unfortunately, many respondents felt they had few or no coping skills to deal with their symptoms. It was also interesting to note that 61 per cent almost always or often had difficulty in making a decision about whether they should or should not go out; clearly this type of approach—avoidance conflict is a significant problem for many agoraphobics.

An interesting finding that warrants further investigation is that 24.5 per cent of the sample reported that there had been difficulties at birth (prolonged labour, prematurity, etc.). Migraine was suffered by 24.8 per cent which confirms the findings of Buglass *et al.* (1977).

It appears that once the agoraphobia developed there was little chance of it completely clearing up. Of the sample 82.4 per cent indicated that the agoraphobia had continued since the point of onset.

SECTION 36 OF THE AGORAPHOBIA QUESTIONNAIRE (BURNS, 1977)

Section 36 consists of seven-point rating scales dealing with a variety of situations which tend to make agoraphobics worse or better (see Appendix IV; pages 150–51). Preliminary findings (see Chapter 6) suggests that this may be a somewhat less satisfactory outcome measure than Section 39. A summary of the main findings of this Section, obtained in the Survey of agoraphobics, is presented below.

Normative data and sex differences

Number of cases = 704; mean = 37.82; standard deviation = 16.29; standard error = 0.61.

There is a highly significant agreement between male and female mean scores of the individual items on Section 36 (Spearman rank correlation co-efficient: $r = 0.99$; $t_{20} = 28.11$; $P < 0.001$). Thus it is concluded that there is no significant difference in mean scores between males and females for Section 36 (see Table 2.7).

Table 2.7

	Males	Females
No. of cases	60	553
Mean	80.03	82.53
Standard deviation	11.09	9.28

$t_{611} = 1.682$; $P = 0.09$

Marital status

An analysis was carried out to determine whether there were any significant differences, as indicated by Section 36, regarding the marital status of the subjects (Table 2.8).

Table 2.8

	Single	Married	Separated	Divorced	Engaged	Remarried	Widowed
No. of cases	33	490	12	13	5	40	20
Mean	82.27	82.38	80.42	83.77	77.00	81.50	69.25
Standard deviation	7.97	9.78	13.40	7.67	6.16	7.56	16.56

Bartlett's Test (equality of variance): $\chi^2_6 = 61.11$; $P < 0.001$

As the variances were different a non-parametric test (Kruskal–Wallis Test) was used to assess any differences between marital status. (Kruskal–Wallis Test (based on ranks): $H = 19.849$. $P = 0.003$.) Thus the P value suggests a significant difference between marital status.

Dunn's Multiple Comparison Test (5 per cent significance level) showed differences between single and widowed; married and widowed; remarried and widowed; and in each instance the widowed group showed greater difficulties as assessed by Section 36.

Employment

In both the case of females ($t_{545} = 3.80$; $P = 0.002$) and males ($t_{58} = 2.2922$; $P = 0.005$) those agoraphobics with a job outside of home feel significantly better in a wide range of situations than those without a job outside of the home.

Parental treatment for nervous disorders

There are no significant differences in mean scores for Section 36 of agoraphobics; (i) whose mother have/have not been treated for nervous disorders ($t_{590} = 0.698$; $P = 0.49$ NS), (ii) whose fathers have/have not been treated for nervous disorders ($t_{575} = 0.384$; $P = 0.70$ NS).

Duration of illness by groups

In order to test whether there was any relationship between the duration of illness and differential responses on Section 36, the sample was divided into six age ranges (1–2 years; 3–4 years; 5–6 years; 7–8 years; 9–10 years; 11 years and over). A Bartlett's test suggested the presence of a significant difference between sample variances ($\chi^2_5 = 38.338$; $P < 0.001$). A Kruskal–Wallis Test was used to test for any differences between groups.

(Kruskal–Wallis Test: $H = 6.632$; $P = 0.25$.) Thus, the P value suggests that there was no significant difference, on Section 36, between groups of agoraphobics where the condition is of recent origin, intermediate or of long standing.

Consultation with local doctors

We reported previously that 95.8 per cent of the sample had consulted their local doctor about their agoraphobia. There were no significant differences between the mean scores for Section 36 of those who had, and those who had not, consulted their doctors ($t_{605} = 0.407$; $P = 0.69$).

Adequate help for the agoraphobia

Section 36 was used to investigate whether there were significant differences between those who claimed they had, or had not, received adequate help for their agoraphobia. Those subjects who reported having received adequate help were less handicapped than those who had not had adequate help ($t_{596} = 2.408$; $P = 0.016$).

SECTION 39 OF THE AGORAPHOBIA QUESTIONNAIRE (BURNS, 1977)

Section 39 consists of five-point rating scales which concentrate on the behavioural functioning of the subject (see Appendix V; pages 152–53). Preliminary findings (see Chapter 6) indicate that it may be a useful assessment procedure.

Normative data and sex differences

Number of cases = 735; mean = 82.52; standard deviation = 20.14; standard error = 0.74.

There is a highly significant agreement between female and male mean scores on the individual items of Section 39 (Spearman rank correlation co-efficient $r = 0.93$; $t_{23} = 12.13$; $P < 0.001$). Thus it may be concluded that there is no significant difference in the mean scores between male and female agoraphobics (see Table 2.9).

Table 2.9

	Males	Females
No. of cases	81	654
Mean	79.51	82.60
Standard deviation	21.39	19.97

$t_{733} = 1.43$; $P = 0.15$

Marital status

The results from the Barlett's Test (equality of variances) gave a P value of 0.096 which indicated that the variances were equal; a one-way analysis of variance was used to test differences between each marital status. There were no significant differences between groups of different marital status (F (6734) = 0.811; P = 0.56).

Employment

Section 39 was used to investigate the reported disruption of everyday functioning of those with and without a job outside of home (Table 2.10).

Table 2.10

	Outside job	No outside job
Males		
No. of cases	41	39
Mean	68.98	89.72
Standard deviation	18.69	18.42
Females		
No. of cases	183	464
Mean	75.22	85.89
Standard deviation	16.84	20.28

Notes:
Male
$t_{78} = 4.996$; $P = 0.001$
The P value indicates that those males with a job outside of the home feel less fearfull/show less avoidance than those without a job.
Female
$t_{645} = 6.835$; $P = 0.001$
The results indicate that those females with a job outside of home feel less fearful/show less avoidance that those who do not have work outside of home.

Those wishing to work

Only one male agoraphobic would not take an outside job if he did not have agoraphobia. Those females with no outside job, and who would take a job were it not for their agoraphobia, show less fear and avoidance (Table 2.11).

Table 2.11

Females	Take a job	Not take a job
No. of cases	366	81
Mean	87.56	79.41
Standard deviation	19.61	21.62

$t_{445} = 3.322$; $P = 0.001$

Family nervous disorder

As we have seen previously, 28.1 per cent of mothers and 13.1 per cent of fathers of agoraphobics had nervous disorders requiring treatment. In comparing the mean scores for Section 39 of those agoraphobics whose mothers had and had not had nervous disorders, the *P* value suggests that there were no significant differences ($t_{704} = 1.29$; $P = 0.20$). A similar finding was obtained in respect of the fathers ($t_{690} = 0.01$; $P = 0.99$).

Duration of illness

The sample was divided into six age ranges (1–2 years; 3–4 years; 5–6 years; 7–8 years; 9–10 years; 11 years and over). A Bartlett's Test (equality of variances) gave $\chi^2_5 = 18.373$; $P = 0.002$ which indicates that there was a significant difference between sample variances. Accordingly, the Kruskal–Wallis Test, based on ranks, was used to test for any differences between the groups ($H = 19.631$; $P = 0.001$). Dunn's Multiple Comparison Test (5 per cent significance level) showed significant differences between the 7–8 years group and the 5–6 years, 9–10 years and 11 years and over groups, with the 7–8 years group being less fearful. There is no ready explanation why the subjects in this group should be less fearful. With this exception there is no indication that subjects with agoraphobia over increasing periods of time respond differently from those with recent onset of agoraphobia.

Consultations with local doctors

We reported previously that a 4.2 per cent sample had never consulted their local doctor about their agoraphobia. There were no significant differences on mean scores for Section 39 of those who had consulted, and those who had not consulted, their doctors ($t_{729} = 0.472$; $P = 0.64$).

Adequate help for the agoraphobia

An analysis was carried out to indicate whether there were significant differences on Section 39 between those who claimed they had, and had not, received adequate help for their agoraphobia (Table 2.12). Thus the *P* value indicates that those subjects reported as having received adequate help feel significantly less fearful/show less avoidance than those who have not had adequate help.

Table 2.12

	Adequate help	Inadequate help
No. of cases	183	537
Mean	78.40	83.88
Standard deviation	20.56	19.86

$t_{718} = 3.195$; $P = 0.001$

CHAPTER 3

Aetiological Factors: Physiological, Personality and Interpersonal Correlates of Agoraphobia

A pervasive and enduring problem in mental health research has been that, although effects of *treatment* techniques for a disorder may be studied in controlled experimental trials, identifying aetiological factors involves correlational data. Unless the researcher is able to *induce* a disorder in the patient by means of some sort of experimental control, thereby allowing cause–effect conclusions to be drawn, he or she has to be content with speculation as to the causes of the disorder. Even if this kind of experimental induction of a problem were possible (and, of course, it usually is not, for ethical and practical reasons), its results would not allow clear conclusions about the problems of people in whom the disorder was not deliberately created in this way. Some attempts have been made to demonstrate, experimentally, the acquisition of behaviours analogous to clinical disorders: Seligman (1975) has produced depressive-like behaviour in normals by means of a 'learned helplessness' procedure; Watson and Rayner (1920) claimed to have produced phobia-like behaviour in a small boy by means of classical conditioning; and Ayllon *et al.* (1965), by showing that an institutionalized female patient could be persuaded to carry a broom around the ward after this behaviour had been specifically reinforced, argued that bizarre behaviour could be understood in terms of such reinforcement contingencies. Of course, perhaps they could; but such demonstrations do not prove that the aetiology of similar disorders found in clinical practice is to be understood in terms of processes like those involved in the experimental procedures. One criticism of the Ayllon *et al.* (1965) demonstration is that it is, at best, a kind of 'behavioural forgery' (Cheshire, 1975).

Because of the correlational and *post hoc* nature of most data bearing on aetiology, current theories and concepts of the aetiology of agoraphobia are tentative, and each approach is heavily influenced by theoretical assumptions that have yet to be fully substantiated. A quotation from Marks' *Fears and*

Phobias is still applicable more than a decade after it was written: 'present insights . . . are necessarily provisional and will have to be modified repeatedly as knowledge increases' (Marks, 1969, p. i). The difficulty is the more understandable in view of the variety of data to be explained: women present agoraphobia for clinical attention up to seven times as often as men; agoraphobic anxiety may sometimes vary inversely with manifest marital difficulties; treatments that have proved successful with other phobias seem relatively unhelpful with agoraphobia; treatments that *have* been successful with agoraphobia involve direct exposure to feared situations, despite the fact that agoraphobia does not seem to improve spontaneously (at least in the short term) with casual, everyday exposure to shops, streets, and crowds; and so forth.

In discussing the aetiology of agoraphobia, behaviour therapy researchers and theorists have devoted much of their attention to hypothesized learning mechanisms in the acquisition and maintenance of phobic anxiety and behaviour; to such a degree, in fact, that our discussion of learning-theory factors merits a separate chapter (Chapter 7). Here, we discuss more general issues: 'background' features of the agoraphobic syndrome (some relatively enduring patient characteristics, individual differences in physiological and life-history factors, and so forth), the interpersonal context of agoraphobia (some personality features, degree of marital conflict, interactions of treatment with domestic relationships, etc.), and, finally, 'interactive' theories of aetiology.

BACKGROUND FEATURES

Physiological factors

Constitutional aspects of human fear are not well understood. Rosenthal (1970) summarizes evidence from twin studies that show greater concordance on various fear-related measures for monozygotic than for dizygotic twins, providing some evidence for a genetic contribution, but Delprato (1980) reviews—and finds inadequate—evidence suggesting that there may be some 'evolutional' components of the fear acquisition process.

Marks (1969) reviews data that seem to indicate different physiological mechanisms in different phobias and anxiety states. Conclusions are that patients with animal phobias show normal electrodermal response (EDR) habituation rate, few spontaneous EDR fluctuations, normal fore-arm blood flow, and speedy acquisition and slow extinction of classically-conditioned eye-blink responses. Agoraphobics show slow EDR habituation, many spontaneous EDR fluctuations, slightly higher than normal fore-arm blood flow, and normal eye-blink conditioning patterns. People with generalized anxiety disorder are similar to agoraphobics but show increased forearm blood flow. Social phobics differ from agoraphobics in that they show quicker acquisition of conditioned eye-blink responses. Systematic desensitization brings most benefit in patients with rapid EDR habituation (see also Mathews, 1977b).

Related to this point, individual response patterns in social phobia have been shown to have important treatment implications. Ost *et al.* (1981) divided forty socially-phobic outpatients into two groups on the basis of their reactions to a social interaction behavioural test. 'Behavioural' reactors, who had shown anxious behaviour but few changes in heart-rate during the behavioural test, responded particularly well to a skills-training approach. 'Physiological' reactors, who showed heart-rate increases but few behavioural signs of anxiety, responded better to applied relaxation training, in which they learned to relax and practised relaxation during a role-play. It is possible that research on agoraphobics may lead to different treatment prescriptions for patients who react physiologically rather than cognitively, for example.

There is some evidence that agoraphobics differ from non-phobic individuals in cardiac functioning. Kantor *et al.* (1980) compared the cardiac functioning of twenty-five female agoraphobics and twenty-three matched non-clinical controls. No subject in either group had any history of cardiac dysfunction that had come to clinical attention. Only patients for whom palpitations were a prominent symptom in panic attacks were selected for the agoraphobic group. There was a significantly higher incidence of mitral valve prolapse (MVP) syndrome in agoraphobics than in control subjects, as assessed by independent cardiologists. For each cardiac symptom, the ratio of agoraphobics to controls was as follows: chest pain (13 : 2), systolic clicks (4 : 0), systolic murmurs (7 : 1), and positive echoes (8 : 2). Kantor *et al.* (1980) note that it is helpful for physicians to reassure patients with palpitations that these are rarely harmful, and the authors conclude that MVP may be a primary source of anxiety for some agoraphobics.

Mitral valve prolapse is apparently a common finding in young women, and this physiological variant may help account for the preponderance of women in agoraphobic samples. However, these results have to be interpreted with caution, because not all agoraphobics complain of palpitations, and a minority (eleven out of twenty-five) of those agoraphobics who complained of palpitations in the Kantor *et al.* (1980) study showed evidence of MVP. Estimates of the incidence of MVP in women in general vary from approximately 6 to 11 per cent, so the discovery of a few cases in female agoraphobic samples would be predictable. The significance of the Kantor *et al.* (1980) data depends on the proportion of agoraphobics who report palpitations as part of their panic attack syndrome. Nevertheless, as Kantor and his co-workers argue, MVP may be a significant aetiological factor in some agoraphobics.

Sex-correlated factors

As we have noted, most self-referred agoraphobics are female. Several hypotheses have been advanced to account for this; all, of course, bearing on the issue of aetiology. Fodor (1978) argues that sex-role stereotyping by society leads women to assume passive, fearful social postures, modelled early in life by characters portrayed in children's story-books, classroom readings, television, and so forth. Fishman (1980) alters the argument a little: because, he argues, times have changed and women are now taking a more active role in industry, the professions, and 'establishment' society, conflict may be created for the woman who feels pressed to succeed occupationally but simultaneously senses a lack of the basic self-assurance that is more easily acquired by men during their upbringing in traditional society (see also Thorpe and Barnes, 1981). Fishman also speculates that men, who might present with agoraphobia if that conformed with sex-role stereotypes, in fact attempt to cover their phobic anxieties by means of alcohol, sometimes presenting clinically as alcoholics, or by developing obsessive-compulsive behaviours. This argument is similar to that of Hallam (1978).

A final theory has to do with the biological state of the organism in the classical conditioning of fears. Asso and Beech (1975) predicted that high levels of unpleasant emotional arousal would make the individual particularly susceptible to acquiring conditioned responses (CRs) to stimuli correlated with a noxious stimulus. Because fluctuations in emotional arousal may be characteristic of the menstrual cycle, Asso and Beech hypothesized that pre-menstrually, women would show more rapid CR acquisition than inter-menstrually. Results of a series of experiments (see Emmelkamp, 1979) were consistent with the hypothesis. In addition, the postpartum period might be expected to produce particular vulnerability to the acquisition of agoraphobia because of the hormonal changes that occur after child-birth; several reports confirm a somewhat high incidence of phobia onset after a pregnancy (Emmelkamp, 1979). Burns (1977) reports that of the 70 per cent of a sample of agoraphobics who reported a clear precipitating event for the onset of the phobia, approximately 8 per cent identified childbirth as the factor. As Emmelkamp (1979) notes, it is impossible to say whether the sufferer developed agoraphobia because of hormonal changes; because of the added responsibility of a new baby and, perhaps, a concomitant sense of being trapped; or because of any of a variety of correlated factors.

Because the data relevant to aetiological issues are correlational, theories are tentative. It may be argued that, because women were traditionally tied to the home and were less motivated to find work, and because their husbands may have commonly reinforced dependent behaviour on their part, women would be more likely to develop agoraphobia. Even if not, they would be more likely to bring agoraphobia to the attention of a health professional than would their male counterparts. Perhaps as society continues to change in the direction of more autonomy for women, more homes in which the bread-winner is a woman, and so forth, the ratio of female to male self-referred agoraphobics may change. Of great interest in this context is the observation by Boulougouris (1976) that, in Greece, most agoraphobics are male.

Personality variables

Agoraphobics have often been described as passive, dependent individuals who have difficulties with the direct expression of thoughts, feelings, or opinions (Chambless, 1978). Although clinical observations lend credence to this (see also Goldstein and Chambless, 1978), such a characterization would not be limited to agoraphobia. Hallam (1978) points out that there are a variety of ways, direct or indirect, to attempt to cope with unsettling disagreements or conflicts, and these include not only agoraphobia but alcoholism, compulsive behaviours, and so on. There is a broad parallel here with the 'hysterical personality' concept that has been held to underlie the spectrum of dissociative and somatoform disorders (Davison and Neale, 1978). The related personality concept of emotional stability has proved a helpful predictor of response to treatment: the more emotionally stable the patient, the better the outlook (see Chapter 6; Mathews *et al.*, 1976). Despite this, few data linking personality attributes to response to treatment are available, and accordingly conclusions are tentative. Attempts to link personality attributes to the development of agoraphobia initially are at this point almost entirely speculative (see below).

THE INTERPERSONAL CONTEXT

Several researchers and theorists have suggested that interpersonal factors are extremely important in the aetiology of agoraphobia and in its maintenance. Goldstein and Chambless (1978) argue that a general tendency to depend on others for support is one of the key indications for the diagnosis of complex agoraphobia, and others note that dependency is likely to be further strengthened in an agoraphobic individual by the nature of the condition (Lazarus, 1966). Goldstein and Chambless (1978) also formulate agoraphobia as in part an effort to resolve or deal with marital or family conflict, and several studies are available which tend to show reciprocal effects of agoraphobic fears and behaviours, on the one hand, and marital difficulties, on the other (e.g. Hafner, 1977a, b). Hafner (1976) presents some evidence that treatment of agoraphobic problems may sometimes be followed by the emergence of interpersonal and other psychological difficulties. Because there is a clear preponderance of women in clinical and research samples of self-referred agoraphobics, Fodor (1978) speculates that this differential incidence may be related to sex-role stereotyping and different cultural conditioning experiences in men and women in contemporary society. Finally, there is evidence that treatment programmes for agoraphobics are improved by the addition of group treatment experiences (e.g. Hand *et al.*, 1974), by the formation of neighbourhood self-help groups (Sinnott *et al.*, 1981), or by the active involvement of the sufferer's spouse in treatment (Mathews *et al.*, 1977). The popularity of self-help groups for agoraphobia (cf. McGennis *et al*., 1977) fits this context, but the impact of the self-help group has so far gone unresearched.

Interpersonal factors, then, have been implicated in the aetiology of agoraphobia in that the upbringing of agoraphobics may produce dependency, or in that agoraphobia may be an indirect attempt at resolution of marital or family conflicts. An important issue in research methodology is that long-term follow-up assessments are required in behavioural treatment research, so that the impact of successful treatment of the phobia on marriage or family life can be assessed. Of equal interest is research attempting to explicate the mechanisms by means of which group treatment approaches can be so strikingly successful.

Family background

There have been few scientific investigations of the family background of agoraphobics. Many research workers (Marks and Gelder, 1965; Roth, 1959; Terhune, 1949) find evidence that agoraphobics come from stable and close-knit families, although Snaith (1968) found an excess of unstable family backgrounds. Buglass *et al*. (1977) observed that agoraphobics tend to come from an anomalous home situation much more frequently than controls; there appeared to be an increased presence of step-parents, step-siblings or adopted siblings. The birth order of agoraphobics is not remarkable (Buglass *et al*., 1977; Marks and Gelder, 1965). There are no significant differences in parental age, family size, parental deprivation (permanent separation from either parent before the age of 15 years) or parental death in childhood (Buglass *et al*., 1977). The incidence of psychiatric disorder in the family ranges from 21 to 40 per cent (Roberts, 1964; Roth, 1959). In the study by Burns and Thorpe (1977a), 13.1 per cent of the fathers and 28.1 per cent of the mothers of agoraphobics were described as having nervous disorders requiring treatment; 34.9 per cent of the sample had at least one sibling requiring treatment. Harper and Roth (1962) found an incidence of neurosis in the families of agoraphobics which was significantly higher than in a control group of temporal lobe epileptics. However, Buglass *et al*. (1977) could find no evidence of excess psychological illness in the parents nor of excessive drinking by the fathers; nor was there any indication of a greater frequency of psychological disorders among the patients' sisters. There was an excess of patients' brothers who were scored positively for 'any psychological illness', chiefly non-phobic. Thirty per cent of the siblings of the agoraphobics had a positive history of psychiatric illness.

Psychological gain

Very little by way of systematic investigation has appeared in the literature on psychological gain in agoraphobics. Shafar (1976) gave an operational definition of psychological gain elements; they were considered to apply where symptoms were used in the furtherance of an aim or as a means towards diminishing those insecurities and anxieties which arose out of neurotic functioning (e.g. where symptoms were seen to have certain values for the patient or to possess an ascertainable protective quality). Shafar (1976) recognizes three types, overt, covert, and conflict-solving gains. The author found that psychological gain operated in 70 per cent of her phobic sample; 39.68 per cent of these had relinquished the gains that had accrued from their phobia at the end of contact. Agoraphobics showed no significant distribution difference from other types of phobics. In the treatment of agoraphobics (a combination of systematic desensitization, graded *in vivo* exposure and supportive psychotherapy), the author found that, in the sample of sixty-eight agoraphobics, psychological gains impeded successful treatment (at least initially) in thirty-seven cases; in a third of the cases this impediment proved to be a permanent obstacle.

Dependency

Emmelkamp (1979) cites studies that support the view that 'dependent' individuals are especially liable to develop agoraphobia. Evidence is equivocal, however, and researchers have found what seems to be a negative and reciprocal relationship between stability of family relationships and dependency. Some (Marks and Gelder, 1965; Roth, 1959; Terhune, 1949) find that the marriages and families of agoraphobics are stable, whereas the agoraphobics are overprotected and dependent. Others (Buglass *et al*., 1977) find that agoraphobics tend to come from unusual home situations, with more step-parents and step-siblings or adopted siblings than control patients; however, the agoraphobics do not differ from controls in degree of dependency (see also Burns and Thorpe, 1977a, b). (Parker (1979) finds that agoraphobics, by contrast with social phobics, do not regard their parents as overprotective, but he does not report on the degree of dependency evidenced by his patients.) There seems to be a relationship, then, between family stability and dependency. If we assume that agoraphobics are dependent, and live in stable families, two hypotheses can be suggested: (i) stable families can be overprotective, and produce dependency; or (ii) agoraphobics develop the phobia so as to preserve the stability of a marriage or family otherwise threatened by divorce or separation (Goldstein, 1970), and the agoraphobic symptoms in turn imply a dependency on family units (Marks, 1970).

The assumption that agoraphobics are dependent individuals could lead to a prediction that they sense an external 'locus of control' (Rotter, 1966). Emmelkamp and Cohen-Kettenis (1975) indeed found support for this in a correlational study (see Emmelkamp, 1979).

Goldstein and Chambless (1978) and Chambless and Goldstein (1980) cite dependency (low levels of self-sufficiency) as one of the four principal characteristics of the complex agoraphobic. This undue dependency on others makes it difficult for the agoraphobic to resolve an interpersonal conflict either by assertive communications with the other person or people involved or by leaving the marriage or family to begin an independent existence. However, it is difficult to circumvent the somewhat circular nature of the Goldstein and Chambless argument (Emmelkamp, 1979): people who are not dependent, and therefore would pose a problem for the argument, are not complex agoraphobics by definition.

Finally, some other recent views have an indirect bearing on the dependency issue. Hallam (1978) argues that agoraphobia is a misnomer, and that individuals diagnosed as agoraphobic are better classified as cases of anxiety neurosis. He cites the difficulty of specifying the relevant phobic stimuli in agoraphobia, and concludes that agoraphobics have to cope with a diffuse tendency to be anxious. Some cope by depending on alcohol or medication, some by avoidance of a variety of potentially challenging situations, and so forth. Mullaney and Trippett (1979) provide some support for this general line of argument by showing that there is considerable overlap between agoraphobia and alcohol dependence.

Although some interesting hypotheses have been advanced about the relationship between agoraphobia and dependency, a clear consensus is lacking. Parker's (1979) recent paper, in which he reports that, whereas socially phobic patients in his survey regarded their parents as overprotective, agoraphobics, if anything, thought they had *less* maternal care and protection, runs counter to the trend. It could always be argued, of course, that if agoraphobics really are extremely dependent, then they could regard even a more than usually protective parent insufficiently caring.

Interpersonal conflict

Several writers have noted that there is a high incidence of marital problems in couples which include an agoraphobic. Webster (1953), for example, examined the closed case records of seventy-five neurotic outpatients, a sample consisting of equal numbers of agoraphobics, anxiety neurotics, and patients showing conversion reactions; conclusions were that agoraphobics had more than their share of marital difficulties. He also noted that the only agoraphobics who showed any sign of improvement were those women whose husbands participated in treatment. In similar vein, Lazarus (1966) stressed the importance of at least interviewing, and ideally treating, the spouse (or perhaps another relative) of the agoraphobic. He argues that it is difficult to live life as a severe agoraphobic without some trusted companion who is willing to accept the inevitable demands of that role. Hand and Lamontagne (1976) observed that two-thirds of a sample of twenty-one married agoraphobics were aware of chronic marital problems, and that, furthermore, seven patients experienced acute marital crises after successful treatment of agoraphobic complaints. Milton and Hafner (1979) note that the 'maritally dissatisfied' half of a group of fourteen agoraphobics responded similarly to couples in treatment for marital problems on a marital adjustment questionnaire; scores were considerably different from the mean of those of untroubled couples. In a survey of fifty members of The Open Door (an association for British agoraphobics), Torpy and Measey (1974) found some evidence of marital problems.

As in the case of the overlapping issue of dependency, findings here are mixed. Marks (1969) concluded that the marriages of agoraphobics tend to be stable, and Buglass *et al.* (1977) found manifest characteristics of the marriages of thirty agoraphobics strikingly similar to those of control patients. It is always possible that in some couples, the presence of agoraphobic difficulties in a partner actually functions to preserve the stability of an otherwise troubled marriage. Goldstein (1970) and Wolpe (1970) have previously argued this point. Complementary to this, it may be that, while the agoraphobic is in a sense behaving in a phobic way in order to deal with an interpersonal conflict, her husband is able to deny any problems of his own that may be contributing to the poor relationship (Hafner, 1977a). This could account for the apparent 'normality' of the husbands of women agoraphobics, as observed by Agulnik (1970), and this view is consistent with earlier discussions by Fry (1962) and Mittelman (1956).

Assortative mating and pathogenic interaction

Because so many investigators have indicated that agoraphobics have an unusually high incidence of marital or family problems, it is clinically and theoretically important, (a) to attempt to validate this notion, and (b) if a relationship exists, to find out what are the mechanisms by which phobic behaviour and marital interactions are linked. Hafner (1977a) outlines two general theories of the interaction of pathology with marital functioning: 'assortative mating', and 'pathogenic interaction'.

In assortative mating, partners initially choose each other on the basis of perceived pathological attributes, presumably at least partly because it would be too threatening for either partner to have a spouse functioning at a much higher level. Implications are that if one of the partners seeks treatment for a mental health problem, improvement would be resisted in some way by the other, so as to maintain the equilibrium of the marital relationship.

By contrast, in pathogenic interaction, the communication between the partners is such that one or both partners may develop mental health problems as a result; and furthermore, the development of a mental health problem in one partner may lead in turn to the onset of pathology of some kind in the other, who would otherwise remain untroubled. On this theory, it could be predicted that improvement in one partner would be followed by improvement in the other.

There are considerable difficulties in attempting to validate or disconfirm these theories, because by the nature of the hypothesized relationships the data are largely correlational. Attempts have been made to shed light on this issue, however, and at least those hypotheses dealing with the effects on the spouse of successful treatment of the partner's problems can be tested experimentally. In this section we will focus on those few studies that have used such experimental manipulations. The effects of problem-oriented treatment of agoraphobia on the patient and the spouse have been extremely varied; for convenience we will discuss research results in terms of four common patterns. It is important to enter a caveat immediately: available research does not allow the general conclusion that successful treatment of agoraphobia leads to the emergence of other difficulties; those patterns we will discuss, each occur in a minority of cases. Hand and Lamontagne (1976), who provide an exceptionally thoughtful discussion early in their paper of 'symptom substitution', incomplete treatment, and so forth, conclude conservatively:

> We cannot find, either before or after treatment, a consistent pattern of interaction between agoraphobia and interpersonal problems, especially with regard to what effect a phobia or its rapid removal has on chronic marital problems. In half of the 14 patients who were aware of their marital problems, phobia removal was not followed by an acute crisis, and sometimes, even led to an improvement. (Hand and Lamontagne, 1976, p. 409)

Effects of agoraphobia treatment on interpersonal relationships

Sequential alternation of agoraphobia and interpersonal difficulties

Hand and Lamontagne (1976) provide a detailed account of the acute interpersonal crises experienced by some of a sample of agoraphobics after successful phobia removal. In two cases, both women, the patients developed orgasmic dysfunctions and became depressed after successful treatment of the agoraphobic fears and behaviours. One of these patients sought an immediate divorce. As it happens she had originally developed agoraphobia immediately after successful treatment of vaginismus and her concomitant sexual rejection of her husband. She decided to remain in contact with her therapist, and managed to resolve her conflict about the marriage (that is, her simultaneous desire for a divorce, and guilt over rejecting her husband; he had been understanding and helpful during her attempts to overcome the phobia) by insisting on a platonic relationship with her husband. In the process of this resolution, she experienced a slight relapse into agoraphobia, but this, too, was overcome.

One male patient became depressed, agitated, and paranoid as his phobic difficulties improved; he had had a long history of paranoid reactions and morbid jealousy. After several sessions of marital therapy, however, his phobic problems began to reappear. Another male patient showed a very similar progression, from successful resolution of agoraphobia to a return to earlier patterns of alcoholism, aggression, and violent jealousy; as he began treatment for depression and entered marital therapy, he gradually relapsed into his phobia. The final patient, a woman, initially regarded her marriage as good, but a few weeks after treatment of agoraphobia, she developed an orgasmic dysfunction, became depressed, and her phobic difficulties returned. Anti-depressant medication successfully controlled the depression and phobia, but the patient remained anorgasmic.

Milton and Hafner (1979) examined treated agoraphobics who tended to relapse, and observed a clear relationship between early relapse and marital dissatisfaction. The more common marital pattern observed in these cases was the 'compulsory marriage' (Fry, 1962), in which the spouse feels obliged to remain in a difficult marriage because the agoraphobic partner is highly dependent on him or her; alternatively, the agoraphobic may feel obliged to remain phobic and married, because if the phobia were removed, then leaving the marriage would be a desirable—but also threatening—possibility. In this pattern, the spouse (the husband in the three cases Milton and Hafner mention) would recognize that the wife was becoming more and more independent and self-confident, and he would therefore act to undermine treatment progress. In another case, the husband of a successfully treated agoraphobic left her 3 weeks after treatment (and after a marriage of 24 years); he had hitherto felt trapped in the marriage by his wife's dependency on him. She developed an acute psychotic reaction 6 weeks later.

These illustrations seem broadly consistent with the assortative mating view. In each case, the patient experienced an alternation between agoraphobia and other (interpersonal) difficulties, apparently consistent with the theory that the spouse will somehow resist successful treatment of the patient.

Concurrent alternation of agoraphobia and interpersonal difficulties

The cases treated by Hand and Lamontagne (1976) that were noted above showed a sequence in the problems; treatment of agoraphobia could lead to the emergence of a different problem focus, and vice versa. In four other cases, these authors refer to a 'vertical' pattern of interaction. These patients were troubled equally by marital and phobic difficulties, and the effect of treatment of agoraphobia was to spark activities on the part of the spouse that undermined treatment effects. There seemed to be a continuing reciprocal influence of one problem on the other, such that a breakdown into sequences was impossible. Again, these illustrations seem to conform with the 'assortative mating' theory.

Alternation of well-being between patient and spouse

Hafner (1977b) sought to gather data bearing on the assortative mating theory by assessing the effects of intensive behavioural treatment for agoraphobia on the patients and their spouses. If the well-being of one partner depends on the disability of the other, then therapeutic change in the latter could be resisted. Hafner reports some examples in which this seemed to be the pattern. One husband, for example, felt useless after his wife overcame her agoraphobia; he made a suicide attempt. Two husbands became depressed after their wives were treated, because this improvement in the wives' functioning brought to the fore the husbands' sexual difficulties. Other husbands became severely jealous as a result of their wives' recaptured freedom, and marital disharmony increased to the extent that the wives reverted partially to their previous agoraphobic behaviour. One husband developed low back pain (presumably functional) which resulted in a curtailment of his wife's outgoing activities. Another developed a florid paranoid psychosis which improved after his wife relapsed into agoraphobia.

Milton and Hafner (1979) report similar findings. In three of the couples of whom the wife was treated for agoraphobia, problems in the husbands became evident after treatment of the wives. The social phobia of one husband was shown to be incapacitating, once the wife could go out again; two husbands displayed sexual problems.

In similar vein, Barlow *et al.* (1981) report that marital satisfaction decreased in two of a sample of six couples after successful treatment of the wives' agoraphobia. Treatment was conducted in a group with the husbands present, and took the form of *in vivo* exposure and cognitive restructuring. All subjects had improved post-treatment, but varying patterns were evident during a 12-month follow-up interval. In the two cases in which the marital relationship worsened, it was the husbands who indicated marital dissatisfaction, yet the wives continued to make good progress in respect of the phobia during the follow-up interval. This seems to count against the view that marital dissatisfaction makes for a poor prognosis in agoraphobia treatment. By contrast, two women suffered phobic relapses during follow-up, despite the fact that increases in marital satisfaction had correlated positively with phobic improvement during treatment. As Barlow *et al.* (1981) acknowledge, husbands played an active role in treatment and therefore may not have had the opportunity to sabotage progress during the period of active treatment.

Liotti and Guidano (1976) describe a pattern in which the wives of fifteen male agoraphobics tended to reinforce anxiety and panic in their husbands. It seems clear that in *some* cases of agoraphobia, the spouse will either resist improvement in the agoraphobic or develop dissatisfaction in him or herself.

Failure to respond to treatment when family relationships are troubled

Hafner (1977b) argues that women agoraphobics whose husbands are troubled have a poor prognosis for treatment of the phobia unless the husbands are treated also. Emmelkamp (1980), however, found no evidence that marital problems (as assessed by a marital deprivation scale) made for a poor prognosis for the agoraphobia with behavioural treatment. Nevertheless,

Emmelkamp conducted a follow-up assessment after 1 month only, whereas Hafner (1977b) has noted that relapses on the part of the patients occurred within four months. Additionally, Hafner assessed the functioning of the husbands with various questionnaires and rating scales (also providing much anecdotal information), whereas Emmelkamp did not, stressing that his was a study of prognosis only, and urging that more studies to test hypotheses similar to those of Hafner need to be undertaken.

Hudson (1974) divided the families of agoraphobics into three categories: well-adjusted (seven cases), anxious-patient (seven cases), and sick families (four cases). Only agoraphobics from the 'well-adjusted family' group had made 'significant improvement' by 3-month follow-up after intensive behavioural treatment, and there was only one exception to this general rule at 12-month follow-up. Although a clinician other than the therapist made the improvement ratings, there seems to have been some contamination of the independence of these ratings (Emmelkamp, 1980).

Bland and Hallam (1981) report similar findings. Twelve agoraphobics were divided into two equal groups on the basis of their responses to a marital satisfaction questionnaire. All responded well to graded exposure treatment, but the less maritally satisfied group tended to relapse during a 3-month follow-up interval; the group difference in ratings of agoraphobia at follow-up was statistically significant. Bland and Hallam conclude that exposure treatment is effective in the short term independent of the level of marital satisfaction, but that marital conflict is associated with subsequent relapse. Similarly, Hafner (1979) describes the deleterious effect on behavioural treatment for agoraphobia in seven women who were married to abnormally jealous men. Conversely, improvement in the agoraphobia on the part of the wives coincided with an increase in the husbands' pathology.

Despite Emmelkamp's (1980) conclusion that marital conflict is not a poor prognostic sign for agoraphobics in behavioural treatment, studies in which a longer follow-up interval than 1 month was used provide evidence of a tendency toward relapse in maritally-troubled patients.

Summary

A number of investigators have reported the presence of serious marital or family problems in a significant proportion of patients presenting agoraphobic symptoms. In addition, it appears that such problems can interfere with the effectiveness of problem-oriented behavioural treatments, leading to partial or complete relapse. Perhaps of more importance is the disruptive effect behavioural treatment may have on the family unit; that is, considerable psychological stress may occur in other family members, the marriage may be severely strained or ruptured, or the patient may experience other problems (e.g. sexual dysfunctions). This latter consideration leads one to search for those predictive signs which might discriminate the patient whose phobia can be treated directly with behavioural methods without such repercussions from those whose treatment will necessarily be more comprehensive.

All of the studies reviewed have found that a rough assessment of marital or family stability (questionnaire or interview) is sufficient to divide groups such that differences in outcome can be observed. However, these methods leave considerable overlap between groups divided on the basis of such measures, and clinical decisions could only be made reliably in extreme cases. This type of discrimination certainly presents challenging areas for research and should be pursued. A related question involves ascertaining the most effective treatment for agoraphobics who are part of a pathological family unit. Should, as Milton and Hafner (1979) suggest, behavioural and marital therapy be used concurrently, or is some form of family therapy alone preferable? Again research is needed to answer such questions.

Long-term follow-up after treatment of agoraphobia

Studies to investigate relationships between treatment of agoraphobia and marital and other difficulties do not permit straightforward conclusions to be drawn. Data are in large part correlational; data supporting the assortative mating view derive from only a minority of cases; and there have been some methodological weaknesses (Emmelkamp, 1980; Hand and Lamontagne, 1976). Of tangential interest here is the report by Stern and Marks (1973b); a woman client's obsessive-compulsive difficulties resisted conventional exposure-based behavioural treatment, only to improve when marital therapy became the major focus of treatment. This report would seem to fit with the general theme of the studies by Hafner and others. However, when a clinical series of maritally-troubled obsessives and phobics were treated in a cross-over experiment (half of the patients had marital therapy first, and exposure second; the others had the treatments in reverse order), the opposite outcome was observed. In fact, exposure seemed a far more effective marital treatment approach than was the so-called marital therapy (Cobb *et al.*, 1980; Marks, 1980).

Careful evaluation of the long-term effects of behavioural treatment for agoraphobia is therefore important in the attempt to understand the aetiological significance of interpersonal relationships in maintaining agoraphobic behaviour. Three reports of extended follow-ups of treated agoraphobics have appeared recently, and these will be taken up next.

Emmelkamp and Kuipers (1979) report follow-up data for agoraphobics treated in four previous trials (Emmelkamp, 1974; Emmelkamp and Emmelkamp-Benner, 1975; Emmelkamp and Ultee, 1974; Emmelkamp and Wessels, 1975). Follow-up data derive from responses to four sets of questionnaires: (1) phobic anxiety and avoidance scales (Watson and Marks, 1971); (2) a depression scale; (3) Rotter's (1966) Internal-External Control Scale; and (4) a social anxiety scale. Data were available from seventy of an original sample of eighty-one agoraphobics, 3.5–5 years after treatment. Statistically significant improvement from pre-test to follow-up was found on the phobic anxiety and avoidance scales and on the depression inventory; improvement from post-treatment to follow-up is significant on the anxiety scale for 'other phobias', and on the depression scale. In general, improvement was not only maintained at an average of 4 years after treatment, but continued improvement during the follow-up interval was evidenced by some measures. This result is consistent with those of Hand *et al*. (1974) for their patients who were treated by direct exposure in structured groups; their observation of continued improvement after formal treatment had ended was the first such report in the literature.

These follow-up results are certainly extremely encouraging. There are some limitations to the conclusions that may be drawn from this, however. First, although all patients in the trials conducted by Emmelkamp and his associates had been treated by exposure methods, some had received imaginal flooding, some *in vivo*, some had observed models, and some had been treated in groups. Follow-up data do not, therefore, permit comparison of different kinds of exposure treatment. In the Emmelkamp (1974) study, some patients (an unspecified number of the twenty subjects participating) had served in a waiting-list control group; it is not clear how many of these were represented in the seventy patients followed-up, nor can it be said how many received treatment subsequent to the controlled trial. Further, Emmelkamp notes in his 1974 report that in five cases, the agoraphobia seemed to play an important part in the sufferer's marital relationship: in one case a husband forced the patient to discontinue treatment, in another the husband refused to acknowledge any improvement in his wife whereas patient and therapist saw clear improvement, and in three cases marital therapy was provided after the treatment of agoraphobia had been concluded. Unfortunately, it is not known what happened to the marriages of the married agoraphobics in the sample of seventy followed-up 4 years or so later. Despite this, the overall results of the follow-up assessment are impressive, perhaps suggesting that if many of the treated agoraphobics had had marital difficulties, they nevertheless went on to maintain progress or improve further in respect of the phobic problems at least.

Johnston and Munby (1980) and Munby and Johnston (1980) report follow-up data from 65 agoraphobics who had been treated in three trials conducted five to 9 years previously (Gelder *et al*., 1973; Mathews *et al*., 1976; Mathews *et al*., 1977). Data consisted of self-report questionnaire responses and results of an interview with one of the original researchers, who rated patients on phobic severity, anxiety, and depression. Thirteen of the patients were also rated by an independent psychiatrist so as to permit a reliability check on the ratings; reliability was satisfactorily high, and the original rater was seen to be rating more conservatively than the independent rater.

Because in the original trials the behavioural treatments had not differed in effectiveness, treatment-groups were collapsed for analysis within each trial. On the phobic rating scales, improvement that had been demonstrated after 6 months was, by and large, maintained at long-term follow-up. Patients rated their anxiety and depression as unchanged from the 6 month follow-up assessment, but the clinician-rater detected some tendency toward a return to pre-treatment levels. There was no evidence for the emergence of new problems after treatment of agoraphobia. No mention is made of any marital or inter-personal difficulties reported by patients in the follow-up interview. A final point of interest is the relative superiority of the progress made by patients from the trial (Mathews *et al.*, 1977) in which treatment was based on exploits into the community from the patients' homes with the support of their spouses; this approach was designed to impart general coping skills. However, these patients had been selected somewhat differently from those in the other trials, and only twelve patients were involved in this study, so general conclusions are hazardous.

Finally McPherson *et al.* (1980) report results of a 4 year after treatment postal follow-up of 69 per cent of a sample of eighty-one patients who had improved with behavioural treatment of agoraphobia. Treatments had included *in vivo* exposure, imaginal desensitization, and a variety of other behavioural treatments. Five ratings were made by each patient: severity of agoraphobia, of other phobic problems, and of depression; adequacy of interpersonal relationships; and occupational adjustment. On all five, improvements from pre-treatment to follow-up were highly significant statistically, with a trend for continued improvement during the follow-up interval; however, this did not approach the degree of continued improvement reported by Emmelkamp and Kuipers (1979) in their follow-up study. There was no evidence of fresh problem emergence, except that one patient reported the development of a new phobia; this responded to behavioural treatment.

None of these three reports of extended follow-up of treated agoraphobics focussed clearly on the possible presence of marriage or family disturbance, so little can be said on this issue. In the report by McPherson *et al.* (1980), patients reported a continued improvement in interpersonal adjustment at extended follow-up as compared to their ratings before treatment; this finding is not, of course, as clearly interpretable as could be wished. Specific assessment of family relationships several years after behavioural treatment of agoraphobia would be a welcome addition to the research literature.

DIRECT INFLUENCES

So far, it is clear that agoraphobia has been regarded as a complex syndrome in which interactions between background factors, the sufferer's personality, and the degree of conflict in his or her interpersonal relationships may be extremely important aetiologically. However, it remains to be explained why the sufferer develops agoraphobia, as opposed to any of a wide range of other mental health problems, as a result of these diverse influences (Hallam,

1978). Behaviour therapists tend to posit conditioning events in the development of phobias; psychodynamic theorists tend to postulate a symbolic relationship between the phobic stimuli and certain underlying conflicts (the 'symptom-symbol' view). First, it is relevant to find out to what extent agoraphobics report precipitating events for the development of the phobia.

Precipitating factors

Roth (1959) indicates that as many as 83 per cent of agoraphobics report a precipitating event. Friedman (1966) on the other hand reports a figure of only 10 per cent—clearly the frequency of precipitating factors varies widely, perhaps because of different definitions of a precipitant. Everyday clinical experience suggests that, in many cases, the condition may begin after some alteration in life style of the individual; events such a serious illness in the patient, bereavement, pregnancy, traumatic events 'down town', etc. have been reported. An event reported by the sufferer need not necessarily have triggered the agoraphobia; such events may have occurred previously without any aversive consequences. However, it may be that the event occurs at a time when the individual is particularly vulnerable to stress (Asso and Beech, 1975).

In the study by Burns and Thorpe (1977a, b), 70.3 per cent of the sample reported a precipitating event, with significantly more females reporting an event than males ($p < 0.01$). Twenty-six per cent of the sample reported a second event. The most frequently reported event is a traumatic experience (for example, 'a car mounted the pavement and nearly knocked me down'; 'I felt faint while queueing in the supermarket'; 'collapsed on the bus when travelling alone'; and so forth). The next most important event was the death of a relative or friend. In 13.1 per cent of cases the agoraphobia is reported to have developed following an illness; in 7.83 per cent the birth of a child and in 1.81 per cent a miscarriage (25 per cent of the female sufferers reported at least one miscarriage). Witnessing to a traumatic event while out was reported by 5.8 per cent of the sample (for example, 'I saw a lady trapped under a bus'; 'the lady in front of me in the supermarket collapsed'; 'when down town I saw a friend have a bad epileptic fit', etc.). The only significant ($p < 0.05$) sex difference was that more men than women reported direct traumatic experiences.

Buglass *et al.* (1977) looked for evidence of background stress (such as physical illness and psychological stress) and discrete traumatic events. Fifteen of the 30 subjects were experiencing 'non-specific' stress before the onset of the agoraphobia; in fact nine of these subjects were suffering from a recognizable neurotic syndrome. Seven subjects reported discrete events at the time of onset of the agoraphobia but only two of these were 'specific' (i.e. an event was reported which occurred in the setting in which the patient was subsequently phobic). The remainder of the sample showed no evidence of either background stress or discrete traumatic events.

Shafar (1976) noted the presence of precipitating factors in 83 per cent of the phobic sample. Relationship problems were seen to be important causative factors in 57 per cent of the cases; 'unhappy childhood' was considered important in 11 per cent; in the remainder of cases (32 per cent) one or more of the following factors seemed important: pregnancy/childbirth, separation from a key figure, change of abode, organic illness/operation, pharmacological factors (poisoning/withdrawal), psychiatric illness, financial stress/loss of or insecurity in employment, accident/assault, sexual guilt, and guilt regarding abortion. Shafar generally found little difference in the distribution of precipitating factors in the various phobias.

Conditioning events

Precipitating events such as those discussed above may or may not help explain the development of agoraphobia (as opposed to a different disorder), depending on one's theoretical perspective. Chambless (1978) notes that one psychodynamic view of agoraphobia is that it represents a conflict over abandonment, and may include chronic, unresolved grief aetiologically. On this view, the report of a bereavement immediately preceding the onset of agoraphobia would be of great theoretical importance (Bowlby, 1973). Learning theorists, by contrast, would be more interested theoretically in reports of conditioning events and so forth.

Recent social learning theory formulations of fear posit four distinct avenues: direct associative experience (for example, being involved in an aircraft hijacking); vicarious experience (watching a television newcast of a hijacking in progress); symbolic instruction (being told that flying is extremely risky); and symbolic logic (reasoning that aircraft are made by people, who are fallible, and therefore aircraft may be unsafe). By extending the list of avenues toward fear beyond direct associative experience, theorists can give an account of phobias in people who have never confronted their phobic object in real life; many flying phobics, for example, have never made a flight (Bandura, 1977; Rachman, 1977).

In an analogue study, Rimm *et al.* (1977) observed that sixteen out of forty-five phobic students were able to relate relevant direct experiences with the phobic situation that could account for the phobia in conditioning terms. Of the remainder, seven subjects reported vicarious experiences or verbal instruction that would be predicted to produce fear. Because these data derive from student volunteers whose participation was solicited in a non-clinical setting, it is unwise to generalize too far from them.

The kind of direct experience that would be of interest to behavioural theorists would be the onset of unpleasant physical sensations resulting from illness while the person is shopping in a crowded supermarket. Classical conditioning procedures of this kind could produce a conditioned response of anxiety; this argument is taken up in greater detail in a later section. It is important to note here that many behavioural theorists have held it irrelevant to focus on external stimuli that could become phobic objects as a result of conditioning procedures; in agoraphobia, what is feared is not so much the external environment, but the internal bodily reaction (Fishman, 1980; Goldstein, 1970; Wolpe, 1969). In terms of this account, the crucial conditioned and unconditioned stimuli are to be found further afield. Zaccheo and Palmer (1980), for example, report a case of agoraphobia in a 31-year-old woman for whom desensitization to external situations brought few gains, but who was successfully treated when she was desensitized to the theme of 'loss of control'.

INTERACTIVE VIEWS OF AETIOLOGY

Phobic behaviour may result from the interaction of constitutional, cognitive, and environmental characteristics. This 'interactionist' view has been stressed recently by cognitive-behavioural theorists such as Mahoney (1980), who argues that analogies from information-processing may be appropriate: one's biological constitution is analogous to the 'hardware' of a computer, imposing certain limits on adaptive capacity and having some 'pre-wired' biases towards certain kinds of response; one's general style of dealing with the environment, that is, one's personality or attitudes, may be compared to the computer programme, or set of rules for reacting to what is presented; and the environmental influences on one's behaviour are similar to the computer's 'input'. The final analogy is between human behaviour and computer 'output'. The hardware, the programme, and the input interact, of course, as do the effects of the agoraphobic's bodily reactions, cognitive appraisals, and surroundings. A clinical example from Evans (1972) serves well to illustrate this interactive view.

A woman client rapidly developed social anxieties in the course of her hitherto normal social activities; the principal source of her embarrassment and distress was her tendency to blush when introduced to a stranger. In terms of Mahoney's analogies, her tendency to react to stress by blushing (as opposed to fainting or developing a duodenal ulcer) is a constitutional influence (her 'hardware'); her view that 'to be seen to blush is extremely embarrassing and undesirable' could be a personality, or attitudinal, characteristic (her 'programme'); and the perceptions that, (a) she is blushing, and (b) people are noticing her blushing, are environmental influences (the 'input'). In this example, the three interact: the attitude ('blushing in public is enormously embarrassing'), coupled with the perception that she *is* beginning to blush, can facilitate physiological anxiety reactions, which include (for her) blushing, which in turn triggers further worrying self-statements, more blushing, further perceptions which confirm the need to engage in worrying thoughts, and so on and so forth.

Relevant to this theme, Marks (1969) notes that:

> innate mechanisms probably do not of themselves produce phobias, but make certain situations prepotent targets for phobias when other condi-

> tions are superimposed . . . illustrated by a woman who developed a phobia of heights for the first time at the age of 40. She suddenly felt dizzy and in danger of falling while on an escalator, shortly after a fenestration operation for deafness. The dizziness subsided but a phobia of escalators started and spread. (Marks, 1969, p. 73).

In agoraphobia, some theorists have stressed the particular importance of an interactionist account of aetiology, and clinical experience with agoraphobics lends credence to the importance of understanding reciprocal influences of, for example, a 'dependent' social posture, marital conflict with a concomitant desire to escape from the relationship, and anticipatory fear of public places and of travel away from home. Fishman (1980) provides a typical interactionist account of agoraphobia. The agoraphobic individual is primarily aware of unpleasant physical sensations, particularly 'lightheadedness', which she fears. In the typical case she is also interpersonally deficient, passive-dependent in social posture, non-assertive, and finds it difficult to express emotion. The sufferer fears abandonment and loss of control, which represents conflicts between dependency and independence; she usually feels trapped in a predicament: an unsatisfying job, for example, or a stale marriage, that cannot easily be escaped.

Because the agoraphobic finds it difficult to recognize or express emotions, the unpleasant sensations deriving from seething, unexpressed hostility become attached to outside surroundings symbolic of the conflict: confining surroundings such as elevators, crowded buses, and so forth. The occasional stirrings of an attitude of independence serve only to bring the conflict to the fore anew. As a result of all this, the agoraphobic wallows in a self-defeating rut: the conflict over dependence versus independence is not fully recognized, and consequently its offshoots—unpleasant physical sensations—may be experienced in surroundings reminiscent of the conflict. Henceforth, contemplating exploits into such surroundings creates anticipatory anxiety, which provides the motivation for their avoidance. This in turn allows the sufferer to dwell on her inadequacy and irrational fearfulness, leading to depression. Attempts to rise above all of this and actively confront the problem situations are likely to fail, because the agoraphobic is by now so sensitive to signals of impending panic that she practically creates them at the drop of a hat. A further cycle of self-denigration and discouragement ensues.

Accounts such as Fishman's (1980) are, of course, difficult to verify, as we indicated at the beginning of the section; nevertheless, the complexity of the agoraphobic syndrome seems to demand a suitably complex aetiological account, even if this poses problems of confirmation. Another, perhaps more detailed, account is provided by Chambless (1978) and Goldstein and Chambless (1978).

Chambless (1978) reviews, and finds inadequate, learning theory accounts of the aetiology of agoraphobia based on classical conditioning and operant learning. Lazarus' (1966) 'broad spectrum' view is more promising, because he suggests that not only could classical conditioning procedures explain specific fears of places, but escape and avoidance responses would be negatively reinforced by anxiety reduction. Most important, the patient's phobic behaviours could also be positively reinforced by attention from other people and reduced responsibilities to the household. Another account that goes a little beyond a straightforward classical conditioning view is that of Goldstein (1970) and Wolpe (1969): In agoraphobia, there is a form of semantic conditioning, in which the sufferer feels trapped in an undesirable life-situation, and hence fears physical surroundings in which he or she could feel trapped (for example, being confined in the dentist's chair, or having to wait in a queue at the supermarket check-out).

Chambless (1978) proceeds to review some of the psychodynamic formulations, and finds these lacking in important respects, not the least of which is that they have not led to effective treatments of agoraphobia. An early Freudian view was that the phobic individual projects 'dangerous' impulses (sexual and aggressive) onto others, and displaces a sense of danger emanating from a significant other person to some aspect of the physical environment. Bowlby's (1973) concept of separation anxiety and the importance of the fear of abandonment seem to fit clinical observations of agoraphobia.

In a 'reanalysis' of agoraphobia, Goldstein and Chambless (1978) argue that a composite of behavioural and psychodynamic views is necessary to give a complete account of the aetiology of agoraphobia. People with uncomplicated fears of streets and public places do not qualify as agoraphobics; they have specific fears that are likely to respond to systematic desensitization. 'Complex agoraphobia', the more common syndrome, applies when the individual displays a constellation of clinical features including a typical personality orientation. The patient is lacking in self-sufficiency and assertiveness, and tends (mistakenly) to attribute unpleasant physical sensations to the immediate surroundings, rather than to the actual source: tensions resulting from interpersonal conflict. The central phobia is of the fear reaction itself, which then, in a secondary process, allows specific surroundings to take on conditioned unpleasantness. The patient is trapped in an unpleasant set of life circumstances, often a troubled marriage, but he or she cannot realistically leave the marriage (because of the lack of self-sufficiency and general dependent posture), or act assertively to resolve the conflict constructively (because of the tendency not to recognize the existence of the conflict, and the general lack of assertive skills). The conflict is resolved, partly, by the agoraphobia, implying an inability to leave the home. Agoraphobic fears are most pronounced in settings in which the sufferer feels physically trapped, which is symbolically reminiscent of the conflict.

There are several criticisms of this formulation which we take up later. However, helpful aspects of this view are that it does provide an account of the link between agoraphobia and interpersonal difficulties, and it does suggest hypotheses for understanding the notorious failure of systematic desensitization to provide effective clinical management of agoraphobia.

CONCLUSIONS

The chief problem with theories of aetiology is in confirming or refuting them. It is always possible to cite case studies in which the sequence of events is consistent with that predicted by the theory; cases which do not accord with the theory can be defined out of contention (Emmelkamp, 1979). Research reviewed in Chapter 5 shows clearly that, as far as treatment is concerned, agoraphobia is very different from simpler phobias, and this may well be reflected in a more complex aetiological picture. Some evidence reviewed here suggests that agoraphobia is intertwined with interpersonal and other difficulties, and evidence from treatment research provides partial support for the idea that treatment of the phobic behaviour *per se* may prove incomplete as broad clinical management of the patient. Nevertheless, the correlational data adduced to confirm theories of aetiology do not, strictly, confirm anything but the existence of a relationship. There is a definite need at this point for an analogue model for agoraphobia, similar to Seligman's (1975) 'learned helplessness' model of depression, that could generate testable hypotheses. Until researchers can prospectively induce agoraphobia-like behaviour experimentally, however, no theory of aetiology can be definitively proven. We can, however, take heart from the fact that general aetiological theories can be *dis*proved, simply by finding a contradictory example. As more evidence accumulates, presumably there is a greater chance of some of the rival theories being disconfirmed.

CHAPTER 4

Assessment of Agoraphobia

CLINICAL AND RESEARCH ISSUES IN ASSESSMENT

Research into the treatment of agoraphobia has mainly been conducted by practising clinicians who are well aware of methodological issues, on the one hand, and clinical realities, on the other (e.g. Emmelkamp, 1979; Marks, 1975; Mathews *et al.*, 1981; see Chapter 5). Yet there have been some understandable differences in emphasis between clinical and research evaluations of agoraphobia in terms of what is assessed and how assessment is conducted. Despite the considerable overlap of assessment issues in these two domains, the clinician has special assessment concerns not always shared by the researcher. For example, regardless of theoretical orientation toward assessment, early considerations for the clinician are usually those of general clinical management: the appropriateness of inpatient, outpatient, or home-based treatment; whether or not the patient presents major difficulties of greater clinical urgency than agoraphobia; and whether what sounds at first hearing like a typical description of agoraphobia turns out on further examination to be a simpler fear of streets or the like (Goldstein and Chambless, 1978).

In terms of the assessment issues involved, there is a contrast between the service-oriented mental health clinic or department, in which practitioners take on 'all comers' who range from the overtly psychotic to the normally troubled, and the research or 'special clinic' setting, in which agoraphobic sufferers may be sought actively and patients with other problems excluded. In the former setting, the practitioner first has to recognise 'agoraphobia'—to discern it from the background of a variety of other clinical problems and syndromes — and then conduct a suitable assessment to lead to an individual treatment formulation. In the research or specialized setting, the clinician already has something of a 'set' for agoraphobia, and the assessment concerns may be matters of subtle detail from the outset. Furthermore, there are differences in terms of the breadth of clinical concern in clinical versus research settings. For the mental health professional in a health centre, the appropriate role may be that of 'case manager'—a perspective from which the total care of the patient is addressed. In this way, referrals to other professionals can be co-ordinated, and clinical reports centralized, by a clinician who oversees the total clinical management of the patient. This broad clinical concern will influence the breadth of the assessment issues addressed.

In the research clinic, the extent of the assessment issues addressed depends on the amount of information available at the time the patient is referred and on the character of the relationship between the research centre and the referring agency. In some instances, the research clinic staff will assume responsibility for complete assessment and total clinical management, but in others the patient may be referred for treatment of specific agoraphobic anxieties while the referring agency provides, for example, for medicinal treatment of depression, and family therapy to help resolve areas of interpersonal conflict. In some cases, then, the research clinician may tend to examine anxiety and avoidance behaviours in great detail, to the relative neglect of the interpersonal context and broader clinical concerns. It is clear that the comprehensive clinical management of agoraphobia requires attention to the broadest spectrum of the patient's areas of functioning (see Chapter 8).

Finally, researchers studying representative groups of agoraphobics to identify effective treatment procedures and key components of the therapeutic process usually perform specific assessment activities at various stages of the research that may be unnecessary for the practising clinician working with a routine referral.

In this chapter we will discuss clinical issues in assessment first, and then proceed to specific research instruments and so forth.

GENERAL ISSUES IN CLINICAL ASSESSMENT

Breadth of assessment

Mental health practitioners vary widely in type of professional training and theoretical persuasions about psychotherapy. Aside from these issues of training and orientation, clinicians assess different aspects of the problem at different times: the patient (in terms of personality, cultural background, etc.); the problem (when and where it is manifested, whether it is based on situational anxiety or lack of appropriate social skills, etc.); and the treatment approach (the extent to which treatment techniques have been appropriately sequenced, the degree to which a certain number of sessions have brought benefit, etc.).

In behaviour therapy, the usual foci are on the patient's current complaints and concerns across several dimensions of functioning (Lazarus, 1976), on the interactions between the person and the environment that provides the context for the concerns (Kanfer and Saslow, 1969), and on the sequence of events surrounding the problem behaviour and which, when assessed, can lead to hypotheses about the functional relationships between these events (Chambless and Goldstein, 1980). Understanding these functional relationships can lead to establishing an efficient plan of action for effecting change, and comprehensive assessment assures that important concerns will not be neglected.

Chambless and Goldstein (1980) and Goldstein and Chambless (1978) have argued that agoraphobia is a complex and multifaceted syndrome that goes far beyond the straightforwardness of simpler phobias. 'Complex agoraphobia', to these writers, is defined by the presence of four characteristics:

1. Fear of the panic attack as the most prominent phobic element (as opposed to fears of streets and crowds themselves)
2. Onset of panic attacks in a climate of interpersonal or other conflict
3. A tendency for the patient to misunderstand the source of his or her panic or anxiety (for example, whereas agoraphobics commonly regard their panic attacks as unpredictable, on analysis it often appears that they follow interpersonal episodes in which certain emotions, like anger, are aroused but quickly suppressed)
4. A tendency for the patient to have difficulties in acting assertively or in mobilizing a sense of self-sufficiency.

This formulation clearly indicates the need for a thorough and broad-ranging assessment.

Further arguments in favour of a comprehensive and detailed assessment are provided by Hallam (1978), who, similarly to Goldstein and Chambless, takes a fresh look at the concept of agoraphobia. To Hallam, agoraphobia is incorrectly labelled as a phobia, because agoraphobics do not unanimously fear a specific object or situation. Instead, they fear general and abstract dangers, such as dying or losing control, and these fears often occur in public places. However, avoidance of streets or crowds does not guarantee freedom from anxiety. Many agoraphobics panic when alone at home, for example. Cues available in public places potentiate the effects of fear from other sources, producing the panic attack. Hallam notes that the popular emphasis on 'phobic avoidance' may have led researchers astray. Concluding that agoraphobia may best be regarded as an occasional feature of anxiety neurosis, Hallam recommends two new approaches to assessment:

1. Examining the 'coping strategies' commonly engaged in by people in general (including staying at home; drinking moderately or to excess; ingesting medication; etc.)
2. Identifying the thoughts or self-statements that precede the anxious or depressed mood.

Each recommendation points to the potential utility of assessing the 'cognitive modality' (Lazarus, 1976; see below) of the patient's functioning.

The multimodal approach as an assessment framework

The multimodal assessment schema introduced by Lazarus (1975, 1976) is an invaluable resource to the clinician as a means to gaining a comprehensive view of the patient's concerns. The 'BASIC ID' acronym (for behaviour, affect, sensation, imagery, cognition, interpersonal relations, and drugs/diet) is a helpful mnemonic and a serviceable checklist. The clinician enquires, in respect of each of the seven modalities, which events the patient is dissatisfied with or would wish to decrease, and which he or she would like to increase. An example from a psychiatric inpatient seen recently by one of us goes as follows.

Behaviour: would like to become more outgoing socially and in general to exert more self-control in terms of planning for the future rather than leaving things to chance. Affect: decrease depressiveness and sadness; deal with anger more appropriately—not necessarily to try to eliminate it, but to express it openly yet not offensively. Sensation: gain a sense of carefree relaxation; reduce migraine headaches. Imagery: develop some positive fantasies about the future; reduce nightmares and occasional waking imagery of her ex-husband abusing her. Cognition: encourage supportive self-statements; reduce defensive attitudes towards people. Interpersonal relations: develop trust in others; decrease suspiciousness. Drugs/diet: start an exercise programme, to include jogging; decide one way or the other about what to do about smoking.

In addition to enquiring about the problem *content* of each modality of functioning, the clinician may also ask about the patient's *ability* to function in each area (Wilkins and Thorpe, 1978). For example, the patient's ability to produce clear visual and other imagery may be decisive in determining whether or not to use systematic desensitization in treatment. Lazarus (1976) suggests also that if a patient fails to mention a particular modality when providing general assessment information, that modality may turn out to be especially important to enquire about; however, this argument is impressionistic rather than data-based (Thorpe and Wilkins, 1977).

As a guide to areas of enquiry in assessing agoraphobia, the multimodal approach is particularly helpful in three ways. First, the cluster of phobic and avoidance behaviours are likely not to be the only issues for the agoraphobic patient. Agoraphobia (meaning, for the moment, its phobia-like manifestations) often presents in a context of depression, marital dysfunction, low self-esteem, and so forth. In fact, the more complex case seems to be the more common referral (Goldstein and Chambless, 1978; Thorpe *et al.*, 1982). The BASIC ID reminds the clinician to enquire into each area. The physiological domain ('drugs/diet') is important in assessment because of the risk that the clinician may overlook problems like hypoglycaemia, which may complicate the clinical picture by masquerading as agoraphobia. Assessing functioning in each of the seven areas guarantees broad coverage.

Second, multimodal assessment is helpful in formulating the phobic nucleus *per se*. Avoiding crowds is a behaviour; feeling 'panicy' is affective, with sensory correlates. Enquiring into imagery and cognitive domains may produce invaluable pointers for treatment planning. For example, if the patient is alarmed by vivid images of becoming psychotic in a crowded place with people jeering and mocking her as she does so, then a similar item could be included in a desensitization hierarchy. If she reports frequently reminding herself 'I will probably never be able to go shopping like a normal person', she could be shown in therapy that this kind of self-statement can be seen as part of the problem, not simply a reaction to the problem. Some form of cognitive restructuring therapy could then be included in treatment planning, for example. If the patient confesses to using alcohol as an aid to confronting challenging situations, or to relying more and more on the minor tranquillizer originally prescribed for occasional use, the degree of dependency on the drug can be assessed by an experimental period of abstinence.

A final advantage of the BASIC ID is that it can be used to assess response to treatment, even if some problem modalities were not directly addressed by treatments presumed to operate through those modalities (Wilkins and Thorpe, 1978). We will try to show in Chapter 5, for example, that some behavioural treatments that appear to ignore cognition in fact turn out to be effective methods of cognitive restructuring.

EVALUATION FOR THERAPEUTIC INTERVENTION

Identifying agoraphobia

Classic clinical descriptions of agoraphobia are provided by Marks (1970) and Westphal (1872); see also Chapter 1. Common features include fears in crowded and/or confined places, difficulties in travelling away from home or a place of safety, and the experience of panic attacks. Of course, not every agoraphobic reports problems in each of these areas: fear of confinement is not always present, and often travel is possible by some means (for example, by car) but impossible by others (often buses or trains). It is important to identify some situational context for the fear, even if, as is true in most cases, few situations guarantee complete freedom from fear. Without a situational component, the syndrome may best be regarded not as a phobia but as an anxiety neurosis (Hallam, 1978). More important is the possibility that a physical disorder is implicated, in which case a medical evaluation is urgently required.

Another important limitation is that agoraphobia is not a specific fear of streets and crowds as exogenous stimuli. Goldstein and Chambless (1978) and Wolpe (1969) regard desensitization hierarchies of scenes to do with streets and shops as irrelevant to agoraphobia (but not, of course, to a specific fear of streets). Zaccheo and Palmer (1980) provide a case illustration in which desensitization was unsuccessful when it focussed on specific external surroundings, but brought clear benefit when the patient was desensitized to an hierarchy with a 'loss of control' theme.

To Goldstein and Chambless, agoraphobia is based on anxiety resulting from interpersonal conflict, but this anxiety is misattributed to external situations. It is therefore missing the point to view anxiety as a conditioned response to streets. The clinician working from this perspective would be likely to enquire carefully about areas of interpersonal conflict in the patient's life, to the relative neglect of details of how long the street, or how capacious the shop, in which anxiety is experienced. Goldstein and Chambless also assume that the agoraphobic lacks a sense of self-sufficiency, and it is accordingly important to assess this. The Sixteen Personality-Factor Questionnaire (16PF; Cattell, 1957) may be helpful here, because some of its categories can help predict favourable response to treatment.

Problem formulation

Treatment plans for agoraphobic patients include procedures ranging from prolonged confinements in supermarkets to sessions of marital therapy, depending on the needs of the individual sufferer. Evidence shows variously that agoraphobics are best treated *in vivo* in groups; assertiveness training may be helpful; treatment of depression may be necessary; and marital therapy is often indicated. It is accordingly helpful not only to determine the extent to which these areas are important to address in the agoraphobic individual, but also to assess the patient's suitability for the procedures involved in these various treatment modes (cf. Wilkins and Thorpe, 1978). The cooperativeness of the patient's spouse can be an important factor, for example.

An essential consideration in treatment formulation is the degree to which the patient's avoidance behaviour masks, manages, or holds in abeyance other problems, such as marital strife or sexual dysfunction (Hafner, 1977b; Hand and Lamontagne, 1976). It is conceivable that agoraphobic behaviour entails a dependence on the spouse that in turn could provide a basis for some sort of relationship in a troubled marriage, for example. Although such features of the problem are commonly labelled 'secondary gain', usually leading to a pejorative general characterization of the patient, it is usually most helpful to enquire quite sincerely about the advantages of being phobic and the problems that may emerge when agoraphobic anxiety is resolved. Avoiding for the moment the difficulty of making statements about causality (let alone the direction of causality—see Hafner, 1977b), the development of agoraphobic behaviour in a marital partner is likely to be associated with some change in the household routine. Such changes are not necessarily pathological or even undesirable, of course, but nevertheless the onset of agoraphobia is likely to pose some potential problems of adjustment for sufferer and spouse. Similarly, then, when agoraphobic anxiety is successfully resolved by means of short-term therapy, new adjustments—for patient and spouse—are probably called for. Even if resolution of agoraphobic difficulties is unequivocally regarded as a change for the better, such significant 'life-changing' events are well known to be, almost by definition, stressful (Holmes and Rahe, 1967).

It follows from this that, (i) for any agoraphobic, some stress may be produced by successful treatment, because of the inevitable change in life-style that results, and (ii) for some agoraphobics, successful treatment of phobia-like anxiety may expose other problems, for example longstanding marital problems, that in a sense had been masked by the agoraphobic anxieties and concomitant dependent behaviours. Treatment would be incomplete if the assessment formulation neglected such important background considerations. This is not to imply, however, that it is necessary to discover all such complicating issues at the outset; it is often unrealistic to expect to. It is commonly at the point that initial treatment of the specific difficulties with crowds and shops has been concluded that further assessment of 'hidden issues' becomes possible. It is in any case important for the clinician to remain as flexible as possible in treatment planning, because there are no clear, general guidelines for either the selection of a 'treatment package' to address the agoraphobic syndrome, or for the appropriate sequencing of the component treatments; and, despite the impressive commonalities in the pattern of problems usually presented by agoraphobics, there is of course an infinite number of combinations and permutations. It is sufficient to note that the agoraphobic syndrome is not always limited to fears in public, confined, and faraway places, but commonly includes less easily-detectable marital conflicts, misattributions, and a non-assertive social posture. These possibilities are important to assess.

The syndrome concept

In our discussion above about some obvious and not-so-obvious 'background' features in agoraphobia, we have raised some issues that psychodynamically-oriented therapists would regard as relevant to the 'symptom-disease' formulation. It may well be that some aspects of a patient's problem (e.g. sexual inadequacy) may in a sense be fundamental to the development of others (e.g panic attacks); this possibility is not disputed. Instead, we take the view that it is an empirical matter to discover what functional relationships exist, and whether or not they are reciprocal, reversible, and so forth.

In medicine, there is a distinction between 'nosographic' and 'nosologic' terms. Nosographic concepts describe a disorder without making any assumptions about underlying causes; nosologic concepts both describe the illness and imply certain aetiological factors (Harzem and Miles, 1978). In our discussion, we will attempt to describe features of agoraphobia nosographically so as to avoid unintended semantic implications or nosologic language. In this way, we can discuss possible interactions between non-assertive social behaviour, marriage or sexual difficulties, or panic attacks, without admitting or denying the possible primacy of any one of them.

An important issue here that is separable from the 'problem versus symptom' issue is that different patterns of clinical problems lead to different predictions of which treatments will be effective. If Goldstein and Chambless (1978) are correct, for example, it is helpful to reserve the term 'agoraphobia' (however inadequate the term may be) to describe the disorder in which sufferers lack a sense of self-sufficiency, are beset by conflict in their important relationships, and who fear fear. Using the term in this way reminds the clinician not only to address the anxiety and panic attacks, but to consider the likelihood that marital therapy and assertiveness training will bring benefit in respect of the difficulty with conflict, and to remember to include in the treatment plan some methods for increasing self-assurance and self-awareness in order to combat the tendency toward misattribution and the general phobic posture.

But not only does the Goldstein and Chambless description of agoraphobia serve as a reminder to look out for all typical features of this disorder, but it also implies, by distinguishing agoraphobia from other phobias in this way, that perhaps different anxiety-reduction treatments are effective with agoraphobia than are helpful with other phobias. In fact, Goldstein and Chambless produced their reformulation in part because of the research evidence that desensitization, effective with many other phobias, is in general inferior to direct exposure methods like *in vivo* flooding in treating agoraphobic anxiety and panic attacks (Mathews, 1977b; Thorpe *et al*., 1982). Hence, diagnosing 'agoraphobia' not only suggests looking into areas of interpersonal conflict and so forth, but also indicates treatment by flooding as opposed to other methods like desensitization. Other patients who fear streets and the like but do not show the other features of the agoraphobic syndrome may be desensitized.

A counter-argument here is that we need only perform a broad-ranging evaluation, using, for example, Lazarus' (1976) multimodal approach, and select a battery of treatments such that each treatment addresses one or more problems. In this way, there would be no need to quibble about the diagnosis and no need to dichotomize people into 'agoraphobic' and 'nonagoraphobic'. If the person fears streets, then a method for reducing anxiety can be sought. If the person has a troubled marriage, appropriate counselling or therapy can be offered. If the person has difficulties identifying or expressing feelings in interpersonal contexts, then this problem can be addressed also.

A key issue here is whether or not it is valuable to regard agoraphobia as a syndrome. 'Syndrome' implies something over and above a list of problems or symptoms (Cheshire, 1975). The argument goes like this: whereas one might prescribe assertiveness training for the individual whose only complaint is of anxiety about speaking straightforwardly to resolve conflicts in close relationships, and desensitization for one who presents a specific fear of shops, *in vivo* flooding could be the treatment of choice for the agoraphobic who has problems with interpersonal conflict *and* experiences panic in crowded places. The patient who presents the fear of streets or shops has 'simple agoraphobia'; the patient who displays these fears in the context of low self-sufficiency and marital conflict suffers from the 'complex agoraphobia' syndrome (Goldstein and Chambless, 1978). More importantly, treatments successful with simple agoraphobia or other phobias will be less effective with complex agoraphobia, and accordingly accurate assessment of the disorder being presented is of crucial importance for treatment planning.

There are difficulties with the syndrome concept. First, it is possible to have disputes about whether or not the patient 'really is' a 'true' agoraphobic, for example, thus tempting the researcher and practitioner to become embroiled in unnecessary reifications. Similarly, it becomes difficult to specify how many, or which, of a cluster of problems one needs to have before one's difficulties are classed as exemplifying the syndrome, and hence considerable heterogeneity within a syndrome or diagnostic class can emerge (Davison and Neale, 1978). Along similar lines, Phares (1967) presents a general critique of conventional practices in psychiatric diagnosis:

> Each new generation of clinicians must learn the three basic lessons of psychiatry:
>
> 1. People within the same diagnostic category are notoriously dissimilar from another.
> 2. Psychiatrists have never been able to agree amongst themselves as to who belongs in which category.
> 3. Categorization of patients has little to do with their treatment or disposition (Phares, 1967).

Despite the criticisms, aspect of the 'syndrome' issue are testable, for example the question: 'Are different treatments effective with agoraphobia than are effective with other phobias?' There are clear indications, from studies specifically designed to answer this question, that *in vivo* flooding is preferable for agoraphobia, whereas desensitization is more helpful with other phobias (Marks *et al*., 1971; Mathews, 1971; see also Chapter 5). However, this was not confirmed in a later experiment by Gelder *et al*. (1973). The research strategy involved is to divide patients into groups on the basis of relevant patient variables (such as 'simple' versus 'complex' agoraphobia, or 'agoraphobia' versus 'other phobias'), and then to divide each group further into subgroups receiving different treatments.

Relevant to this, Marks and Bebbington (1976) describe a 'space phobia' which is some ways resembles agoraphobia but in other ways does not. Age of the patient at onset is 30 years later in space phobia; the fear in space phobia is of fainting or falling when no physical support is available; and in this disorder public places occasion only mild fear. Exposure *in vivo*, a familiar treatment for agoraphobia, was used in two of the four cases reported, apparently with some success. Marks and Bebbington caution that it is too early to make confident recommendations about treatment in other cases. If later research shows *in vivo* exposure to be generally helpful for space phobics, then the syndrome issue will be relatively unimportant (at least for treatment selection). If a different treatment turns out to be more helpful, then identifying the syndrome will be of great importance in treatment planning.

The clinical interview

The clinician is acting conventionally in diagnosing agoraphobia when the major presenting features are fear of leaving home, crowds, confined places, public transport, and fear of fear. The presence of marital discord, low self-sufficiency on the part of the patient, and a tendency to deal with interpersonal conflict indirectly further substantiate the diagnosis. Chambless and Goldstein (1980) provide some helpful illustrations of 'simple' versus 'complex' agoraphobia by presenting brief transcripts from interviews, in which it becomes plain that patients describing clear situational contexts for the fear with a plausible rationale for anxiety are the 'simple' agoraphobics, whereas the 'complex' agoraphobics tend to report inexplicable, 'out of the blue' panics that began without any apparent rhyme or reason. Careful, open-ended questioning may reveal some connections between the onset of agoraphobic problems and certain life events—connections that have, previously, eluded the patient. The fact that this pattern (the patient not recognizing some apparently obvious connections) is quite typical in agoraphobia is consistent with the Goldstein and Chambless theory that agoraphobics find it difficult to account for feelings of tension or apprehension otherwise than by attributing them to specific fears of their immediate surroundings or to vague fears about madness or death (Hallam, 1978).

The patient's spouse is usually available for interview, because agoraphobics often have difficulty attending clinics alone (at least at the initial assessment stage). It is desirable to include the spouse in assessment at some point because the spouse will often play a part in treatment: first, because the marital conflicts that are often implied by the diagnosis of agoraphobia in one partner may be most directly addressed by means of couple counselling; and second, because home-based practice exercises may be facilitated by spouse involvement (Mathews *et al*., 1977), and accordingly it is helpful to assess the spouse's level of interest and motivation for participating in such a treatment approach.

Other areas for assessment are the kinds of coping strategy usually attempted by the patient in confronting anxiety, and the extent to which the patient recognizes and understands his or her emotional reactions to interpersonal ups and downs. These issues are important in identifying areas that need treatment, and in selecting specific treatments for their remediation.

Interview-based behavioural assessment is characterized by enquiry into specific details of the problem behaviour and its antecedents and consequences (Kanfer and Saslow, 1969; Lick and Katkin, 1976). For example, elucidating the patient's conception of 'nerves', 'panic', or 'anxiety' may involve listing bodily sensations, emotional feelings, self-statements, and avoidance behaviours in several situations, and identifying crucial time-intervals between stimulus and response. It may be helpful to ask the patient to attempt a venture into the feared environment with the therapist present, so as to enable the clinician to witness the problem behaviour *in situ*.

Agoraphobia commonly presents in the context of several other complaints or difficulties, including, as noted above, depression and interpersonal problems. These interpersonal problems seem at least correlated with (and may even be attributable to) the patient's sense of low self-sufficiency and his or her tendency to respond indirectly to interpersonal conflict. Assessment of the patient's social skills may lead to the recommendation that assertiveness training be included in the treatment plan (Chambless, 1978). Because assertiveness both entails forthrightness and implies self-assurance, assertiveness training may be doubly appropriate (see McFall and Twentyman, 1973, for behavioural approaches, and Thorpe, 1975, and Wolfe and Fodor, 1977, for cognitive-behavioural methods of assertiveness training).

Questionnaire measures

Questionnaires have the advantage of eliciting many data in a standard, structured form. Administering a questionnaire can save a great deal of interview time, and this is especially helpful when agoraphobia is involved because of the generality of the anxieties and the tendency for many aspects of the patient's life to be affected. Questionnaires on marital adjustment, interpersonal assertiveness, depression, and self-sufficiency may produce important prescriptive information. Inventories of agoraphobic behaviour (tendency to escape or avoid, or act defensively in, shops, streets, buses, etc.), and questionnaires about situational anxiety, to include assessment of social anxiety, are helpful in identifying specific problem areas efficiently and in providing a baseline against which to measure progress in treatment. Phobic rating scales have been an important feature of therapy outcome research in agoraphobia, and they have also been helpful in clinical practice; however, we will defer discussion of these rating scales until a later section on research instruments.

Marital adjustment

Apparently the most relevant questionnaire index of marital adjustment used in agoraphobia research has been the Marital Questionnaire devised by Crowe (1976, 1978) and subsequently revised as the Maudsley Marital Questionnaire (Crowe and Golombok, unpublished information). Scores on the earlier version of this measure have been used by Milton and Hafner (1979) both as an independent variable (to divide patients into groups on the basis of their degree of marital maladjustment) and as a dependent variable (to assess for beneficial changes in marital harmony after treatment). On this measure, the most maritally-troubled patients are likely to be those most at risk for relapse after successful treatment. However, there is no evidence to identify any broad treatment approach that is more helpful to maritally troubled versus untroubled agoraphobics; without such evidence, it seems best to offer marital therapy as a part of the whole treatment approach to those agoraphobics and their spouses who score as most disturbed on Crowe's questionnaire. Other inventories of this kind are discussed by Stuart (1980).

Other instruments that have been used by agoraphobia researchers also seem to bear on the issues of troubled interpersonal relationships and their role in maintaining agoraphobia. The Hostility and Direction of Hostility Questionnaire (HDHQ; Caine *et al*., 1967) and the Maudsley Hospital Questionnaire (MHQ; Crown and Crisp, 1966) have been used by Hafner (1977a, b), Hafner and Marks (1976), Hafner and Milton (1977) and Milton and Hafner (1979). The Hysteroid/Obsessoid Questionnaire (HOQ; Caine and Hope, 1967) has been used by Hafner and Milton (1977), and Milton and Hafner (1979). Research results with these measures are not simply summarized (see Chapter 3 for a fuller discussion), and it therefore seems best to use extreme scores to call attention to the possibility that concerns suggested by them could be addressed in therapy as part of the total approach.

Assertiveness and self-sufficiency

No specific assertiveness inventory has apparently been evaluated with agoraphobics. Inventories in common use include the College Self-Expression Scale (Galassi *et al*., 1974) and the Rathus Assertiveness Schedule (Rathus, 1973); the latter has been evaluated with psychiatric (Rathus and Nevid, 1977) and correctional (Heimberg and Harrison, 1980) groups.

The Bernreuter Personality Inventory Self-Sufficiency Scale (see Wolpe, 1969) has been a popular index of self-sufficiency despite the fact that it has not emerged unscathed from factor-analytic work (Gathercole, 1968). Another measure that has been used in several controlled trials with agoraphobics is the Sixteen Personality-Factor Questionnaire (16PF; Cattell, 1957).

Inventories like the Rathus, the Bernreuter, and the 16PF are broad-ranging and seem to measure general personality traits. At a more specific level, Bandura and Adams (1977) advocate the situational assessment of self-efficacy expectations on the rationale that this kind of 'microanalysis' can predict individual differences in treatment progress. Because this kind of assessment has been used more commonly in research trials than in clinical practice to date, and because inventories for general use have not yet been developed, we will discuss this topic more fully in a later section on research assessment methods.

Depression

Again, no measure has been evaluated specifically for agoraphobics. The Beck Depression Inventory (Beck, 1978) is widely available and in common use in many mental health facilities.

Inventories of agoraphobic behaviour

Specific questionnaires about agoraphobia have not been widely available. Representative inventories are those compiled by Burns (1977; see also Burns and Thorpe, 1977a, b) and Chambless (1978). These inventories each have several components: a section eliciting general demographic information, rating scales (for example, five-point scales of affective reaction to various phobic situations; Burns, 1977), and open-ended questions (for example, the patient is asked 'what runs through your mind' during a panic attack?; Chambless, 1978).

A general inventory of fears and phobias is the Fear Survey Schedule (Wolpe and Lang, 1964), which has been used widely in research on agoraphobia. An advantage of this instrument is that 'secondary phobias' can be assessed before and after treatment of agoraphobia as generalization measures (see Chapter 5). A similar inventory of fifty-five commonly feared situations has been used in survey research by Marks and Herst (1970) and factor-analysed to show, among others, a cluster of agoraphobic fears by Hallam and Hafner (1978).

Responses to the agoraphobia questionnaire designed by Burns (1977) provided the data reported in Chapter 2, and parts of the questionnaire are used as outcome measures in the experiment we describe in Chapter 6. Section 39 of the questionnaire is the important one here; it lists twenty-five agoraphobia-relevant situations, and patients rate each one on a five-point scale of level of fear and tendency to avoid. Data from the National Survey (Chapter 2) have recently been reanalysed by Johnston *et al*. (1982) so as to assess the possibility of forming a *cumulative* scale of agoraphobic fears.

Existing scales and self-report inventories are scored so as to give equal weight to each situational fear. A disadvantage of this is that two patients with the same score may have very different patterns of problems or of situations avoided. Johnston *et al.* (1982) divided National Survey respondents into three arbitrary cohorts of 200, 198, and 161 agoraphobics. Principal component analysis was performed on cohort 1 and replicated on cohort 2. Two factors emerged: an agoraphobia factor and a claustrophobic factor, the two cohorts producing strikingly similar results. 'Agoraphobia' accounted for 35.1 per cent of the variance in cohort 1, and 39.2 per cent in cohort 2; 'claustrophobia' accounted for 9.2 per cent (cohort 1) and 8.6 per cent (cohort 2).

Next, Guttman cumulative scaling techniques were applied to cohort 1 and the validity of the resultant scales was assessed by imposing them on the responses of cohorts 2 and 3. Results indicate that cumulative scales can be derived from the original questionnaire, and they are internally consistent and clearly replicable.

An advantage of these scales is that knowing a respondent's score on one of them allows a reasonably confident prediction of his or her profile of avoidance behaviours. Direct comparisons may be made between patients, and the scales are helpful in charting progress. Empirically, the scales are likely to be extremely useful in comparisons of graduated with confrontive exposure treatment; the scales will not only help in establishing a graded hierarchy of problem situations, but they also offer testable predictions about the dimensions along which therapeutic generalization takes place.

Prognostic indicators

Some relatively enduring patient characteristics are appropriate assessment targets because of their predictive potential (quite aside from indications mentioned above such as marital dysfunction). High 'extraversion' as measured by the Eysenck Personality Inventory (EPI; Eysenck, 1964) correlates with favourable response to behavioural treatment in some studies, and so do elevated Factors A and C on the 16PF (see Chapter 5). Data we present in Chapter 6 confirm these findings and reveal that high scores on 'neuroticism' (EPI) and the Fear of Negative Evaluation Scale (FNE; Watson and Friend, 1969) are negatively related to performance on a behavioural approach test relevant to agoraphobia. None of these measures leads to the prescription of one behavioural treatment technique as opposed to another, unfortunately. In fact, no data are available from prospective treatment trials to show that agoraphobic patients with certain descriptive attributes do better with certain treatments. One study is available in which the experimenters sought to manipulate 'expectancy of benefit' in an agoraphobic research sample, but outcome was not affected by 'expectancy'; nor is it even certain that a high expectancy was, in fact, induced by the procedure (Gelder *et al*., 1973).

In studies of clinical groups other than agoraphobics, *post hoc* analyses have sometimes produced data to suggest that treatments can be matched to patients on the basis of specific patient attributes. Speech-anxious volunteers who show high general social anxiety as measured by the Social Avoidance and Distress Scale (SAD; Watson and Friend, 1969) respond better to a cognitive-behavioural treatment, self-instructional training, than to systematic desensitization (SD), and conversely, the less generally-anxious subjects do better with SD (Meichenbaum *et al*., 1971). In chronically institutionalised male psychiatric patients, the older patients became more assertive after a 'socioenvironmental' treatment than in response to SD or relaxation training (Weinman *et al*., 1972). Other interactions of patient variables with treatments have been identified (DiLoreto, 1971; see also Lick and Katkin, 1976).

Self-monitoring and behavioural observation

Observation of the patient's behaviour in the feared situation for *assessment* purposes is more typical of controlled research programmes than of routine clinical practice (of course, patients are often observed in their feared surroundings in the course of routine clinical work, but this is rarely undertaken purely for assessment purposes). However, *self*-observation by the patient, in the form of making daily diary entries about home-based practice exploits, is (we hope) becoming more and more common in case management. In this kind of procedure assessment and treatment become difficult to distinguish, because these records not only provide data on progress but they tend to have a beneficially reactive effect in reminding the patient of the desired goals of treatment and actual progress towards them. Coupled with the fact that direct exposure to feared situations actually reduces anxiety, it is clear that this kind of *in vivo* self-observation is multiply helpful in assessment and treatment (Jannoun *et al*., 1980; Leitenberg *et al*., 1975; Mathews *et al*., 1977). A daily record of phobia-relevant activities was a component of the assessment battery used in the controlled trial we report in Chapter 6.

Cognitive assessment can take many forms, including the assessment of imagery, cognitive style, beliefs, expectations, attributions, and self-statements, and the sampling of thoughts *in vivo* (Kendall and Korgeski, 1979). *In vivo* thought sampling may be very helpful for agoraphobics, who can record not only their emotional reactions to *in vivo* exploits, but also their 'automatic thoughts' and possible 'rational' alternatives to the unhelpful ones. Coleman (1981) has devised a 'Daily Record of Dysfunctional Thoughts' specifically intended for use by agoraphobics, and this kind of assessment seems to be extremely promising; no data are available yet.

EVALUATION OF THERAPEUTIC OUTCOME

What to measure

It is important to note at the outset that it is not obvious what to take as the final criterion for deciding that treatment of phobic anxiety and behaviour has been successful. Behavioural approach/avoidance tests may provide compelling objective evidence of improvement, for example, whereas the patient may report continuing to feel extremely fearful. The resolution most favoured by researchers has been the one suggested by Lang (1968); that is, to measure the patient's responding within each of three response modes: verbal-cognitive, motor, and physiological. These, of course, form three of Lazarus' (1976) modalities (Wilkins and Thorpe, 1978). Triple-response-mode assessment has been used commonly in anxiety and phobia research on the rationale that events in each domain could serve to define 'anxiety'. The consistent observation that these three response modes do not often produce correlated outcome data has been taken to be both a rationale for the use of this multimodal assessment and a conceptual difficulty in the definition of anxiety (Cone, 1979; Nelson and Hayes, 1979).

Since Lang argued for triple-response-mode assessment of anxiety in 1968, other arguments in its favour have emerged. Wolpe's (1958, 1969) theoretical formulations, for example, placed great emphasis on the physiological mode, and he has defined anxiety simply in terms of autonomic responses (see also Lick and Katkin, 1976). Since then, Bandura (1977) has offered an important theoretical critique of two-factor theory; that is, the view that 'anxiety' (physiologically defined) *mediates* avoidance behaviour. Therefore, Bandura adds an important justification for multimodal assessment: defensive behaviour and subjective anxiety are correlated effects of expectancies of harm; hence, those originally correlated effects may well be at variance after treatment unless treatment addresses the causal expectancies. It is quite conceivable, for example, that a treatment procedure could beneficially inspire changes in overt behaviour without ameliorating autonomic 'anxiety', and *vice versa*. So as to provide data bearing on more than one theory, and to ensure comprehensiveness of assessment in treatment and research, multimodal assessment is clearly desirable.

Asynchrony among response measures

Researchers have found it particularly important to assess anxiety by self-report *and* behavioural *and* autonomic measures because these measures do not always correlate well. If self-report, behavioural, and autonomic observations invariably produced consonant results, then each measure would be concurrently valid with respect to each other, and only one kind of assessment would be necessary. This kind of synchrony is not usually observed. Barlow *et al*. (1980) illustrate the desynchrony of measures of heart rate and the self-report of anxiety in three moderate to severe agoraphobic women who had made clear behavioural gains from treatment. One patient who showed dramatic improvement on behavioural and self-report criteria (and who terminated treatment early because of her good progress) nevertheless showed increased heart rate post-treatment during a behavioural test; she had relapsed completely on the other measures 1 month later.

An important issue is whether or not Lang's three response modes are independent. The data (and the folklore) say they are (Lang, 1971), but there is a difficulty in interpretation here; low correlations among the three modes could mean *either* that they represent independent processes *or* that they are manifestations of the same process, but they are not being measured comparably. The contrasting concern is 'whether two behaviours are "really" related, or whether they are merely made to appear so because of the use of a common methodology' (Cone, 1979, p. 88). A further complication is that events described in terms of the three modalities can have reactive effects upon each other. For example, in Chapter 6 we report that patients who showed more avoidance (i.e. did not walk very far on a behavioural test of agoraphobia) showed less self-reported anxiety than patients who walked further; thus, patients showed 'anxiety' in one response mode but not in another. Presumably, walking only a moderate distance produced few phobic stimuli, and hence only slight self-reported anxiety. It is clear that, in this case, different things are being measured by the 'self-report' and 'behavioural' indices. For the self-report index to measure the same thing as the behavioural test, the inventory would have to be modified to enquire not 'how anxious did you feel while walking?' but, instead, 'how far did you walk?' (cf. Kazdin, 1979a). To Cone (1979), by thus examining the *content* as well as the *behaviour* (e.g. pulse rate, approach behaviour) and the *method* (e.g. self-report, observation by rater) involved in assessment, misleading system-method confounds can be eliminated.

Rating scales and self-report indices

Phobic rating scales

Marks and his colleagues (Gelder and Marks, 1966; Marks and Mathews, 1979; Watson and Marks, 1971) have found rating scales of phobic severity very helpful in research evaluations of treatment effectiveness (Emmelkamp, 1979). Typically, these scales have been completed by patient, therapist, and an independent assessor before and after treatment and at follow-up.

The original five-point rating scales of Gelder and Marks (1966) included questions about phobias, general anxiety, depression, obsessions, and depersonalization. Fear and avoidance aspects of phobias were combined on a given scale. Watson and Marks (1971) separated fear and avoidance ratings, but correlations between them were typically so high that later researchers have reverted to the combined scale (Marks and Mathews, 1979). Watson and Marks (1971) used nine-point scales (0–8), but this does not really contrast with those of Gelder and Marks (1966) because those five-point scales allowed half-points to be recorded. Nine-point scales seem optimal in phobic rating scales (Mathews *et al*., 1981).

Marks and Mathews (1979) describe a brief self-rating form that can be used to monitor progress in phobic patients. The rating form was compiled by researchers from three centres in England, and is recommended by the authors for general use in research to facilitate comparability of results from different trials. Patients rate the severity of a 'main target phobia', which they identify for themselves by writing in a description of the phobic situation. Other components of the rating form are 'global phobia' (a disability rating); a fifteen-item 'fear questionnaire' which divides into five items each on agoraphobia, social phobia, and blood-injury phobia; and 'anxiety-depression', referring to five common non-specific neurotic complaints. The fear questionnaire resulted from a series of factor-analytic studies (e.g. Hallam and Hafner, 1978; see also Marks and Herst, 1970), and the items represent the three most common phobias. The patient who does not have a blood-injury phobia but does suffer from a different specific phobia (as opposed to agoraphobia or social phobia — see American Psychiatric Association, 1980) can simply write it in, so the rating form is applicable to any phobic patient.

The ubiquity of the Gelder and Marks (1966) and Watson and Marks (1971) rating scales in clinical research in England and Holland has enabled Teasdale *et al*. (1977) to compare several reported studies and consequently to evaluate treatment effectiveness across studies. Nevertheless, researchers in different settings and countries continue to use a variety of measures that are difficult to compare. Another difficulty has been that different patients have been rated for different phobic concerns in some studies even when the same rating scales have been employed; this has made for difficulty in comparing the progress of different patients in the same study (Emmelkamp, 1979). In order to render future studies with agoraphobia more comparable, Emmelkamp recommends the use of the Watson and Marks nine-point anxiety and avoidance scales for five standard situations: walking away from clinic or hospital; a walk in a busy street; a journey by bus; entering a supermarket; and entering a restaurant. As it happens, all except the first of these situations are represented in the Marks and Mathews (1979) rating form (not available to Emmelkamp, of course, in preparing his 1979 chapter), and that item could easily be written in by a researcher. It is worth noting at this point that these situations are reasonably transferable cross-culturally: they seem at least relevant to European agoraphobics, and those who live in urban areas of the United States. The 'bus journey' item would not be relevant to many American rural areas; a reasonable substitute in some areas of the country could be a drive along a limited-access highway, in which situation many agoraphobics experience that sense of being 'trapped' and away from safety that is central to the phobia.

Behaviour therapists have tended to use self-report indices as dependent variables in research while retaining mixed feelings about their validity. It is clear that self-report measures are vulnerable to demand characteristics, for example (Bernstein and Nietzel, 1977; see below). Nevertheless, Lick and Katkin (1976) have summarized evidence that self-report indices of anxiety or fear may correlate well with independent behavioural observation. In general, the greater the specificity with which the questions on the inventory identify potential problem situations, the greater the relationship with observed avoidant or defensive behaviour.

Self-efficacy scales

Bandura (1977) has stressed the importance of assessing the patient's sense of personal effectiveness in dealing with a phobic situation. These efficacy expectations correlate well with behavioural indices of phobic severity, leading Bandura to conclude that a central mechanism in effective treatment is the enhancement of self-efficacy perceptions.

Self-efficacy scales used in the experimental treatment of eleven agoraphobics are described by Bandura *et al*. (1980). Each scale took the form of a hierarchy of fear-relevant exploits, in which each item would refer to the general properties of a challenging environment rather than to specific locations. Each item could be rated on a hundred-point continuum. *Level* of self-efficacy is represented by the number of tasks the patient judged he or she could accomplish; *strength* of self-efficacy is reflected by the average rating given each item on the hundred-point scale. Bandura *et al*. (1980) were careful not to enhance the correlation between self-efficacy and performance spuriously (which could have resulted if ratings had been made immediately before behavioural tests, if specific behavioural test items were rated, etc.). Fear-arousal (before and during performance) was, as predicted, closely correlated with strength of self-efficacy.

Self-efficacy scales may be used clinically in conjunction with ratings of fear and avoidance, although this kind of assessment is less formal than the research procedures of Bandura *et al*. (1980). Ratings of self-efficacy take two forms in a project currently in progress at the University of Maine (Thorpe *et al*., 1982).

Agoraphobic patients treated by group exposure *in vivo* routinely complete fifteen-item individual anxiety hierarchies. Confidence ratings are made by patients for each hierarchy item at various stages of treatment. These ratings are made on nine-point scales in response to the question: 'How confident do you feel about your ability to handle this situation successfully?' Scores range from 0 ('not at all confident') to 8 ('perfectly confident').

A second kind of rating is made by the patient immediately before and after tackling a phobia-relevant situation *in vivo*, and ratings of fear and avoidance are made at the same time (see Table 4.1).

Table 4.1. Situational confidence ratings*

BEFORE/AFTER NAME:——————————
SITUATION: DATE: ——————————
Please circle one number on each scale.

How confident do you feel about your ability to handle this situation?

Not at all confident	0	1	2	3	4	5	6	7	8	Perfectly confident

How anxious do you think you will be/were you in this situation?

Not at all anxious	0	1	2	3	4	5	6	7	8	Extremely anxious

How much would you prefer to avoid this situation?

Not at all	0	1	2	3	4	5	6	7	8	Very much want to avoid

*From Thorpe *et al*., 1982, Research in progress.

Behavioural observation

As Kazdin (1979a) has pointed out, the emphasis placed by most behavioural researchers on the potential situational specificity of behaviour is a double-edged sword. If we measure behaviour in specific situations because of our unwillingness to rely uncritically on its generality to other, even similar, situations, then we are at the same time posing grave problems for ourselves in ever making statements about treatment-produced generalization from one situation to another; 'if performance is specific to the situation in which it is assessed, current assessment practices for behavioural treatment evaluation may be severely limited' (Kazdin, 1979a, p. 57). A solution to this problem is to assess the problem behaviour in its natural environment, so that improvements detected by the assessment procedure are *ipso facto* improvements in the environment of greatest relevance to the patient. In the case of agoraphobia, the kind of behavioural test described by Emmelkamp (1979) and others is ideal—as part of the procedure to assess progress, the patient confronts the very surroundings in which the problem is evident in real life.

Behavioural tests take several forms. Observations by others of the patient's behaviour in the feared environment are usually taken to constitute the most relevant and valid data (Lick and Katkin, 1976). In agoraphobia, relevant behavioural approach tests (BATs; Lang and Lazovik, 1963) involve asking the patient to walk away from safety and recording how far the patient is able to progress. Such situations include walking away from home, entering and walking around in large shopping centres, or making trips by public transport. In any of these cases, data bearing on Hallam's (1978) hypothesis—that, for the agoraphobic, being away from safety is the crucial phobic element—are available. Researchers have recorded the duration of walks away from home or clinic (Emmelkamp, 1979) and distance actually walked (Watson *et al*., 1973). In other studies, researchers have assessed how far a patient can proceed within an hierarchy of *in vivo* exploits (Mathews *et al*., 1977), or records of progress within the most challenging phobic environments have been made (Hand *et al*., 1974; Teasdale *et al*., 1977).

Limitations of behavioural tests: demand characteristics

Despite the understandable popularity of performance-based behavioural tests, there are two major limitations: demand characteristics, and reactivity. Emmelkamp (1979) makes the point that not only is there a general 'demand' for the patient to do better after treatment than before, but different treatments may create different demands. A patient who has received confrontive direct exposure to the phobic situation in treatment may react differently to the instruction on a BAT to 'walk until anxious' from the patient who has been carefully desensitized. Similarly, 'waiting-list' control groups improve differentially on post-treatment behavioural tests with different experimental rationales for their status (Bernstein and Nietzel, 1977). It is important not to overstate this argument, as Bernstein and Nietzel acknowledge; in any event, in studies of agoraphobia, researchers have by now largely abandoned 'no treatment' comparison groups.

An issue commonly raised in discussing behavioural tests is the fact that researchers, not only the patients, may have certain expectations about treatment efficacy; indeed, researchers are *expected* to make specific predictions about the outcome of an experiment in advance of carrying it out (Cheshire, 1979). It is the usual practice for researchers who have made predictions about the outcome of the experiment not to participate in behavioural test sessions unless they have been 'kept in the dark' about the details of each subject's treatment. Otherwise, experimenters could unwittingly convey different demands to members of different experimental treatment groups by subtle facial cues, and so forth. This issue is not as clear-cut as it appears to be at first sight, however. One concern, that the researcher may influence the subject to act according to the former's expectation, may well be significant in respect of a self-report response, but of relatively minimal importance in the case of phobic avoidance *in vivo*. The latter may well be very resistant to this kind of subtle social influence. The related concern, that if the rater or observer has made a prediction of outcome, then his or her rating is automatically suspect and not to be trusted, has been challenged recently by Cheshire (1979, 1980). Nevertheless, conventional procedure includes the use of the 'experimentally blind' assessor (Thorpe, 1979).

Reactivity

The reactivity problem entangles three issues. One is the ubiquitous 'Hawthorne effect', in which observation by an experimenter has a general effect in altering behaviour in the desired direction (provided that a certain direction is 'desired' by experimenter and subject, of course). Another is increased familiarity with the assessment procedures, particularly when the same test is repeated after treatment and at follow-up assessment. An example would be a series of requests made by means of a tape-recording to an unassertive volunteer. The subject's simply knowing better 'what to expect' can produce more poised performance, creating the illusion that assertiveness has increased in an externally-valid way. The remaining, and the most problematic, concern is that behavioural tests which require agoraphobics to confront feared situations in fact constitute treatment. Hence, 'placebo treatment' comparison groups (and even 'no treatment' groups), the members of which are retested in a behavioural approach situation, actually receive treatment; as it happens, perhaps the best treatment available! Emmelkamp (1979) concludes that limits need to be placed on how often a research patient is behaviourally retested.

Other limitations on the external validity of studies with behavioural approach tests, summarized by Lick and Katkin (1976), include the fact that such tests are conducted in a 'safe' environment, and only a small sample of feared situations is examined. The use of behavioural tests in the natural environment, and especially with unobtrusive observation, counteracts these concerns (Kazdin, 1979a).

Psychophysiological assessment

Psychophysiological monitoring of heart rate or the electrodermal response has been a helpful feature of several studies (Lick and Katkin, 1976; Thorpe *et al*., 1982), but interpretation of such data is traditionally difficult. Indeed, some of these difficulties in interpretation have emerged only recently, because theoreticians have turned from early Wolpean formulations citing the primacy of autonomic reactivity toward theories challenging the 'anxiety-as-mediator', two-factor theory (Bandura, 1977; Franks and Wilson, 1978; Hineline, 1977; see Chapter 7). Reduction of autonomic anxiety is of course extremely helpful as part of the resolution of the problem, but there is no guarantee that reduction of autonomic anxiety *per se* changes phobic behaviour in other response classes.

In an uncontrolled series of ten patients with simple phobias, Watson *et al*. (1972) were able to show that physiological improvement (in terms of heart rate and skin conductance reduction) paralleled clinical improvement. However, as we have noted earlier, Barlow *et al*. (1980) report that an agoraphobic patient who improved in all respects except heart rate reduction in feared surroundings relapsed soon after treatment. Because more data are needed to clarify the relationships among self-report, behavioural, and physiological indices of clinical improvement, it is recommended that researchers assess their patients in all three areas wherever possible.

CHAPTER 5

Behavioural Treatment Research

Agoraphobia may be assessed and formulated in a variety of ways, and behaviour therapists have explored a similar variety of treatment approaches. Numerous case illustrations, clinical series, and controlled trials have been reported in which behavioural and quasi-behavioural treatment techniques have been pursued with agoraphobics. These treatments include paradoxical intention (Ascher, 1981), biofeedback (Chiari and Mosticone, 1979), cognitive restructuring (Coleman, 1981; Mancini *et al*., 1977), multi-faceted group treatment (Linder, 1981), thought-stopping (O'Brien, 1979), physical activity (Orwin, 1973), multimodal behaviour therapy (Popler, 1977), and supraliminal and subliminal exposure to phobia-relevant cinematic films (Tyrer *et al*., 1978). Other approaches include withdrawing social reinforcers held to maintain avoidance behaviour, investigating marital dysfunction and interpersonal conflict, helping the patient deal with panic attacks, and reducing situational anxiety directly by combinations of behavioural, cognitive, and pharmacological treatment strategies (Thorpe *et al*., 1982). The most systematic research programmes have focussed on identifying the important procedural parameters of situational anxiety-reduction techniques, and methods in which the patient is exposed to phobic stimuli in imagination or *in vivo* have received by far the most attention. These methods seem to rely theoretically on behaviour theory concepts of extinction or habituation (Marks, 1972a, b).

DEFINITIONS

Patients can be exposed to phobic material in fantasy or in real life, in graded steps or all at once, and protectively or confrontively. Exposure may be controlled by patient or therapist, and anxiety during exposure may or may not be attenuated by muscle relaxation or ingestion of a tranquillizing drug. Systematic desensitization (SD; Wolpe, 1958) involves the graded presentation of phobic material to the patient's imagination while he or she is deeply relaxed, for example, whereas *in vivo* flooding (Marks, 1972b) confronts the patient in real life with highly anxiety-provoking situations until fear responses eventually diminish. Although these procedures seem to be polar opposites in terms of the parameters mentioned above (Marks, 1969; Wilkins, 1973), it may nevertheless be more helpful not to dichotomize the techniques but to regard SD and flooding as lying at extremes of a continuum on these dimensions. Intermediate procedures are imaginal flooding (or 'implosion'; Stampfl and Levis, 1967), in which confrontation is in fantasy rather than in real life, and graded practice (Burns, 1977; Mathews *et al.*, 1977), or graduated exposure to real phobic situations with progress determined by the patient.

It is, therefore, somewhat arbitrary to attempt sharp distinctions between techniques labelled SD, graded practice, imaginal flooding, and *in vivo* flooding. In some studies, for example, patients are 'flooded' *in vivo* to successive situations within a graded hierarchy. Procedural parameters—imaginal versus *in vivo*, and so forth—are more important than the general labels. We will use the term 'flooding' to refer to unprotected or confrontive exposure to phobic stimuli, real and imagined. 'Exposure' is now the preferred term to describe confrontation by real phobic stimuli (Marks, 1981a, b), but we will retain the earlier term, flooding, in this review for convenience in classifying procedures. We can then discuss the advantages of *in vivo* over imaginal flooding, for example, in less cumbersome language.

SYSTEMATIC DESENSITIZATION

Early clinical and research reports

Marks (1969) has reviewed early reports of treatment of agoraphobia by SD. These reports were usually limited to uncontrolled case studies and clinical series, and results suggest that SD has been sometimes—but not reliably—more helpful than (undefined) individual and group 'psychotherapy'. However, outcomes have not been very impressive. Systematic desensitization treatment takes a lot of time (80 h per case in one report; Meyer and Gelder, 1963); does not always produce better results than ill-defined non-behavioural comparison treatments (Gelder and Marks, 1966); superiority of SD to such other treatments, where found, has diminished over follow-up intervals up to 2 years (Gelder *et al.*, 1967); and generalization of gains from treated to non-treated situations has been poor. Some reports were 'retrospective' studies of closed clinical records, data from which are extremely difficult to interpret. Finally, several reports of clinical series have confounded SD with graded practice methods.

It has been argued that SD has been unhelpful in the treatment of agoraphobia because the wrong hierarchy items have been selected. Usually, patients have been desensitized to situations—shopping centres, buses, and so on—whereas what they really fear is panic. Wolpe (1969) regards the former kind of hierarchy as irrelevant, and Goldstein and Chambless (1978) have reiterated this point: appropriate hierarchy items would describe sensations of fear and panic rather than the correlated environments. Zaccheo and Palmer (1980) give a relevant case-report. However, systematic research in this area—desensitization to fear and panic sensations—has not been reported with conventional SD. It is possible that imaginal and *in vivo* flooding, and graded practice methods, operate on the desensitization principle; in any case they are in general more helpful clinically than SD (see below).

Recent clinical research

Better-controlled studies of SD and agoraphobia in the 1970s have produced some encouraging results. An excellent study by Gelder *et al*. (1973) showed that SD was as effective as imaginal flooding, and both were superior to a credible comparison condition in which neither desensitization nor flooding procedures were implicated. This study is reviewed in more detail in a later section. Few treatment effects were found in a study by Evans and Kellam (1973), who compared therapist-administered SD with a semi-automated SD procedure. Twenty-four phobics, of whom twelve were agoraphobic, received sixteen half-hour treatment sessions. No behavioural test was used, and assessment consisted of self-report indices and global ratings of fear by a psychiatrist. No difference was found between the two SD variants. This study is unhelpful because conventional SD did not produce important clinical gains, and to argue that semi-automated SD performs as well as SD does not offer much assistance to the clinician.

Another procedural variation studied recently has been the role of muscular relaxation in SD. In an experiment with a 'cross-over' design, eight phobics (two of whom were agoraphobic) were desensitized, in one condition with, in the other without, muscle relaxation. Rating scales and physiological measures revealed no difference between conditions (Benjamin *et al*., 1972). This study is of limited significance because of the absence of behavioural assessment and the small number of participants. A more conclusive study by Gillan and Rachman (1974) used thirty-two phobics (comprising agoraphobics and 'specific' phobics), behavioural tests in addition to self-report and psychophysiological indices, and two comparison conditions: 'pseudotherapy' (SD to an irrelevant hierarchy) and 'psychotherapy' (insight and rational therapy). Systematic desensitization to a relevant hierarchy—with or without muscle relaxation—produced results superior to those derived from the comparison conditions, although behavioural test results did not clearly differentiate the groups. This study is important because it replicated with a clinically phobic group Davison's (1968) well-known analogue study of SD processes, and produced different results: the groups without muscle relaxation did as well as the standard SD group.

GRADED PRACTICE

Early reports of studies with single-subject designs have indicated that when agoraphobic patients are asked to walk away from the clinic until they become anxious, feedback and praise (social reinforcement) from the therapist have a clearly beneficial impact on progress (Agras *et al.*, 1968; Leitenberg *et al.*, 1968). Any beneficial effect resulting purely from the instruction to walk until anxious was transient, and in the baseline and reversal periods of the 'ABAB' design patients reported feelings of depression and made self-defeating statements. When praise was reinstated, 'lost' behaviour was rapidly reacquired, and the cognitive and affective discomforts were eliminated. Praise had a specific impact on 'distance walked' and 'time away' from the clinic, depending on which criterion was used for reinforcement. Practice in the real phobic situation was essential to the procedures (Leitenberg *et al.*, 1970). Relevant to this point, Marks (1972b) quotes Freud as follows:

> one can hardly ever master a phobia if one waits till the patient lets the analysis influence him to give it up . . . one succeeds only when one can induce them through the influence of the analysis to . . . go about alone and struggle with the anxiety while they make the attempt (Marks, 1972b, p. 129).

Despite the limitations of single-case studies and series, the use of reversal designs and the inclusion of severe agoraphobics allows some confidence to be placed in the results of these studies. Because urging real-life practice and then delivering feedback and praise for incremental gains do not conflict with the other behavioural strategies reviewed, the routine use of such encouragement, feedback and praise seems desirable as part of the clinical approach to agoraphobia. In particular, there is evidence that feedback of progress in the early stages of treatment is more important than praise for successful performance in encouraging initial gains (Leitenberg *et al.*, 1975), although in this study continuing time-in-therapy was confounded with the addition of feedback.

In an important controlled trial to evaluate effects of 'successive approximation' and 'self-observation' in sixteen agoraphobics, Emmelkamp and Ultee (1974) used a cross-over design in which patients received six 90-min sessions of each treatment. Successive approximation consisted of delivering praise and feedback for increasing time spent in the phobic situation; self-observation entailed self-recording by the patients of time spent outside without feeling tense (i.e. no praise or feedback was given by the therapist). Significant clinical gains were made on several variables; the two techniques compared did not differ in short-term effectiveness. This seems to confirm that practice in feared situations is the important variable. Nevertheless, feedback—therapist-delivered or noted by patients themselves—remains important. Feedback may remind the patient of the specific behavioural objectives of therapy, and slight but beneficial changes in target behaviour, otherwise unrecognized, may be detected and provide encouragement (and, possibly, perception of self-efficacy—Bandura, 1978) that facilitates further gains.

Studies of graded practice have largely involved single-subject methodology, with the exception of the cross-over trial just noted. Neither kind of study has produced long-term follow-up data corresponding to specific techniques, and research in this area is neeeded. Similarly, little is known about generalization effects. Available research allows us to conclude that graded practice, especially with feedback and social reinforcement, is genuinely helpful to severe agoraphobics even in isolation. Feedback is particularly helpful in initiating progress, consistent with Mathews' (1977b) view that treatments are successful to the extent that they promote real-life practice. It is also important to note that some studies of SD which produced beneficial results in the short term incorporated graded practice into the procedure (Gelder *et al*., 1967), a procedure strongly recommended by Agras (1967). For severe agoraphobics tested individually, real-life practice is an important feature of treatment. Research to be reviewed in a later section strongly indicates the inclusion of the patient's spouse in self-directed real-life practice (Mathews *et al*., 1977). Until research matching specific patient characteristics to response to specific treatments is available, the general recommendation derived from the experimental literature is for patients to enter feared situations in a graduated progression with encouragement, praise and feedback from therapist and significant others as an important component of treatment. A major advantage of involving the spouse in treatment is that professional time is curtailed, results comparable with clinic-based treatments are found, and continuing improvement has been noted in follow-up intervals up to 6 months. These issues are taken up again later.

FLOODING

A preliminary study by Boulougouris and Marks (1969) set the stage for a programme of research in this area by Marks and his colleagues. The paper reports the results of imaginal flooding and practice in a series of four phobic patients, including two agoraphobics; 'lasting improvement' resulted. Watson *et al*. (1971) treated ten patients with chronic phobias by prolonged *in vivo* exposure; patients were asked to confront the feared objects until anxiety diminished. The therapists abandoned attempts to maximise anxiety in treatment because this soon seemed to be counter-therapeutic. Modelling and social reinforcement were provided. All patients showed marked reduction of their phobias on clinical and physiological (heart rate and skin conductance) measures. Treatment lasted 6 h on average, and this brought benefit greater than that usually found after flooding in fantasy for a similar period of time, or indeed than over twice as much exposure to SD. These conclusions, of course, derive from a clinical series rather than from a controlled comparative trial.

More recently, Emmelkamp (1974) has emphasized the teaching of generalizable coping skills by means of self-directed *in vivo* exposure; and Mathews *et al.* (1977) report on an uncontrolled home-based treatment programme for agoraphobics. The patients took the responsibility for conducting self-directed exposure sessions, with the support of at least one other member of the family. Wherever possible, patient and spouse were given a comprehensive treatment manual from which to work. Spouses (invariably husbands) were given an additional manual with suggestions about support and encouragement. Results with eleven women agoraphobics were comparable with those of agoraphobic outpatients in treatment, and also to those of patients treated in groups. Improvement continued during a 6-month follow-up period. Progress was assessed by the patient and an independent assessor, and a behavioural test was used; the three ratings produced the same results. This study has since been successfully replicated by Jannoun *et al.* (1979).

These informal and uncontrolled demonstrations do not, of course, produce findings as reliable or revealing as the controlled trials to be reviewed; however, it is noteworthy that Watson *et al.* (1971) and Mathews *et al.* (1977) have been able to offer informal comparative data from other similar populations they have treated (and, more importantly, researched) using similar protocols and measures. The latter study in particular assumes importance in the context of studies of *in vivo* flooding in groups (to be reviewed below).

Finally, in the most recently-reported study (but one which in many ways fits a much earlier theoretical context), Greist *et al.* (1980) found that *in vivo* exposure instructions brought significantly more benefit to phobics than did instructions to avoid feared stimuli. The cross-over trial included seventeen patients (four obsessive-compulsives, thirteen phobics—five of these agoraphobics). This is clear evidence that actual exposure to phobic situations—at least when patients are instructed to confront such situations so as to *'learn . . . to tolerate your fear until it disappears'* (Greist *et al.*, 1980, p. 4, original italics)—is more effective than avoidance in reducing fears.

Relevant versus irrelevant stimuli in flooding

Watson and Marks (1971) treated ten agoraphobics and six patients with specific phobias by means of imaginal flooding. In an experiment with a 'cross-over' design, half of the patients received eight sessions of imaginal flooding to stimuli related to the phobias, followed by eight sessions of imaginal flooding to irrelevant fear cues, such as being mauled by a tiger (no 'psychodynamic' themes were employed). The other eight patients had the same treatments in the reverse order. If flooding operates by means of a specific extinction process, then flooding with relevant phobic stimuli would predictably bring greater benefit than the irrelevant fear cues. Surprisingly, phobias improved during each treatment phase, as measured by clinical and attitude scales, and by heart rate and skin conductance during phobic imagery. Different mechanisms appeared to be functioning in the treatments, because

1. In irrelevant fear flooding the outcome was better for those patients showing greater fear within sessions, whereas this was not true for phobic cues
2. Greater physiological arousal before treatment was associated with better response to 'relevant' flooding, but was unrelated to outcome with irrelevant fear
3. In the group which received relevant flooding first, this procedure appeared to protect the patients from excessive anxiety in the subsequent irrelevant fear sessions

No comparable effect was observed in the second group. These findings suggest that habituation plays a part in flooding procedures (Marks, 1972a).

A major difficulty with the experiment—which indeed applies to all similar 'cross-over' trials—is that follow-up data produce limited information. Although improvements were maintained at least up to 6 months after treatment, the only procedural difference between the groups at follow-up was the order in which treatment had been given; no follow-up data bearing on the relative long-term effects of the two treatments are available.

Brief versus prolonged flooding

Stern and Marks (1971, 1973a) sought to examine the relative merits of brief and protracted flooding. Sixteen agoraphobics were treated by either imaginal flooding (in 10- versus 80-min episodes) or *in vivo* flooding (in 30- versus 120-min episodes). Overall exposure-time was equated for 'brief' and 'protracted' conditions. Prolonged flooding *in vivo* was significantly more effective than brief flooding *in vivo*; within-treatment measures showed that greater anxiety-reduction (as measured by heart rate and self-reported anxiety) took place in the second hour. Imaginal flooding produced minimal change regardless of condition (brief or prolonged). As a result of these findings, Marks (1972a) suggests that flooding *in vivo* is the more recommended procedure, and for periods protracted beyond 1 h; he recommends that exposure be continued until the patient no longer experiences anxiety in any response mode (self-report, behavioural, or physiological).

There are at least analogue data to suggest that prolonged *imaginal* flooding is significantly more effective at lower levels of arousal, however. In a study with spider phobics, a single session of imaginal flooding was given by Mathews and Shaw (1973). Variables were continuous versus intermittent flooding, and high versus low anxiety during the imaginal exposure. The most helpful procedure was continuous, low-anxiety imaginal themes, in response to which subjects imagined themselves successfully coping with the feared situations. These results add to the consensus (cf. Hand *et al.*, 1974) of findings to the effect that the arousal of high anxiety during flooding is unnecessary. This concept has implications for the treatment of agoraphobia by means of a combination of behaviour therapy (flooding) and medicinal treatment (anxiety-reducing drugs); this material is reviewed in a later section.

With treatment-time equated, protracted flooding *in vivo* brings greater benefit than briefer exposure episodes. Foa *et al.* (1980) have recently provided data on the related issue of the distribution of treatment sessions when the sessions themselves are of equal length. Eleven agoraphobics were divided into two groups, in which twenty sessions of discussion (30 min) plus *in vivo* exposure (2 h) were given. The difference between treatment conditions was that in one, ten daily sessions were followed by ten weekly sessions, and in the other, ten weekly sessions preceded ten daily sessions. Assessments, made before treatment, at crossover, and after treatment, consisted of interviews with an independent assessor and nine-point rating scales of fear and avoidance. Massing of practice brought significantly more benefit than spaced sessions, particularly on the avoidance ratings.

Results of earlier trials which were not designed to address the hypothesis of Foa *et al.* (1980) are difficult to interpret because of the confounding of massing of practice with increased number of treatment sessions. Nevertheless, Foa *et al.* (1980) find indications that, for a given total treatment time, the greater the number of sessions, the better the outcome. Clearly, there has to be a limit to the brevity of treatment sessions, as indicated by the data of Stern and Marks (1973a) discussed above. A defensible conclusion is that, provided that sessions are protracted for at least two hours, it is desirable to offer treatment sessions as frequently as possible.

Imaginal versus *in vivo* flooding

Several other studies have compared imaginal with *in vivo* flooding. Emmelkamp and Wessels (1975) studied twenty-six agoraphobic patients, of whom seven had dropped out by the time of the mid-treatment assessment. Treatment conditions were prolonged exposure *in vivo*, imaginal flooding, and a combination of imaginal and *in vivo*, each for four 90-min sessions. All patients subsequently underwent eight 'self-observation' sessions, in which they exposed themselves to a graduated series of anxiety-arousing situations. Although imaginal flooding produced slight benefit, prolonged *in vivo* flooding was markedly superior, at least in terms of the therapists' ratings. 'Self-observation' brought great benefit to 'imaginal flooding' patients, but not to those who had had *in vivo* flooding. After the self-observation phase of the study, the groups were indistinguishable, at least up to 1 month after treatment. Mathews (1977b) notes that the flooding sessions in the study were completed in just over one week, and that the patients were not specifically advised to practise between sessions; these features of the study permit

Mathews to maintain his view that imaginal flooding is effective to the extent that it encourages the patient's own efforts to practise *in vivo*, which in turn brings benefit in the long term. This view also helps account for the fact that, in a study designed to answer similar questions to those of Emmelkamp and Wessels, Mathews and his associates found discordant results.

Mathews *et al*. (1976) sought to compare imaginal and *in vivo* flooding. A specific hypothesis was that imaginal flooding might facilitate later *in vivo* exposure, either by means of an immediate but temporary reduction in anxiety, or by an eventual extinction of anxiety, facilitating or potentiating *in vivo* exposure thereafter. The researchers tested this hypothesis by comparing a group in which *in vivo* exposure exercises followed each imaginal flooding session, with a group for whom a course of imaginal flooding was completed before real-life exposure was programmed. A third group of patients received real-life exposure only throughout the study. All patients had sixteen sessions of treatment. Thirty-six agoraphobic women took part in the study (twenty-one others had been assessed but did not participate in the whole study for various reasons), and three therapists conducted the treatment sessions. Assessments were made before treatment and after eight and sixteen sessions; a final assessment was made 6 months after that. The mid-treatment assessment (after eight sessions) allowed the researchers to compare the effects of eight sessions of imaginal exposure with the effects of the same number of *in vivo* exposure sessions, and also with eight sessions of combined imaginal and *in vivo* exposure. The immediate post-treatment assessment permitted comparisons of sixteen sessions of real-life exposure with two kinds of combined treatment: eight sessions of imaginal followed by eight sessions of *in vivo* exposure, versus sixteen sessions in each of which *in vivo* participation for 45-min followed 45-min of imaginal exposure.

Various conventional statistical analyses of the data were performed, none of which detected a treatment-group difference at any assessment session. Two variables analysed *post hoc* were predictive of favourable response to treatment: 'emotional stability', as measured by Factor C of the Sixteen Personality-Factor Questionnaire (Cattell, 1957), and a 'total expectancy score' (a composite of expectancy ratings about future performance on a phobic hierarchy). Neither variable interacted significantly with treatment-group. Conclusions offered by Mathews *et al*. (1976) include the recommendation that the clinician select a treatment technique in terms of its convenience, although *in vivo* exposure may be preferable because imaginal flooding was generally disliked by patients and therapists. It is important to note that, in this study, 'imaginal flooding' involved presenting to the patient scenes of the most feared situations *and* of the most feared *outcome* of being in such a situation, despite the graduated presentation of such scenes. By contrast, *in vivo* exposure, also graduated, progressed at the pace of the patient: therapists gave help in some cases where this was essential, and they gave simple reassurance and coping instructions. Another observation was that the least effective therapist in the study was male, and was relatively less experienced clinically.

The study was well-designed and executed, and included several measures: rating scales by patients, independent assessors, and therapists; psychometric tests; psychophysiological monitoring (heart rate and skin conductance); and behavioural tests. The lack of a comparison group that did not receive the specific treatments tested is a limitation, although comparisons with earlier similar studies seem to indicate that the outcome exceeded benefit attributable to unmeasured and pervasive features of treatment in general ('non-specific' effects). In any case, the tendency to include 'attention-placebo' or similar comparison groups as a matter of routine without a specific rationale has been criticized recently by Kazdin (1979b). The researchers placed considerable responsibility on the patients for home-based practice, keeping a diary of fear-related exploits, and so forth. The patients themselves attributed beneficial outcome first, to the therapists' encouragement and sympathy, and second, to practice and learning to cope with panic.

The researchers conducted an analysis of within-treatment data in order to investigate possible ephemeral anxiety-reduction or exposure-facilitating effects (Johnston *et al*., 1976). The only significant treatment-condition difference was that on semantic differential ratings of the hierarchy item to be approached next, *in vivo* exposure subjects recorded a significant positive change that was not evident for 'imaginal' subjects. A conclusion is that there are reliable, positive short-term effects of real-life exposure that are not apparent in the case of imaginal exposure. These analyses are, of course, *post hoc*, which limits any predictive interpretations. Johnson *et al*. (1976) found no evidence that imaginal flooding facilitates later exposure. Their general conclusions are reiterated by Mathews (1977b): although imaginal and *in vivo* exposure may differ in short-term effectiveness, they both facilitate practice between sessions; it is this practice that actually 'does the trick' in eventually helping the patient to overcome agoraphobic difficulties.

Individual treatment versus flooding in groups

Another procedural variant in flooding—imaginal and *in vivo*—is treating patients in groups as opposed to individually. A sample of nineteen agoraphobic women took part in a crossover study conducted by Watson *et al*. (1973). Treatment was given in three group sessions for a total of 9 h; three separate groups of subjects were involved. The sequence of events for a given group each treatment day was:

1. One hour of either imaginal or *in vivo* exposure to phobic situations ('imaginal' exposure involved scenes of feared phobic outcomes presented by means of a tape-recording; 'exposure'—i.e., *in vivo* participation—included modelling and shaping from the therapist, and progress was determined by the patient);

2. One hour of the alternative treatment;
3. After a one-hour lunch break, one hour of *in vivo* exposure.

Assessment methods included the phobic self-rating scales of Watson and Marks (1971), ratings of the anxiety-arousing potential of five phobic situations, a behavioural test (a walk from the hospital, divided into eight ranges of progress), and semantic differential ratings of the behavioural test assignments. These assessments were made at each session (the behavioural test was given twice—before and after—each session) and at a follow-up interval that averaged 5 months across patients. Significant improvement was noted in 'total phobic scores' (a composite of anxiety and avoidance ratings) from beginning to end of each session, and also from 'before' to 'after' treatment and 'before' to 'follow-up'. Notably, there was also a significant worsening between the end of the first session of treatment and the beginning of the next, and between the end of treatment and follow-up. From within-treatment measures it was apparent that *in vivo* treatment brought more benefit than imaginal treatment in general, although *in vivo* was least effective with the most depressed patients (seven patients were on regimens of antidepressant medication before treatment), and also with those with more frequent panic attacks and 'free-floating' anxiety. *In vivo* exposure was most helpful for patients with the most negative initial phobic attitudes. The general outcome at follow-up was that six patients were 'symptom-free', five were improved but with significant remaining phobic difficulties, and eight were unimproved.

Hand *et al.* (1974) treated twenty-five outpatients with chronic agoraphobia in six groups of four or five patients each. Each patient had 12 h of *in vivo* flooding spread over 3 days of 1 week; each session involved 4 h of continuous flooding *in vivo*. Three of the groups were structured so as to increase social cohesion in general and specifically during flooding sessions; the other groups were not so structured. Ratings given by the patients confirmed that in the structured groups, more social cohesion was perceived than by subjects in the unstructured groups. On the rating scales and behavioural tests outcome for all groups after treatment was comparable to that in earlier trials with individual therapy. The most striking finding was that members of the 'structured' groups demonstrated a continuing improvement over the follow-up interval (6 months) which was true neither for the 'unstructured group' patients nor, indeed, for patients in any earlier trial. A further benefit derived from the study was that the therapists' time was used more economically than in comparable, 'individual' treatment studies.

Hand *et al.* (1974) had originally hypothesized that structured group treatment *in vivo* would save therapist time and increase patient motivation via group cohesion and reinforcement. They had also expressed doubt as to the direction of possible modelling influences: a 'successful' patient could serve as a coping model for others, but a patient who showed great difficulties might exert a negative influence. In fact, one patient in one of the structured groups made histrionic threats during some sessions, but this apparently did not have a deleterious effect upon other patients: rather, group support seemed to help her, and she progressed well throughout the study thereafter. Certainly no 'group panic' was observed, although some patients did experience 'horror' reactions and suffered some depression between sessions.

In a particularly interesting discussion section, Hand *et al.* (1974) note that the strategy of coping with anxiety *in vivo* (i.e. accepting the likelihood of experiencing anxiety; attending to the cues that precede anxiety; noting how long it takes for anxiety to subside), which was the paradigm of the group exposure sessions, is aimed not at total extinction of anxiety but at managing it and coping with it. Their discussion of the interaction between a patient's behaviour in the feared situation and the 'cognitive set' they adopted has some invaluable tips for the clinician. For example, it appeared that procedural details (e.g. whether or not to permit a patient to leave a situation while still anxious) were less important than the self-statements emitted by the patient (see section on cognitive-behavioural treatment below). Finally, it is important for clinicians to note that in this study, as in others like it, patients actually did experience panic attacks *in vivo*. Their efforts to cope with these panics seemed an important aspect of the whole therapeutic procedure.

In a study to be reviewed more fully in a later section, Hafner and Marks (1976) treated fifty-seven agoraphobics *in vivo* either individually or in groups (medicinal treatment via diazepam was another variable studied). Group exposure produced greater therapeutic change than individual, and gains were maintained, but not enhanced, at six-month follow-up assessment. Similar findings were reported in an attempted replication of the Hand *et al.* (1974) study by Teasdale *et al.* (1977). Intrigued by the successful results of Hand and his co-workers, Teasdale's team examined all studies of agoraphobia that had used the assessment methodology of Gelder and Marks (1966) or the modification thereof by Watson and Marks (1971). In this way, the outcomes of various studies could be compared, at least broadly. The result of this examination was that the *in vivo* exposure in structured groups reported by Hand *et al.* (1974) brought more benefit than any other technique in any study reviewed, largely because of the continuing improvement during the follow-up interval of the 'cohesive group' subjects. However, Teasdale *et al.* (1977) note that the follow-up data reported by Hand *et al.* (1974) were incomplete: only two of the three structured groups were examined in the analysis.

In this replication study, Teasdale *et al.* (1977) omitted any general comparison group ('control' group—as had Hand and his co-workers), neither did they replicate the unstructured group treatment. The other difference in the replication study was that, while Hand's team had had three structured groups, each with four or five patients, and data were reported for only two of these groups (seven patients), Teasdale and his co-workers had three groups: of five, five, and eight patients, with follow-up data complete for all groups. In all other respects, the design was that of the earlier study.

Results were that, first, 'social cohesion' was rated by patients at a level intermediate between the ratings of the Hand *et al.* (1974) 'structured' and 'unstructured' patients; and second, in terms of change in agoraphobic responses, the continuing improvement of Hand *et al.*'s patients during the follow-up interval was not replicated. Although treatment was cost-efficient and effective in the short term, the overall improvement was less than that reported in the earlier study, and in fact was not superior to treatments reported in other studies using the same assessment methodology. Teasdale's team speculate that Hand *et al.*'s group that was not re-assessed at follow-up may have had more severe agoraphobics than the other groups, the results of which were therefore artifactual. It is also possible that the greater social cohesion in Hand *et al.*'s subjects was an extremely important factor; notably, Hafner and Marks (1976) also had only 'moderately cohesive' groups on the criteria of Hand *et al.* (1974). It seems likely that, while variables such as individual versus group treatment are readily manipulable by the researchers, a factor such as group cohesion in a sample of research patients may be less controllable by experimenters. It would be interesting to read of attempts to evaluate different methods of achieving this kind of cohesion in groups of agoraphobics.

Finally, in a study of twenty-four agoraphobics treated in groups, Jones *et al.* (1980) compared group *in vivo* exposure, group discussion plus counselling of significant others, and a combined treatment group. Results after 11 weeks of treatment and at 3-month follow-up showed superior performance of the 'combination' group on a behavioural test measure.

Patient-controlled versus therapist-guided exposure

Another procedural variation that has been evaluated in *in vivo* exposure methods is the extent to which the patient may elect to retreat from a feared situation. Everaerd *et al.* (1973) compared imaginal plus *in vivo* flooding with 'successive approximation'. In the latter, patients were asked to approach a phobic situation (e.g. a walk along the street) until they began to feel uncomfortable, at which point they were to return home immediately. Twenty-one patients applied for the programme, but seven refused to continue when they learned the nature of the treatment offered. There were two male patients in the final fourteen. Patients each received both treatments in a cross-over design. No difference was recorded between the two treatments, although those subjects who had flooding before successive approximation showed more phobic anxiety after each session. In general, the two treatments were indistinguishable.

On a similar theme, a study relevant to the issue of therapist-initiated *in vivo* exposure as opposed to self-exposure on the part of the agoraphobic patient was reported by McDonald *et al.* (1979). Patients either planned outings relevant to their fears or discussed general life difficulties. Self-report and independent-assessor data showed that 'self-exposure homework' subjects showed significantly fewer phobic responses on two of three measures post-treatment and at follow-up 1 month later. It thus appears that exposure instructions alone have a therapeutic effect.

It is surprising that uncontrolled self-exposure was so helpful in these two studies, because the patients could have easily avoided the most challenging situations, or could have retreated during a period of high anxiety. The instructions to the Everaerd *et al.* (1973) 'successive approximation' group—to return home as soon as discomfort is experienced—would be countertherapeutic if we accept a treatment rationale based on extinction or habituation (Marks, 1972a). Despite this, Hand *et al.* (1974) noted that in their study of group *in vivo* exposure, a patient's 'cognitive set' was more important than certain procedural details (e.g. retreating from a situation when still anxious). It is, of course, conceivable that subjects in the Everaerd *et al.* (1973) and McDonald *et al.* (1979) studies mobilized the correct set without explicit instruction from the therapist.

Ascher (1981) reports a study that has a direct bearing on the issue of cognitive set during self-exposure. He treated ten agoraphobics by means of self-initiated gradual exposure or paradoxical intention. The experimental design was a partial cross-over in which five patients initially underwent graduated exposure for six sessions, and then used paradoxical intention; the other five patients received paradoxical intention instructions only. In gradual exposure, patients withdrew from a situation when discomfort was experienced (cf. Everaerd *et al.*, 1973); in paradoxical intention, patients were encouraged to become as anxious as possible and then to remain in the situation until fear had subsided. On the basis of behavioural approach test scores, it was clear that 'paradoxical intention' subjects made significantly greater progress than gradual exposure patients. Ascher speculates that the Everaerd *et al.* patients may have reached 'ceiling' on the dependent measures, so that possible differential treatment effects were not given the chance to emerge. In any event, Ascher's initial results with paradoxical therapy seem most promising, and the study clearly merits replication in other centres.

Home-based exposure treatment, in which patient and spouse are given detailed manuals of procedure from which to work, holds substantial promise for agoraphobics (Jannoun *et al.*, 1979; Mathews *et al.*, 1977; Mathews *et al.*, 1981). Although no prospective comparative trials have been reported, Mathews *et al.* (1977), by comparing the results of several studies using the same assessment methodology, have been able to show that home-based treatment produces at least as much benefit as do other behavioural treatments, and with considerably less expenditure of the therapist's time. The continued improvement observed during follow-up is paralleled only by the results of the Hand *et al.* (1974) study, which was in any case incompletely analysed (Teasdale *et al.*, 1977).

A unique combination of home-based and group exposure treatment has been described by Sinnott *et al.* (1981). Group exposure treatment was effective in itself, but benefits were enhanced when members of a treatment group were selected because of the geographic proximity of their homes. These 'zoned' groups brought added benefit because patients could use each other's home as a target for *in vivo* expeditions, the added social contact was helpful, and 'homework' exercises were thus facilitated.

COMPARATIVE STUDIES

Flooding versus systematic desensitization

Mathews (1971) treated six phobic patients in fifteen weekly hour-long sessions. After three preliminary sessions, patients received treatment in three conditions: imaginal flooding, systematic desensitization (SD), or a 'control' group in which patients produced free associations to phobic imagery. The final four sessions for each group consisted of graded *in vivo* exposure, a common element which one might predict would mask differences between the groups (Marks, 1972b). However, flooding and SD produced significantly more improvement than free association. On a clinical rating of 'main phobia' on an avoidance test, and on self-reported anxiety, flooding was more effective than SD, especially with agoraphobic subjects. Six patients, of course, do not constitute an impressive basis for generalization.

Sixteen patients with various phobias were treated by Marks *et al.* (1971), who sought to compare the short-term effects of flooding and SD. Each patient received six sessions of imaginal flooding and six sessions of SD in a balanced, cross-over pattern (accordingly, any follow-up data do not correspond differentially to SD or flooding). The last two sessions for each group included *in vivo* exposure for the last hour. Assessment comprised clinical scales completed by subjects and psychiatrists, and measures of heart rate and skin conductance during phobic imagery. Flooding was significantly superior to SD on rating scales and on autonomic indices, although flooding and SD both produced significant improvement in the main phobia. Flooding produced more improvement in agoraphobia specifically, whereas SD produced more improvement in other phobias; and patients who were initially the most anxious responded particularly well to flooding. Anxiety within the treatment sessions did not correlate with outcome.

Crowe *et al.* (1972) compared imaginal flooding, SD, and graded practice in a cross-over study of fourteen phobics, including four agoraphobics. Each patient received 4 h of treatment by each method. Short-term effects of each treatment were assessed by a behavioural avoidance test and by rating scales completed by patient, therapist, and an independent assessor. Graded practice was significantly more effective than SD on the behavioural test, with the effects of flooding intermediate. However, on the rating scales, flooding and SD brought more benefit than graded practice. The discrepant results with the different measures may be attributable to the fact that only in graded practice were patients exposed to phobic situations *in vivo*. In general, therapeutic effects were small, possibly because of the few sessions devoted to each treatment. It is also important to note that it would be misleading to conclude that flooding proved inferior to another technique in this study—the 'graded practice' procedure could well have been labelled a form of *in vivo* flooding by other researchers. The 'imaginal' versus '*in vivo*' exposure issue seems to be the important one.

Flooding and graded practice approaches, then, seem more helpful to agoraphobics than SD. In a trial with twenty severe agoraphobics, Gelder and Marks (1966) found SD to produce disappointing results: subjects who received 're-educative psychotherapy' improved no less than SD subjects, despite the fact that SD has an extremely good record with 'simple' phobias. To provide more data bearing on this point, Gelder *et al*. (1973) conducted a controlled trial of flooding versus SD versus 'associative psychotherapy'—essentially a free-association procedure. These authors argued that SD seems relatively ineffective with agoraphobia; imaginal flooding has a mixed press with volunteers in analogue studies, although with agoraphobia it seems superior to SD (Marks *et al*., 1971); yet there is some variability in the results of 'flooding' studies (cf. Hussain, 1971; see below). Gelder *et al*. (1973) hypothesized that expectancy effects may be particularly important in flooding, and that subject variables such as level of anxiety may account for much of the variance. Some evidence for the latter point is provided by Boulougouris *et al*. (1971) and by Marks *et al*. (1971). A difficulty with the latter study is that the cross-over design prevented clear interpretation of the follow-up data.

In the experiment by Gelder *et al.* (1973) the following variables were manipulated in a factorial design: treatment condition (flooding, SD, and control); type of phobia (eighteen agoraphobics, eighteen specific and social phobics participated); and expectancy level (half of the subjects in each treatment group were exposed to an interview designed to maximize expectation of benefit). All patients were genuinely phobic; all had been phobic for at least 1 year, and showed sufficient avoidance behaviour to have difficulty with a behavioural assessment. Patients whose phobic condition was not the primary problem to them, and those taking medication other than minor tranquillizers, were excluded, as were those who had no difficulty with the avoidance test; it is not clear how many potential subjects were eliminated on these criteria. All patients constructed an anxiety hierarchy; flooding was imaginal, avoiding psychodynamic themes, but including some frightening imagery that went beyond the bounds of what was realistically likely to happen *in vivo*. In each group, this 'fantasy' stage of treatment was followed *in vivo* participation. Fifteen weekly outpatient sessions were followed by assessments after 1, 3, and 6 months.

Results indicated few differences between SD and imaginal flooding, but these treatments were significantly more effective than the comparison-treatment group on several measures. Flooding was superior to control on the bahavioural test (flooding and SD were not significantly different on this measure), and this pattern was also true for the psychiatric rating scales.

Overall, flooding recorded some significant gains over control that were not made by SD, but the clearest effect was for flooding and SD to prove superior to control, which was particularly ineffective for agoraphobic subjects. No other effects associated with 'type of phobia' were apparent, except that an independent clinician rated SD patients as showing more 'self-satisfaction' than their counterparts in flooding. The 'expectancy' variable did not differentiate the outcome, but semantic differential information indicated that the manipulation may have been ineffective. The major conclusion from this impressively well-designed study is that imaginal exposure to phobic stimuli, by means of either the repeated presentation of graded scenes or the continous presentation of frightening imagery, is more effective in reducing fear than a plausible treatment that provided practically everything but these kinds of imaginal exposure. It is quite conceivable, as Mathews (1977b) argues, that the non-agoraphobic patients responded better to the 'non-specific' treatment than the agoraphobics because the former were more susceptible to 'placebo' effects and to encouragement to practise non-phobic behaviour *in vivo*.

Mathews *et al*. (1974) examined the data of the Gelder *et al*. (1973) study for within-treatment effects of the treatments and for pre-treatment data that might prove predictive of success in treatment. With respect to the latter question, there was a positive correlation of Eysenck Personality Inventory extraversion scores and favourable response to SD or flooding, but no measure predicted success with one treatment as opposed to the other. Within-treatment autonomic measures did differentiate SD from flooding—in SD, heart rate tended to decline gradually during each session and overall, whereas in flooding, heart rate increased initially, and then decreased across sessions. Additionally, significant improvement on a rating scale of predicted anxiety *in vivo* occurred only after *in vivo* treatment had begun, whereas on a similar rating of anxiety while *thinking about* a phobic situation, improvement occurred early in the fantasy stage of the treatment. In any case, none of these differences actually enables prediction of the more appropriate treatment.

Rudestam and Bedrosian (1977) hypothesized that SD and flooding might operate through the common mechanism of habituation. Since agoraphobics habituate slower to repetitive stimuli than do other phobics (cf. Mathews, 1977b), it seems possible that prior conditioning of anxiety might be crucial in 'specific' phobics, but general over-arousal may be the case with agoraphobics. College undergraduates reporting specific ($n=16$) or social phobias ($n=16$; including agoraphobia) were treated by SD or imaginal flooding. Self-report and autonomic data—in the context of viewing colour slides of phobic objects—were recorded. Autonomic changes (for the better) were greater in flooding for the 'specific' phobics, whereas self-report responses by patients and ratings by therapists favoured SD. It is by no means clear, however, that the subjects included severe agoraphobic patients, or even agoraphobics at all as clinically defined. It may be more helpful to regard this study as an analogue investigation with college volunteers than as a trial with a clinical population.

Flooding versus cognitive-behavioural approaches

Consistent with Lazarus' (1976) plea for broader-ranging assessment and intervention strategies in clinical behaviour therapy, the 'cognitive' (more precisely, covert verbal) behaviour of subjects and patients has been examined and modified in recent years in the context of a variety of studies with non-clinical volunteers: unassertive (Thorpe, 1975; Wolfe and Fodor, 1977), speech anxious (Meichenbaum *et al*., 1971; Thorpe *et al*., 1976), and test anxious (Meichenbaum, 1972) subjects (for reviews, see Ledwidge, 1978, and Meichenbaum, 1977). Evaluations of cognitive-behaviour modification (CBM) in application to agoraphobia have been both few in number and disappointing in results, provided CBM is defined (as it conventionally is) as a verbal procedure in which subjects are encouraged to dispute unhelpful attitudes, rehearse more productive self-statements, or participate in Meichenbaum's (1977) 'stress inoculation', which involves a variety of procedures including relaxation, imaginal exposure to phobic stimuli, and the rehearsal of coping self-statements in programmed stages. As noted earlier, Marks (1972a) observed that patients who had received *in vivo* flooding occasionally reported beneficial changes in their thoughts, to the extent that for some, this 'cognitive modification' seemed to be the most notable change to occur during therapy. It is accordingly of interest to evaluate the effects of CBM as compared with flooding, or CBM plus flooding, in treating agoraphobia.

In an analogue study, Mathews and Shaw (1973) used imaginal flooding in a single session with spider-phobic volunteers. As noted above, the variables of interest were massed versus spaced flooding practice, and high versus low anxiety arousal during treatment. The optimal effect was derived from continuous exposure to phobic imagery in the context of which subjects imagined themselves coping successfully. This 'coping imagery' strategy seems very similar to procedures used by Meichenbaum (1977), and is also quite clearly consistent in thrust with self-efficacy theory (Bandura, 1978). Of course, a treatment which seems to be aimed at encouraging a beneficial sense of self-efficacy may not necessarily achieve this ambition. In any case, a trial of CBM with agoraphobics certainly seems warranted, especially so since the Mathews and Shaw results seem reliable in analogue populations: Mathews and Rezin (1977) confirmed the earlier results in a study using dental phobics.

It is entirely possible that the patients treated in the 'structured' groups of Hand *et al*. (1974; see also Franks and Wilson, 1975) experienced at least a form of CBM treatment. First, the rationale given was to stay in the feared situation until fear dissipated, and to observe the context and focus on imagery and feelings when anxiety was experienced; and second, 'structured group' patients seemed to help each other cope with panics, as illustrated by an episode in which a patient who displayed 'negative modelling' did not elicit sympathy for this, but rather her attempts at coping were reinforced by others in the group. Hand *et al.* (1974) offered the conclusion from their observations of patients in this study that for a patient to leave a feared situation while still anxious was not necessarily deleterious: it depends on the 'attitude' adopted by the patient, an important caveat for clinicians (Franks and Wilson, 1975, 1978). As Franks and Wilson (1978) put it, self-efficacy theory would predict that what is important is that exposure continues until appropriate expectations of efficacy have been established.

In the most direct comparison yet available, Emmelkamp *et al.* (1978) used a cross-over design in which twenty-one agoraphobics were exposed to 'cognitive restructuring' and prolonged real-life exposure. Each technique was implemented in a group context. Patients were randomly distributed among four groups, two of which received cognitive restructuring, and the remaining two of which had *in vivo* flooding; after five 2-h sessions, each group received the alternate treatment for the same number of sessions. Assessments were made pre-treatment, at cross-over, post-treatment, and 1 month after treatment, and consisted of a behavioural test, self-report inventories, and rating scales completed by the patient and an independent clinician.

In all, each patient received ten 2-h group therapy sessions, each of which was led by two therapists. Cognitive restructuring comprised a 'relabelling' phase in which an explanatory rationale was given, discussion of 'irrational beliefs' in a rational-emotive therapy (RET; Ellis, 1962) format, and self-instructional training, in which productive self-statements were practised in a stress-inoculation context (Meichenbaum, 1977). 'Prolonged exposure' involved remaining in phobic situations until anxiety declined. Patients and therapists walked into town as a group initially, but as treatment progressed patients became more independent. In general, all four therapy groups showed improvement from pre- to post-test on almost all variables, and no sequence effect was detected. Prolonged exposure produced significantly more improvement than cognitive restructuring on a behavioural test and on many self-report and rating scales. Results of the assessment at 1-month follow-up were almost identical to those immediately post-treatment. *In vivo* exposure was generally, consistently, and significantly superior to cognitive restructuring despite the fact that the latter included more than one CBM technique. It is of great interest that Emmelkamp *et al.* (1978) noted that a number of clients reported that exposure produced greater cognitive change than cognitive restructuring, and the authors remark that designating a technique 'cognitive restructuring' does not necessarily mean that the desired effect is thereby induced in the patients. It makes good semantic sense to say that *in vivo* exposure is a better cognitive modification technique than the CBM procedures used in this study. Predictably enough, Ellis (1979) responded to the authors of this study to confirm the importance of real-life 'homework' exercises in the practice of RET, which Emmelkamp *et al.* (1978) indeed acknowledge in their paper.

Related to this, Biran and Wilson (1981) report the results of a controlled trial of guided exposure and cognitive restructuring with specific phobias. Twenty-two patients with phobias of heights, travelling in lifts, or darkness were selected from fifty people who had responded to newspaper advertisements. Mildly phobic individuals were excluded. Assessment procedures were behavioural approach tests, including post-treatment tasks different from those used before treatment so as to allow assessment of generalization of gains; rating scales of anticipatory and performance fear; self-efficacy scales; questionnaires about other situational fears, and inventories of depression, social anxiety, and irrational beliefs; and measures of heart rate and skin potential.

In guided exposure, patients attempted encounters with real phobic situations, first with the help of the therapist and with various other supports, and then while the supports were gradually withdrawn. Patients were encouraged to practise between sessions. Cognitive restructuring procedures replicated those of Emmelkamp *et al.* (1978), and included cognitive relabelling, discussion of irrational beliefs, and self-instructional training.

Guided exposure was significantly more effective than cognitive restructuring in reducing avoidance, subjective fear, and physiological reactivity. Behavioural gains closely matched increases in level and strength of self-efficacy. Comparable results derived from a 1-month follow-up assessment, after which cognitive restructuring patients were offered guided exposure treatment. These patients made progress similar to that of the original exposure patients. Six months after treatment, progress had been maintained. On some measures, exposure patients had made further gains during the follow-up interval.

These results are entirely consonant with those of Emmelkamp *et al.* (1978), and serve to underline Wilson's (1981b) point that, whereas cognitive restructuring techniques are less helpful for clinical phobias than performance-based treatment, cognitive mechanisms are important in the therapeutic process by which exposure brings behavioural benefit. In the Biran and Wilson (1981) study, guided exposure prompted greater changes in perceived self-efficacy than did cognitive restructuring.

Bandura *et al.* (1980) have recently extended self-efficacy research to agoraphobia. No particular treatment innovations were offered in this programme, which included preparatory group sessions, and individual *in vivo* ventures in which patients were initially accompanied by field therapists who included some former agoraphobics. What is novel in this study is the assessment of self-efficacy expectations, which closely paralleled behavioural gains from treatment.

It can always be said in criticism of self-efficacy theory that increases in confidence are a well-known correlate of successful treatment of phobias, and that, in studies like those of Bandura *et al.* (1980) and Biran and Wilson (1981), ratings of perceived self-efficacy simply constitute an additional dependent variable of the same class as ratings of phobic severity. Alternatively, however, it can be argued that the assessment of self-efficacy expectations is vital in checking on the completeness and adequacy of treatment. Last, Barlow and O'Brien (1981) present a case report in which an agoraphobic male made substantial gains from exposure treatment on behavioural, anxiety self-report, and autonomic indices. However, thoughts of avoidance and escape increased over the four treatment sessions, coping thoughts declined, and, in general, 'negative' thoughts were more prominent than 'positive' thoughts by the end of treatment. The patient was followed up for a year, at which point some behavioural relapse had occurred.

This result is reminiscent of that of Barlow *et al.* (1980), who report that an agoraphobic woman who improved in all respects except heart rate (which increased in phobic situations) later relapsed. Practical conclusions are that treatment is best continued until optimal gains have been established in *all* response classes, including perceptions of personal efficacy.

COMBINED BEHAVIOURAL AND PHARMACOLOGICAL TREATMENT

Some researchers and clinicians have used medication in the routine clinical management of agoraphobia. The aims are commonly to control generalized anxiety, dysphoric mood, or physiological correlates of the panic attack, for example palpitations. Other writers, perhaps in response to the generally discouraging results of early studies and clinical reports of SD with agoraphobia, describe combined treatment approaches, in which drugs are used with behaviour therapy. In these combined approaches, medication has been used, (a) in place of instructed muscular relaxation in SD, (b) to suppress anxiety during exposure to phobic situations, or (c) to control panic attacks while behavioural techniques are used to control anticipatory anxiety.

It is difficult to mark a clear distinction between the use of a drug with behavioural treatment and the routine use of a drug for general clinical management. Some patients who are given medication as their principal treatment are encouraged to practise entering feared situations, for example. For this reason we will first discuss some reports and trials of drugs that may be used alone, and second, we will review some studies of the combined use of medication with behaviour therapy.

Clinical management by means of medication

Wolpe (1973) notes that he has occasionally used chlorpromazine, meprobamate, and codeine in the treatment of agoraphobia. Some patients who have used these medications consistently before entering feared situations have been able to confront them subsequently without reliance on the drug. This suggests that such treatment is not necessarily only palliative. Usually, however, these patients have used the medication for protracted periods before being able to face the phobic environments unaided. Wolpe also cites unpublished work by others who have prescribed minor tranquillizers (chlordiazepoxide and diazepam) for *in vivo* desensitization purposes; patients would enter the phobic surroundings during the peak effect of the medication.

The effects of phenelzine were evaluated by Tyrer *et al.* (1973) in a double-blind study with two groups of agoraphobics and social phobics: one group took phenelzine, the other placebo, for 2 months. The only behavioural treatment component was the instruction to the patients to expose themselves to phobic situations gradually. No behavioural test was used; assessment comprised ratings by patients and therapists. Overall ratings, and ratings of subsidiary phobias, gave the advantage to phenelzine, but there was no group difference in terms of specific concerns related to the main phobia. General improvement was similar to that reported in early (and disappointing) studies of SD (e.g. Gelder *et al.*, 1967), and was not comparable to the more impressive results from *in vivo* flooding (Marks *et al.*, 1971). At 1-year follow-up, the only group difference was that placebo patients had required more additional treatment since the end of the experimental phase of the study (Tyrer and Steinberg, 1975). Tyrer *et al.* (1973) had noted that patients who discontinued the drug in the 'phenelzine' group tended to relapse, and this was also found by Solyom *et al.* (1973). In that study, patients who had been treated by means of SD, aversion relief, or flooding had the advantage over 'drug' patients at 2-year follow-up.

Phenelzine is a monoamine oxidase inhibitor, a class of drugs commonly used in the management of depression. Imipramine, a tricyclic antidepressant, has also been evaluated in the treatment of agoraphobia. However, as is the case with phenelzine, imipramine used alone as treatment for agoraphobia has been characterized by relapse on the part of the patient when the drug is discontinued (Klein and Fink, 1962). Imipramine will be discussed further in a later section.

Barbiturates and imaginal exposure

In an ambitious study, Lipsedge *et al.* (1973) treated sixty agoraphobics by means of standard SD, methohexitone-assisted SD, or management via iproniazid (a monoamine oxidase inhibitor). These treatments were assessed in various combinations, allowing the researchers to conclude that iproniazid had relatively disappointing effects: it reduced patients' reports of anxiety, but it did not seem to reduce avoidance behaviour. Methohexitone-assisted SD brought more benefit than SD alone, and the most successful treatment overall was the combination of iproniazid with drug-assisted SD. The experiment is flawed in some respects: groups were not strictly equivalent before treatment, and there was no saline-injected group to control for expectancy or attribution effects. No behavioural test was used. Two-year follow-up data were collected for all participants (an impressive feature of the study); the assessment consisted of rating scales completed by patients and an independent clinician. No treatment-group difference was obtained at follow-up, and this is probably attributable to the fact that three-quarters of the patients had been given additional drug treatment between the end of the experimental phase of the study and the follow-up assessment. Results very similar to those of this trial of iproniazid were found for alprenelol by Ullrich *et al*. (1972).

In a cross-over trial with forty agoraphobics and social phobics, Hussain (1971) compared imaginal flooding plus intravenous thiopental with SD plus intravenous thiopental; in the other phase of the study, the same behavioural treatment was given, but saline solution was injected instead of thiopental. Patients had six 45-min treatment sessions, two meetings per week. Assessment consisted of ratings made by patients and therapists. In a cross-over trial, long-term follow-ups can only compare groups in terms of the order in which they received the treatments, of course. In the short term, then, drug-assisted flooding produced marked improvement, SD with or without thiopental brought moderate benefit, and flooding plus saline solution was associated with slight improvement. The lack of a behavioural test is an unfortunate limitation here, because, as noted above in respect of iproniazid, a drug can reduce self-reported anxiety without facilitating approach to the phobic situation (Lipsedge *et al*., 1973).

Chambless (1978) and Chambless *et al*. (1979) report a trial in which twenty-seven agoraphobic outpatients received imaginal flooding, imaginal flooding with intravenous methohexital sodium, or an attention-control procedure. Although no group difference emerged in behavioural test data, patients' self-ratings suggest that imaginal flooding is more effective without the drug. The authors conclude that patients may benefit from experiencing anxiety during imaginal flooding. The experimental effect, although only observed on self-ratings, is particularly striking because some patients who received methohexital sodium nevertheless experienced anxiety during treatment.

It is important to be cautious in interpreting the results of this and other similar studies. The rationale for this kind of study is that it may be helpful to attenuate anxiety during behavioural treatment, and therefore an anxiety-reducing drug is used within treatment for some subjects. However, there are two links in this chain of reasoning: (i) the drug reduces anxiety; and (ii) anxiety-reduction may be beneficial. Finding that treatment is not beneficial (for 'drug' patients) could mean that anxiety-reduction in the sessions is countertherapeutic, or it could mean that the drug did not succeed in adequately reducing anxiety. This latter point can always be raised in appraising studies like this, unless there is independent evidence that the drug did what it was intended to do in reducing anxiety.

Minor tranquillisers and flooding

The combined use of orally-administered diazepam and *in vivo* flooding for patients with specific phobias was evaluated by Marks *et al.* (1972). Eighteen patients were treated in a single 2-hour session. Flooding treatment was conducted 1 or 4 h after the ingestion of diazepam or placebo. All groups improved significantly, but the group that experienced flooding 4 h after taking diazepam (i.e. while the effect of the drug was waning) made the most progress.

Johnston and Gath (1973) argue that a perennial problem with pharmacological treatment is that patients may attribute any improvement to the drug rather than to their own efforts, and this would be less favourable in the long term because the patients would acquire no sense of personal control. This argument is entirely in line with the later hypothesis by Bandura (1978) that a sense of self-efficacy on the part of the patient is crucial to a successful outcome. Johnston and Gath predicted, for other reasons, that the effect of flooding would be greater if anxiety were kept low during treatment, and also that this effect would be lesser or more short-lived if anxiety-reduction were attributed to the drug by the patient. In an ingenious procedure in which patients could be misled as to whether a tablet or a syrup (both of which were taken in all conditions) could contain the real medicine or the placebo, Johnston and Gath created four treatment groups by manipulating, (a) whether the patient received diazepam or placebo, and (b) whether the patient's belief (that diazepam or placebo had been given) was true or false. If it is important for anxiety to be kept low during flooding, then the groups receiving diazepam would predictably make greater progress. If attributing success to the drug impairs the effectiveness of treatment, then the most successful group would be the one in which patients actually take diazepam but are unaware that they have taken it. The least successful group would be the one in which patients think they have taken a drug but, in reality, have not.

Six severe agoraphobics were treated as inpatients for 30 days; data from only four of these patients were available at the end of the study. Behavioural test data were consistent with the first, but not the second, hypothesis: diazepam was clearly helpful, but any differential attribution effects seemed irrelevant.

Hafner and Marks (1976) combined diazepam with *in vivo* exposure in groups. Although diazepam seemed effective, the benefit brought by group treatment was great enough to mask any improvement attributable to the drug. Within the sessions, patients who took diazepam reported less distress than 'placebo' patients. This effect could possibly have been negative, in that the patients whose discomfort was controlled by diazepam had less opportunity to learn to cope with anxiety and panic (cf. Chambless and Goldstein, 1980; Franks and Wilson, 1979).

Hafner and Milton (1977) conducted a similar study, except that there were two therapists with each group during flooding rather than one, treatment was more condensed and the sessions longer, and propranolol (not a psychoactive drug) was the drug being evaluated. Propranolol was selected because it is often indicated in conditions in which palpitations are prominent.

The outcome was that propranolol had an adverse influence (possibly because of a waning effect during the latter part of each treatment session).

Antidepressants and behaviour therapy

Zitrin *et al*. (1976) compared a combination of SD, assertiveness training, and homework assignments (with and without imipramine) with supportive psychotherapy plus imipramine. 'Supportive psychotherapy' included encouragement to practise. Agoraphobics responded more favourably to imipramine than to placebo; with imipramine there was no difference in outcome between 'behaviour therapy' and 'supportive psychotherapy'. The same results were obtained after more patients had progressed through the procedures in this continuing study (Klein *et al*., 1977).

As Franks and Wilson (1975) have pointed out, there is the possibility that 'behaviour therapy' patients in the Zitrin *et al*. (1976) study reached ceiling on outcome measures because of the potency of imipramine treatment, and therefore could not be clearly differentiated from 'psychotherapy' patients. The latter were, in any event, given quite directive therapy in which behavioural performance was stressed.

More recently, Zitrin *et al*. (1980) report the results of a trial in which agoraphobics were treated by means of group *in vivo* exposure, with and without imipramine. Patients received either imipramine or placebo for four weeks before the exposure treatment began, and this took the form of ten weekly 3–4-h sessions (consisting of 45 min of discussion, then *in vivo* exposure) led by psychiatric social workers. In this sample of seventy-six agoraphobic women, 29 per cent of each group stopped attending before treatment was concluded. Imipramine patients were more improved than placebo patients after treatment and at 12-week follow-up. The authors note that the effect of imipramine was on the panic attacks, not on depression. They recommend imipramine to control panic attacks, and group exposure to reduce anticipatory anxiety; both treatments are necessary for complete treatment.

Commenting on this study, Marks (1981c) suggests that, granted that imipramine did not operate by means of reducing clinical depression in the agoraphobics, it still could have reduced the patients' dysphoric mood, thereby bringing indirect benefit in encouraging enthusiasm for treatment.

In a study similar to that of Zitrin *et al*. (1980), Solyom *et al*. (1981) evaluated phenelzine with and without individual *in vivo* exposure. The experiment took the form of a factorial design in which four conditions were produced by the manipulation of exposure and phenelzine. Forty phobics (agoraphobics and social phobics) participated. Assessment involved clinical ratings, patient self-ratings, and patients' daily records of progress. Exposure proved the more important therapeutic ingredient (exposure-plus-phenelzine and exposure-plus-placebo groups performed better than the phenelzine and placebo groups that had no exposure). Two months after treatment, the phenelzine-plus-exposure and placebo-no exposure groups had relapsed.

Of great theoretical interest is the authors' comment that phenelzine did successfully reduce anxiety during treatment, suggesting that anxiety-reduction within treatment may be countertherapeutic (cf. Chambless *et al.*, 1979).

SUMMARY

There has been a tradition in behaviour therapy circles to the effect that SD is best for simple phobias, and is less effective with agoraphobia, particularly when there is much generalized anxiety (Gelder *et al.*, 1973; Gelder and Marks, 1966). Methods involving direct exposure to phobic stimuli are, in general, more helpful to agoraphobics. Early reports on SD with agoraphobia—case studies, clinical series, and prospective trials—suggest that it brings greater benefit than comparison conditions such as 'psychotherapy', but this has not been a reliable finding, and in any case SD seems to produce fewer gains with agoraphobics than with other phobics, and effects of treatment may be transient (Eysenck and Beech, 1971). SD seems no less effective without muscle relaxation and when the procedure is partly automated, although the latter conclusion is not well founded.

Real-life practice, or exposure to feared situations regardless of procedure, is generally beneficial as contrasted with continued avoidance or imaginal or symbolic methods of treatment. The addition of practice to methods like SD may make all the difference to successful treatment, recognizing that SD may sometimes be preferred to prolonged exposure when the patient initially refuses this. Similarly, whereas *in vivo* flooding is superior to imaginal flooding, the addition of self-directed practice to the latter—at least when treatment is lengthy—makes up the difference. Home-based practice is particularly recommended. The effects of practice are enhanced by the addition of feedback and praise by the therapist, particularly in the early stages of treatment. The effects of praise are specific to the behavioural dimension attended to, so praise is ideally given for a variety of component behaviours such as time spent away from home or clinic, distance walked, and so forth. Praise and feedback for successful performance have been found to counteract brief episodes of depression and discouragement during treatment. The inclusion of the patient's spouse in self-directed practice efforts from home is strongly recommended, and this seems to promote continued improvement after formal treatment has ended (this suggests that the therapist does not have to 'keep going' until all signs of phobic behaviour have been completely eliminated; spaced follow-up contacts will suffice if the spouse is actively involved). Patients report that particularly valuable aspects of therapy are praise and encouragement from the therapist, and learning to cope with anxiety by means of practice.

Self-directed practice without feedback and praise from a therapist may still be helpful provided that *in vivo* sessions are prolonged, and the patient stops proceeding before significant tension is experienced. If the patient does push the practice too far and experience anxiety or panic *in situ*, and retreats before anxiety diminishes, this may not be deleterious provided the patient mobilizes the most helpful 'cognitive set': that is, emits self-statements reflecting a positive expectancy of gain and a reassuring attitude. The addition of specific training in coping skills seems to enhance the results of self-directed exposure, although experimental comparisons have not confirmed this. In the most successful study reported, which involved group exposure *in vivo*, coping strategies recommended to patients may have been an important component of treatment. A helpful rationale and instruction to patients has been 'learn to tolerate your fear until it disappears'.

Prolonged exposure (*in vivo* flooding) in which patients remain in a phobic situation until fear dissipates entirely is more beneficial than imaginal exposure (a reliable finding), and seems to have a general effect in habituating fear responses. Procedurally, it is important to prolong flooding until anxiety diminishes in all response classes, although premature retreats are not necessarily disastrous, as in the case of graded practice. It does not seem necessary to attempt to maximize anxiety during treatment, but the recent report by Ascher (1981) suggests that paradoxical intention, in which the patient tries to experience anxiety to the full, is an extremely promising approach. Replications of this study are needed. The addition of modelling and praise to treatment by *in vivo* flooding may be helpful, but conducting flooding sessions with structured and cohesive groups of agoraphobics has produced results rivalling the best in the literature, with continued improvement noted during long follow-up intervals. This finding has not been fully replicated, but a less successful replication study still produced results similar to the most effective programme studied.

CBM procedures produced disappointing results for agoraphobics when tested against *in vivo* exposure. It has been noted above that cognitive modification may be an important component of other procedures which do not appear at first sight to be 'cognitive' at all—they may operate by means of cognitive changes produced indirectly, consistent with self-efficacy theory (Bandura, 1978). In studies of *in vivo* flooding, coping strategies have been recommended to patients as part of the treatment procedure (such as: 'focus on the situation when you feel anxious'; 'watch your anxiety dwindle with time'; and so on), and it is therefore premature to dismiss the 'cognitive modality' from treatment consideration. In any case, CBM alone would not be realistic as a total approach to treatment; Ellis (1979), a cognitive therapist *par excellence*, regards it as essential to include active homework. Research comparing *in vivo* flooding in isolation versus in combination with CBM is in need of expansion.

Results of trials of behaviour therapy combined with medicinal treatment have been inconclusive, and there are some special difficulties in this line of research which may contribute to problems in arriving at clear conclusions: difficulties in measuring effects of drugs independent of their effects on phobic behaviour; difficulty determining optimal dosages, and how soon exposure should begin after ingesting the drug; and so forth. There are also problems in determining whether drugs labelled 'tranquillizing' in fact have that effect. The original hypothesis tested in some studies that anxiety-suppression during treatment is helpful has received some support, although this does not necessarily mean that the experience of anxiety during treatment is harmful. To the extent that tranquillizers facilitate *in vivo* exposure, they can be recommended in clinical practice as part of a comprehensive treatment programme, in particular for those patients who refuse flooding *in vivo* and for whom graduated practice is a severe challenge. Anxiety-inhibition by medication can be helpful in facilitating the direct exposure to feared situations that seems to be the important procedure. The issue of adding medication to behaviour therapy in agoraphobia continues to be controversial, however. Emmelkamp (1977) points out that many studies included relatively few agoraphobics; and in the well-controlled study by Hafner and Marks (1976), no group difference was found at follow-up between patients who received diazepam and those who had placebo. The use of medication will best be determined by an assessment of the individual patient; it is available for those who will not contemplate exposure methods, and for whom SD produces disappointing gains.

CONCLUSIONS

Treatment of agoraphobic avoidance by prolonged *in vivo* exposure to feared situations has produced the most beneficial outcomes in general. Many patients reject this approach, however, and for them realistic alternatives include *in vivo* exposure in groups, graduated practice (preferably with the support and active encouragement of a spouse or significant other), or systematic desensitization to reduce anticipatory anxiety in the early stages of treatment. The use of tranquillizing medication can be considered when it is difficult to encourage direct exposure otherwise. Imaginal flooding does not seem advantageous clinically, and cognitive therapy has yet to prove itself in the treatment of agoraphobia.

The agoraphobic syndrome sometimes includes marital dysfunction, which, when present, is not always clearly apparent early in treatment. Marital difficulties make for a poorer prognosis in some patients. Treatment of problems in marital interaction may accompany treatment of agoraphobic avoidance. Effects of the addition of assertiveness training to behavioural treatment regimens for agoraphobia have not been evaluated systematically.

Comprehensive assessment may reveal depression, general anxiety, or lack of self-assurance in the patient. Problems identified by a broad-ranging assessment may be addressed concurrently or sequentially by a battery of procedures, but there are few guidelines as to the optimal ordering of these treatments.

Investigation of relationships between patient characteristics and response to particular treatments is needed to enable prescriptive recommendations to be made for the individual agoraphobic. A difficulty here is that traditional group designs do not usually allow treatments based on an individual behavioural analysis to be offered. Finally, because few studies have been conducted in which treatment components have been systematically added to assess their incremental utility, and because the combination of exposure with cognitive-behavioural techniques has largely gone unresearched, there is scope for prospective trials of behavioural and cognitive-behavioural methods using an 'additive' research strategy.

CHAPTER 6

Additive Effects of Behavioural Techniques—A Controlled Trial

RATIONALE FOR THE PRESENT STUDY

When the present study was designed the main behavioural methods being applied to the treatment of agoraphobia were systematic desensitization (in imagination and *in vivo*), graded practice (which may also have included feedback, social reinforcement, etc.) and flooding; the value of the latter technique was only beginning to be established.

Most of the research in the behavioural treatment of agoraphobia was, and still is, based on the 'narrow band' approach where one technique is compared with another. Although this approach is of value, particularly within a research context, Lazarus (1971) and others have vigorously assailed this particular conception of behaviour therapy as being rigid and even therapeutically sterile. Few well-controlled studies have attempted to combine several treatment methods whereby the subjects are given two, three or four types of treatment following each other within the same treatment session.

Although Lazarus' (1971) criticisms were directed at the behavioural school, most of the major therapeutic approaches not infrequently concentrate on one modality. For example, considerable emphasis is placed on cognitive-affective processes in the psychoanalytic school; thus this approach can be seen to be severely limited for penetrating insights *per se* cannot be expected to result in effective functioning in patients with deficient behavioural repertoires, say in social skills; these patients, through faulty learning, lack of appropriate opportunity, etc., would appear to require explicit training, perhaps involving role playing and shaping techniques, for the acquisition of adaptive social patterns of behaviour. The neo-Reichian school of bioenergetics (Lowen, 1967), concentrates on behaviour in the form of 'body language' involving the sensory-affective dimension. Gestalt therapists employ role playing and imaginary techniques. Ellis's theory of rational emotive therapy (Ellis and Harper, 1961) is derived directly from a theory that assumes that psychological disorders arise from faulty or irrational patterns of thinking; considerable emphasis is placed on the modification of the self-defeating and unproductive patterns of thinking.

It is clear that the agoraphobic syndrome is very complex with manifestations at the cognitive, psychophysiological and behavioural levels; it is apparent that the agoraphobic sufferer has to contend with many specific problems at different levels. It is likely that most clinicians would agree with the pragmatic assumption that the more a patient learns in therapy and the more coping skills he acquires the more progress he is likely to make and the less likely he is to relapse after the termination of treatment. Blake (1965) argued that an alcoholic receiving only aversion therapy is more likely to relapse than one who had also received relaxation training; additional treatment methods such as assertive training and family therapy together with vocational guidance would be likely to further increase benefits. Thus the degree of improvement and lasting change may be seen as a function of combined techniques and strategies.

Lazarus (1975, 1976) has advocated a multimodal approach to deal with complex disorders. Although this approach has value from a clinical point of view there is little empirical evidence to support his BASIC ID framework. An alternative approach is of the type advocated by Meichenbaum (1973); this strategy involves starting with an existing behaviour therapy technique (systematic desensitization) and adding a cognitive element (stress inoculation); a comparison is made of the effects of the single technique with the combined techniques. A similar additive research strategy has been adopted by McFall *et al.* (1973) involving assertive training.

By piling treatment methods on top of one another any differences which may occur in the outcome measures between groups of subjects may be informative about the effects of this approach, provided the treatments are not incompatible. This chapter describes a research project in which the authors used this additive model to investigate the effects of a range of techniques in the treatment of agoraphobics; the approach is relatively new and, although the available literature on this model is limited, beneficial results were obtained in the studies quoted.

Two experiments were undertaken. In the first experiment four main treatment methods were used: behavioural counselling, systematic desensitization, reinforced graded practice and stress inoculation; a description of the methods will be provided later. There were four treatment groups. For all subjects each session consisted of an interview and relaxation training; in addition subjects received the following treatments:

Group I: Behavioural counselling.
Group II: Behavioural counselling and systematic desensitization.
Group III: Behavioural counselling, systematic desensitization and reinforced graded practice.
Group IV: Systematic desensitization, reinforced graded practice and stress inoculation.

It can be argued that the stress inoculation method may aid the implementation of the graded practice, etc., and that the graded practice may aid systematic desensitization, etc.

The second experiment consisted of one group of subjects (waiting-list controls) and was designed to monitor fluctuations in untreated agoraphobia.

HYPOTHESES

Experiment 1

1. Subjects in Group II (behavioural counselling and systematic desensitization); Group III (behavioural counselling, systematic desensitization and reinforced graded practice) and Group IV (systematic desensitization, reinforced graded practice and stress inoculation) will show significant improvement at the end of the treatment programme, on the various outcome measures, over subjects in Group I.
2. Subjects in Group I will show minimal and non-significant improvement on pre-treatment measures at the end of treatment.
3. Subjects in Groups II, III and IV will maintain at the 3-months, 6-months and 12-months follow-ups the gains they had acquired by the end of treatment.
4. Subjects in Group I will show minimal and non-significant improvement on pre-treatment measures and on 3-months, 6-months and 12-months follow-up.
5. There will be no significant differential effects at the end of treatment attributable to the therapists.

Experiment 2

1. Subjects in Group V (waiting-list controls) will show no significant improvement over the equivalent period of time that the subjects in the other groups received treatment.

EXPERIMENT 1

Definition of Agoraphobia

For the purpose of this research, agoraphobia was defined as a condition in which the sufferer could not normally proceed unaided in public places beyond a certain point without experiencing intense anxiety and panic; thus the condition put a restriction on the subject's movements and the sufferer was dissatisfied with these limitations. (See Appendix I). The diagnosis of agoraphobia, if appropriate, was confirmed at the end of the second assessment session.

Subjects

Source of referrals

The research programme was advertised by means of the press and local radio in Manchester and Rochdale, by circulars to consultant psychiatrists and general practitioners in the area and through the Phobics Society (Manchester). It was made explicit to potential volunteers that referrals had to be made through a doctor.

Selection criteria

A total of thirty-two subjects participated in the research programme. An agoraphobic was automatically incorporated into the programme as referred provided the following criteria were met:

1. The diagnosis of agoraphobia was confirmed by the therapists.
2. The subject was available for treatment twice weekly.
3. The subject was not completely housebound and was able to attend the Clinic (for example, by ambulance, car, etc.).
4. The subject had no incapacitating psychiatric illness such as a psychotic reaction, alcoholism, etc. However, subjects with depression were not specifically excluded.
5. The subject was prepared to sign a contract undertaking to complete the treatment programme (see Appendix II).
6. The subject had no incapacitating physical illness.
7. The subject had not received any previous behaviour therapy treatment.

Subjects continued with any medication they were taking at the start of the programme; the chronicity and extent of the problem were not impediments to inclusion in the project.

A total of thirty-nine subjects were referred for the research programme; six were rejected either before or immediately after the commencement of treatment. Of the five who were excluded after the initial assessment, three were rejected on the grounds of availability, that is they could not attend regularly for treatment, one on the grounds that the diagnosis of agoraphobia could not be confirmed and one on account of alcoholism. Protracted physical illness was the reason for rejecting one subject immediately after the commencement of treatment.

Drop-outs from the project

One subject, a non-severe agoraphobic in Group IV, for reasons unknown, broke her contract and opted out of treatment after her fourth treatment session; a replacement subject was obtained. All other subjects continued in the project until 1-year follow-up.

Characteristics of subjects

Of the thirty-two subjects taking part in Experiment 1, twenty-eight were female. The age range was 18–59 years with a mean age of 34.97 years (standard deviation was 9.88 years). This confirms Marks *et al.* (1966) finding that the mean age of treatment is 34 years. Most subjects were receiving medication: seven subjects in Group I, six each in Groups II and III and eight in Group IV. The medication was mainly Valium and Librium.

A more detailed account of all the subjects of Experiments I and II is given in Appendix III. For comparative purposes characteristics of the 963 subjects taking part in the National Survey of Agoraphobics are also shown.

Therapists

The authors, Dr L. E. Burns and Dr G. L. Thorpe, who were well experienced in the behavioural treatment approach, were the main therapists. A nurse therapist, Mrs J. Hawkrigg, who was specifically trained by the therapists, administered, under supervision, some of the treatment and used the following techniques: relaxation training, systematic desensitization, reinforced graded practice and stress inoculation.

Researchers

The researchers consisted of the two therapists, the nurse therapist and an independent clinical psychologist, Mr R. H. Curtis. Mr Curtis was well experienced in the treatment of agoraphobics; he was unaware of the treatment procedures being used or which group each subject was in.

Assessment

A number of measures were taken during the project, details of which are given below. In addition, interviews were held covering other aspects of the patient's functioning such as the inability to work, intake of drugs, etc.

Pre-treatment measures

Descriptive and generalization measures

1. Assessment of General Intellectual Functioning—The Standard Progressive Matrices (SPM) (Raven, 1960).
2. Assessment of General Verbal Functioning—The Mill Hill Vocabulary Scale (MHV) (Raven, 1965).
3. The Agoraphobia Questionnaire (excluding Sections 36 and 39—see next section (Burns, 1977).
4. The 16 Personality Factor Questionnaire—Form A, 1967–8 edition (16PF) (Cattell, 1946).

5. The Social Avoidance and Distress Scale, (SAD) (Watson and Friend, 1969).
6. Fear of Negative Evaluation Scale (FNE) (Watson and Friend, 1969).
7. The Eysenck Personality Inventory—Form A, (EPI) (Eysenck, 1964).

Self-report, expectancy and behavioural measures

1. Agoraphobia Questionnaire, Sections 36 and 39, (Burns, 1977).
   (a) Section 36 consists of seven-point rating scales dealing with a range of situations which tend to make agoraphobics worse or better, (for example, having to queue in a shop, having a definite appointment, etc.) (see Appendix IV).
   (b) Section 39 consists of five-point rating scales which concentrate on the behavioural functioning of the subject (for example, precisely what the subject is or is not able to achieve in the natural environment) (see Appendix V).
2. Expectancy Rating: Subjects were asked to rate themselves on a seven-point scale to the question 'How much benefit do you expect to derive from the treatment?'
3. Behavioural Test—Unaccompanied Walk: Each subject was asked to walk unaided during daylight hours along a predetermined route from the clinic to the back of Woolworths in the centre of Rochdale, a distance of 4240 feet. The distances from the clinic to seventeen landmarks along the route were obtained with the help of the Surveyor's Department, Rochdale Corporation. Subjects were instructed to stop and return following the onset of *severe* tension or panic. In view of the fluctuating nature of agoraphobia this test was administered on each of two days and the mean distance noted. The subjects reported how far they had been able to walk. Occasionally, on a random basis, subjects were discretely monitored by observers; in no case was a discrepancy found between the self-report and the report of the observer.

   The following measures were taken on this test:
   (a) The distance travelled.
   (b) The time taken.
   (c) A rating by the subject on a five-point scale (from 0 = no anxiety to 4 = maximum anxiety).

Continuous measures during treatment

Benefit rating

At the end of each treatment session subjects were asked to rate themselves on a seven-point scale to the question 'How much benefit have you derived from the treatment to date?'

Mid-treatment measures

Descriptive and generalization measures

1. Social Avoidance and Distress Scale (SAD).
2. Fear and Negative Evaluation Scale (FNE).
3. Eysenck Personality Inventory—Form A. (EPQ).

Self-report, general benefit rating and behavioural measures

1. Agoraphobia Questionnaire—Sections 36 and 39.
2. General Benefit Rating. Subjects were asked to rate themselves on a seven-point scale to the question 'Overall, how much benefit have you derived from the treatment?'
3. Behavioural Test—unaccompanied walk.

Post-treatment measures

Generalization measures

1. Social Avoidance and Distress Scale (SAD).
2. Fear of Negative Evaluation Scale (FNE).
3. Eysenck Personality Inventory—Form A (EPQ).
4. 16 Personality Factor Questionnaire—Form A (16PF).

Self-report, general benefit and behavioural measures

1. Agoraphobia Questionnaire—Sections 36 and 39.
2. General Benefit Rating—a seven-point scale on the overall benefit that had been received from the full treatment programme.
3. Behavioural Tests
   (a) Unaccompanied walk.
   (b) Top three hierarchy items. In this test the subjects attempted the three most difficult items in their anxiety hierarchies.
   (c) Visit to Arndale Centre, Middleton. Subjects were taken by car, on an individual basis, to a large shopping complex. Times of remaining unaccompanied in the centre and anxiety ratings (five-point scale) were obtained.

Independent measures

1. Assessment by a clinician
   (a) Ratings of the severity of the agoraphobia were made, on a five-point scale, by an independent clinician; the ratings were made on the basis of

four standard questions (see Appendix VI) supplemented by further questions as necessary.

(b) PD Scale of the Symptom Sign Inventory (SSI) (Foulds and Hope, 1968).

2. Assessment by a relative; The assessment was carried out by means of a questionnaire containing seven-point rating scale on sixteen behavioural and symptomatic items of which agoraphobics frequently complain. There was also provision for obtaining other information (see Appendix VII).

Follow-up measures

Follow-up assessments were carried out at 3, 6 and 12 months. The same procedures were given to the subjects as those used at the post-treatment assessment except for the following: the 16 Personality Factor Questionnaire, the General Benefit Rating and two behavioural tests (visit to Arndale Centre and top three hierarchy items).

A summary of the assessment procedures used during the project is provided in Table 6.1.

Treatment methods

Interview

A short, 5-min interview preceeded each treatment session; the purpose of this interview was to provide the subject with a brief opportunity to report progress and to raise any problems which may have occurred between therapy sessions. Subjects in all groups were encouraged to get out and about as much as possible.

Relaxation training

Relaxation training was given to all thirty-two subjects by means of tape recordings. The method used was basically Jacobsonian (1938) in nature and involved the systematic contraction and relaxation of groups of muscles; a detailed description of the techniques is provided by Beech *et al.* (1982); Burns (1981b).

Behavioural counselling (modified)

Behavioural counselling may be defined as the process of helping people to learn how to solve certain interpersonal, emotional and decision-making problems (Krumboltz and Thoreson, 1976). In this definition the key word is 'learn'. Considerable emphasis is placed on helping clients assume control of their own anxieties and become more self-sufficient; the goal is achieved through counselling, based on learning principles, so that the clients may develop appropriate skills for altering their own behaviours.

Table 6.1. Summary of assessment procedures

Method	Pre-treatment	Continuous during treatment	Mid-treatment	Post-treatment	Follow-up 3, 6, 12 months
Progressive Matrices	×				
Mill Hill Vocabulary	×				
Agoraphobia Questionnaire (excluding Sections 36 and 39)	×				
Agoraphobia Questionnaire—Sections 36 and 39	×		×	×	×
16 Personality Factor Questionnaire—A	×			×	
Social Avoidance and Distress Scale	×		×	×	×
Fear of Negative Evaluation	×		×	×	×
Eysenck Personality Inventory—A	×		×	×	×
Expectancy Rating	×				
Benefit fo Treatment Rating		×			
General Benefit Rating			×	×	
Behavioural Tests					
(a) Unaccompanied walk: Distance	×		×	×	×
Time	×		×	×	×
Anxiety	×		×	×	×
(b) Arndale Centre: Time				×	
Anxiety				×	
(c) Top three hierarchy items				×	
Independent ratings					
(a) Clinician's PD Scale SSI				×	×
Clinician's Agoraphobic Rating				×	×
(b) Relatives				×	×

During the modified behavioural counselling sessions concern was focussed on three main areas:

1. A behavioural analysis of the day-to-day functioning of the subject, particularly with regard to the agoraphobic behaviour; thus the experiences of the individual in the natural environment were discussed in considerable detail; approximately one-third of each counselling session was taken up with this area.
2. Another third of the session was devoted to a discussion of the subject's experiences, in terms of learning and conditioning principles; the basic concepts of respondent and operant behaviour, positive and negative reinforcement, self and covert reinforcement, operant and classical conditioning, generalization, extinction, modelling, etc. were described and applied to agoraphobic behaviour in general and the subject's behaviour in particular.
3. The final third of the counselling session involved helping the subject to think about the principles and the particular problems experienced, and to use this understanding to combat anxiety. The therapist did *not* give specific recommendations or set specific exercises for the subject to accomplish. Thus, having understood the principles involved and having gained insight into the nature and maintenance of their agoraphobia, subjects were encouraged to utilize this knowledge.

Systematic desensitization

The systematic desensitization used was the traditional kind (Wolpe and Lazarus, 1966). Individual hierarchies of sixteen items were constructed for *each* of the subjects. Thus, the subject, while deeply relaxed, proceeded through an imagined hierarchy of anxiety-provoking situations, beginning at the lower end of the fear gradient. The presence of anxiety was signalled by having the subject raise a finger. Two items from the hierarchy were presented for visualization at each treatment session except for session 16; accordingly, in the first treatment session, items 1 and 2 were presented; at the second session items 2 and 3 and so on. At session 16, the sixteenth item was presented on four occasions. Visualization lasted 15 s and the inter-trial interval was 30 s. Subjects had to visualize each item on four consecutive occasions, without experiencing anxiety, before proceeding to the next item.

Reinforced graded practice

Subjects receiving reinforced graded practice had various exercises to attempt from the clinic; for example, to walk a certain distance, to buy something in the local shop, to travel certain distances on a bus, etc. In the case of a severely handicapped subject the nurse therapist was permitted to accompany the subject for the first exercise or two but this support was withdrawn as soon as possible. On the satisfactory completion of the goal, the subject was socially reinforced by the nurse therapist and another therapist. If the subject failed to achieve the goal no comment was made.

Stress inoculation

The stress inoculation approach has been described in a series of papers by Meichenbaum (1973, 1975a,b,c, 1976), Meichenbaum and Cameron (1974) and Meichenbaum and Turk (1975). As the name of the training procedure implies, subjects are provided with a prospective defense or set of skills to deal with future stressful situations.

Operationally, stress inoculation involves three phases:

1. Educational phase: The subject is provided with Schachter's (1966), or a similar, conceptual framework for understanding the nature of stressful reactions. Accordingly, the subject is informed that fear reactions seem to involve two major elements:

   (a) A heightened autonomic arousal (increased heart rate, rapid breathing, sweaty palms, etc.)
   (b) a set of anxiety producing avoidant thoughts, images and self-defeating statements.

   The therapist then indicates that treatment will be directed towards:

   (a) helping the subject to control the physiological arousal
   (b) substituting positive coping self-statements for the unproductive self-statements which habitually occupy the mind under stress conditions.

   The final aspect involves a discussion centering on the subject viewing the phobic reaction, not as one massive panic reaction, but as a series of four phases: preparing for a stressor, confronting or handling a stressor, possibly being overwhelmed by a stressor and, finally, reinforcing oneself for having coped.
2. Rehearsal phase: The rehearsal phase is designed to provide the subject with coping techniques (relaxation and positive self-statements) which can be employed at each of the various phases of the coping process. The coping self-statements are intended to help the subject assess the reality of the situation; to control negative thoughts and self-statements; to acknowledge, use and possibly relabel, the arousal experienced as well as to prepare for the direct confrontation of the phobic situation.
3. Application phase: After training in the clinic the subject tests out and practises the coping skills by actually employing them while in stressful situations.

Procedure

The scheduling of assessment and therapeutic sessions is shown in Appendix VIII. When subjects were referred to the project, two sessions were devoted to assessment (PRE A and PRE B). Having met the selection criteria subjects were allocated to the treatment groups. Certain procedural difficulties were occasioned by the fact that not all thirty-two subjects were referred at the start of the project; subjects were, in fact, referred over a period of 2 years. In the first instance, twelve subjects were available for the project. They were ranked on the result of the behavioural test (unaccompanied walk—distance). Each subject was randomly assigned to one of the treatment groups.

As more subjects were incorporated into the research programme, they were allocated to the treatment groups in essentially the same way, except that care was taken to ensure that, in each group of eight subjects, four would fall above and four below the estimated final sample mean on the behavioural measure. (The final mean, of course, could not be known until the final subject was taken on for treatment.) Thus, eventually, each group would consist of four 'severe' and four 'non-severe' subjects, severity being arbitrarily defined in terms of whether the subjects came below or above the total group mean on the behavioural test. Clearly, as more subjects were taken on for treatment, the mean altered unpredictably, so that the shifting value of the mean had to be taken into account.

In the case of the first subjects to be allocated to the groups early in the project, assignment to the groups was random except for matching on the behavioural test. As more subjects were taken on there was less choice as to which group the subject would belong: thus, as the number of subjects increased, allocation was more arbitrary than random; in either case no systematic bias could have been introduced into the allocation procedure. Together with the above considerations it was ensured that one male subject was placed in each group.

Thus, subjects were allocated into the four treatment groups with the following restrictions:

(a) There should be eight subjects in each of the four groups (seven female and one male).
(b) Subjects were matched on the behavioural measure in the manner described above and, thus, it was ensured that, in each group, four subjects would fall above and four subjects below the mean of the sample on the behavioural test measure.

In the case of the final subject for the research programme, there were no degrees of freedom left and the behavioural test score of the subject had to fall within a certain range; fortunately, the subject concerned fell in this range.

Table 6.2 summarizes the interview and treatment methods which the subjects in each group received; the durations of each procedure are also given.

Treatment manuals (see Appendices IX, X, XI and XII) were drawn up by the two therapists in an effort to standardize procedure and therapeutic methods as far as possible. Particular care was taken over the behavioural counselling. The therapists exchanged tape recordings of their behavioural

Table 6.2. Treatment groups and timings

Group I		Group II		Group III		Group IV	
5 min	Interview	5 min	Interview	5 min	Interview	5 min	Interview
10 min	Relaxation	10 min	Relaxation	10 min	Relaxation	10 min	Relaxation
		10 min	Systematic desensitization	10 min	Systematic desensitization	10 min	Systematic desensitization
50 min	Behavioural counselling	40 min	Behavioural counselling	20 min	Reinforced graded practice	20 min	Stress inoculation
				20 min	Behavioural counselling	20 min	Reinforced graded practice

counselling sessions; also, the nurse therapist, who sat in with the therapists during treatment, was able to provide liaison.

Following the allocation of subjects to the treatment groups, all subjects received two pre-treatment sessions TR A and TR B (see Appendix VIII), in which full descriptions of the therapeutic programme and the rationale for it were given; subjects accepted the treatment offered and agreed to sign the contract. At the conclusion of the pre-treatment sessions the subjects' expectations were assessed by means of rating scales.

During these two pre-treatment sessions the construction of anxiety hierarchies was begun. Training in relaxation was commended; for this purpose a 10-min tape recording had been made by the first therapist (Dr L. E. Burns); the second therapist (Dr G. L. Thorpe), whilst listening through an ear piece to this recording, made his own tape; thus the two tapes were identical with regard to context and duration of instruction. All subjects were instructed to practise relaxation at home each day for 20 min. Subjects in Groups II, III and IV, whilst relaxed, received practice in the visualization of a neutral stimulus (a flower); the item was presented at each of the pre-treatment sessions on four occasions for 15 s visualization, with an inter-trial interval (of relaxation) of 30 s. In addition, subjects in Group IV received training in the stress inoculation procedure.

The treatment programme now commenced. Each therapist provided individual treatment for four subjects in each of the four treatment methods. As mentioned previously, the nurse therapist, under supervision, administered relaxation training, systematic desensitization, reinforced graded practice and stress inoculation; the nurse therapist, however, did not take an active part in the behavioural counselling sessions although she sat in some of these sessions as an observer. The nurse therapist assisted the two therapists approximately equally and treated subjects in all four treatment groups. The treatment programme consisted of sixteen sessions administered twice weekly. The duration of each treatment session was kept constant as far as possible and was scheduled to last for 65 min. Clearly the times of the individual components of the treatment programme varied somewhat due to signalling of anxiety during systematic desensitization and the nature of the reinforced graded practice exercises, etc., but the overall period was rarely exceeded by more than a few minutes. Occasionally it was not possible to administer treatment on a twice-weekly basis due to a subject's illness, etc. No major procedural problems were encountered during the treatment programme.

As will be observed from Appendix VIII, in addition to the two pre-treatment and one mid-treatment assessments, three sessions were devoted to post-treatment assessment. During the post-treatment assessment and in addition to the formal assessment procedures used previously, several new assessment methods were introduced. The independent clinician, (Mr R. H. Curtis), administered the PD Scale of the Symptom Sign Inventory in order to assess any remaining psychological disturbance; on the basis of standard questions (supplemented as necessary by further questions) each subject was rated on a five-point agoraphobic scale. As mentioned previously, the clinician was unaware of the treatment group within which the subject fell or the treatment methods being used. The subject's spouse (or, if this was inappropriate, another close member of the family) was given a questionnaire to complete; this questionnaire was completed independently of the subject and was returned, by mail, to the therapists.

Two new behavioural tests were introduced at the post-assessment period; each subject, accompanied by the therapist, was taken by car to a large shopping centre (the Arndale Centre in Middleton), where they were asked to walk around unaccompanied for 30 min. The time the subject remained in the centre was recorded by the therapist as was a rating of the anxiety (on a five-point scale) experienced by the subject. The second behavioural test consisted of asking the subjects at the first post-treatment session (Experimental Session 22), to attempt, during the next 10 days, that is by Experimental Session 24, the three most difficult items from their anxiety hierarchies. Examples from the hierarchies included 'Sitting in the hairdressers having my hair done', 'Walking around the centre of town on a Saturday afternoon by myself' and 'A fifteen minute bus journey in the rush hour on my own'. Very occasionally it was inappropriate for the subject to attempt some item, (for example, attending a school function); in this case the next most anxiety-engendering item was to be attempted. The therapists relied on the self-report of the subject as to whether or not they achieved their goals.

Follow-up assessments were carried out at 3, 6 and 12 months by one of the therapists (Dr L. E. Burns), the nurse therapist (Mrs J. Hawkrigg) and the independent clinician (Mr R. H. Curtis), Dr Thorpe having left the department. Unfortunately, at the end of the treatment it was clear that a few of the subjects required further help; flooding (2.5 h sessions) was offered to those who felt they would derive further benefit from treatment. Subjects in Group I who requested further treatment received a mean of 9.5 h flooding; in Group II 7.3 h; in Group III 8 h, in Group IV 7.3 h. Clearly this additional treatment needs to be borne in mind when considering the follow-up results.

EXPERIMENT II

The purpose of this experiment, which was begun shortly after the final subject in Experiment I had completed the post-treatment assessments, was to monitor fluctuations in untreated agoraphobia over an equivalent 10-week period. The same definition of agoraphobia, sources of referral and selection criteria applied as in Experiment I. Ten subjects were immediately available for the experiment—six severe and four non-severe—agoraphobics; two of the severe agoraphobics were rejected using random tables. Seven of the eight subjects were receiving medication for their agoraphobia; as in Experiment I the medication was mainly Librium or Valium.

All the selected subjects agreed to participate in the research project having been informed that it would not be possible to offer them treatment for 10 weeks but that assessments would be carried out at intervals of approximately 4 and 8 weeks. Subjects were not asked to sign a contract; there were no drop-outs from the experiment.

The experiment was run by one of the therapists (Dr L. E. Burns), and the nurse therapist, (Mrs J. Hawkrigg).

The scheduling of the assessment sessions and the methods of assessment were exactly the same as in Experiment I (see Appendix VIII) except for the following omissions:

1. Equivalent pre-treatment period: expectancy ratings.
2. Continuous: benefit ratings.
3. Equivalent mid-treatment period: general benefit ratings.
4. Equivalent post-treatment period: general benefit ratings; spouse rating questionnaire; behavioural test, Arndale Centre, independent assessment by psychologist.

There were, of course, no follow-up assessments.

The subjects were offered behavioural treatment as soon as the equivalent post-treatment period assessments had been completed.

RESULTS

The results are presented separately for Experiments I and II.

Experiment I

In the first instance one-way ANOVAs were calculated for the pre-treatment scores on each measure, in order to ascertain whether the treatment groups were initially different. Results were then analysed by means of the repeated measures analysis; where this analysis indicated treatment group differences in any measure the Newman Keuls' test (comparison of group means) was normally used.

Pre-treatment measures

Descriptive and generalization measures

Pre-treatment group differences were non-significant on the following measures: Standard Progressive Matrices; Mill Hill Vocabulary Scale; Social Avoidance and Distress Scale; Fear of Negative Evaluation Scale; Eysenck Personality Inventory–Form A. The only significant treatment group difference in the 16 Personality Factor Test was Factor Q2 ($F(3,28) = 2.95$, $P = 0.05$). Group 1 had a significantly higher score ($P < 0.01$) on Self Sufficiency than Groups II, III and IV. The responses of the subjects, along with those in Experiment II, to the Agoraphobia Questionnaire are shown in Appendix III.

Self-report, expectancy and behavioural measures

No significant pre-treatment group differences were found on the following measures: Agoraphobic Questionnaire (Sections 36 and 39), Behavioural Tests—unaccompanied walk (distance, duration or anxiety measures). Expectancy ratings were presented after each of two preliminary treatment sessions (TR A and TR B). At the TR A session there was no significant difference between the four groups on expectation of success. When considering TR A and TR B repeated measures analysis showed no significant difference between the groups although the subjects recorded more enthusiastic expectations on the second presentation of this measure ($F\,(3,28) = 9.78$, $P < 0.005$).

Continuous measures during treatment

Benefit rating

This measure was administered after each treatment session (TR1 to TR16). The results indicated that, regardless of the treatment group, the subjects recorded progressively greater benefit from treatment as the number of sessions increased ($F\,(15,360) = 14.30, P < 0.001$). Subjects in Group IV rated themselves as having derived greater benefit than did subjects in the other groups ($P < 0.01$).

Outcome measures

Descriptive and generalization measures

1. Social Avoidance and Distress Scale: The results indicate a general reduction in reported anxiety ($F\,(5,120) = 16.18$, $P < 0.001$) not associated with differential treatment effects.
2. Fear of Negative Evaluation Scale: There was a significant reduction ($F\,(5,120) = 5.09, P < 0.001$) in anxiety as assessed by this measure but it was not related to differential treatment effects.
3. Eysenck Personality Inventory (Form A).
   (a) Neuroticism Scale (N): There was a significant difference between treatment groups ($F\,(3,24) = 6.39, P < 0.005$). Group II had significantly lower scores ($P < 0.01$) than the other treatment groups. There was also a significant decrease ($F\,(5,120) = 5.10$, $P < 0.001$) in neuroticism scores over trials.
   (b) Extraversion Scale (E): There was a significant increase in the E scores over trials which was not associated with differential treatment effects ($F\,(5,120) = 3.71$, $P < 0.005$). There was also a significant interaction ($F\,(5,120) = 2.30$, $P < 0.05$) between severity of agoraphobia and trials.

(c) Lie Scale (L): There was a significant increase in L scores as a function of time, not associated with treatment group effects (F (5,120) = 7.57, $P < 0.001$).

4. The 16 Personality Factor Test.
The following significant results were obtained:

Factor H: There was a general reduction in shyness and threat sensitivity (F (1,24) = 4.63, $P < 0.05$) not associated with differential treatment effects.

Factor I: There was a significant interaction effect (Treatment × Severity) (F (3,24) = 5.52, $P < 0.005$).

Factor M: Two interaction effects were noted, Treatment × Severity (F (3,24) = 3.62, $P < 0.05$) and Treatment × Trials (F (3,24) = 3.69, $P < 0.05$).

Factor O: There was a general reduction in Guilt Proneness (apprehension, worrying) not associated with differential treatment effects (F (1,24) = 7.18, $P < 0.025$).

Factor Q1: A Severity × Trials interaction was observed (F (1,24) = 4.91, $P < 0.05$).

Factor Q3: There was an increase in Self-Concept Control over time not associated with treatment effects (F (1,24) = 15.83, $P < 0.001$) and a Severity × Trials interaction (F (1,24) = 4.80, $P < 0.05$).

Factor Q4: A Severity × Trials interaction was noted (F (1,24) = 4.51, $P < 0.05$).

Self report, general benefit rating and behavioural measures

1. Agoraphobic Questionnaire

(a) Section 36: The results indicate a general improvement in the ability of the subjects to handle difficult situations in the natural environment but it was not associated with differential treatment effects F (5,120) = 5.99, $P < 0.001$).

(b) Section 39: Similar results were obtained on Section 39 indicating a reduction in self-reported anxiety in a variety of situations not associated with differential treatment effects (F (5,120) = 20.00, $P < 0.001$). A significant difference on severity was noted, the severe group reporting more anxiety and avoidance (F (1,24) = 5.76, $P <$ 0.025).

2. General benefit ratings
These measures were taken at the mid- and post-treatment assessment sessions. There were no significant treatment group differences. However, there was a general increase in reported benefit from mid- to post-treatment (F (1,24) = 6.51, $P < 0.025$).

3. Unaccompanied Walk

   (a) Distance: Subjects walked progressively further over the assessment sessions ($F\,(5{,}120) = 6.95$, $P < 0.001$) but this was not associated with differential treatment group effects. The severe subjects walked a significantly shorter distance than non-severe subjects $F\,(1{,}24) = 46.87$, $P < 0.001$). Interaction effects (Treatment and Severity: $F\,(3{,}24) = 3.67$, $P < (0.05)$ and Severity × Trials: $F\,(5{,}120) = 4.25$, $P < 0.005$) are. noted.
   (b) Time: The results indicate that the subjects remained for increasingly long durations during the walk but, again, this was not associated with differential treatment group effects ($F\,(5{,}120) = 9.38, P < 0.001$). The severe groups remained on the walk for significantly shorter times than the non-severe groups ($F\,(1{,}24) = 49.79$, $P < 0.001$).
   (c) Anxiety: There was a significant reduction in anxiety ratings over time not associated with differential treatment group effects ($F\,(5{,}120) = 7.44$, $P < 0.001$).

Top three hierarchy items

This assessment was given on only one occasion, at post-treatment. There were no significant treatment group differences ($F\,(3{,}28) = 0.18$ NS)

Visit to Arndale Centre, Middleton

Similarly, this test was given once, at post-treatment. No significant group differences were found on either measure: time ($F\,(3{,}28) = 0.44$ NS); anxiety ($F\,(3{,}28) = 0.39$ NS).

Independent measures

Assessment by a clinician

Independent assessments were carried out at post-treatment and at the three follow-up intervals by a clinical psychologist.

1. Clinician's agoraphobic ratings: A general improvement on the agoraphobic ratings from post-treatment to 6-month follow-up with a slight deterioration at 12 months was observed ($F\,(3{,}72) = 7.00$, $P < 0.001$), but differential effects due to treatment were not noted. A significant difference is noted on severity in that the severe subjects were rated as having more agoraphobic tendencies ($F\,(1{,}24) = 7.75$, $P < 0.025$). An interaction effect, (Treatment × Severity), is also noted ($F\,(3{,}24) = 3.57$, $P < 0.05$).
2. Symptom Sign Inventory (PD Scale): the results reveal only a Treatment × Severity interaction effect ($F\,(3{,}24) = 3.10$, $P < 0.05$).

Assessment by a relative

At the same time as the clinician's ratings above, the spouse, close relative or a friend completed a questionnaire. There were no significant effects.

Analysis of therapists' effects

The study was designed so that an assessment of the differential effects after treatment attributable to the therapists is possible; the statistical analyses take the form of two-way analyses of change scores, post- minus pre-treatment, with factorial combinations of treatments and therapists; arbitrarily, the following measures were chosen for analyses: (a) Social Avoidance and Distress Scale; (b) Fear of Negative Evaluation Scale; (c) Eysenck Personality Inventory—N and E; (d) Agoraphobia Questionnaire—Sections 36 and 39; (e) Behavioural Test—Unaccompanied Walk (Distance, Time and Anxiety); (f) Benefit Ratings. There were no significant differential therapist effects on any of the measures.

Experiment II

In this experiment the results of the new control group are combined with those of Experiment I; thus, the five groups are compared on all appropriate measures using one-way ANOVAs, repeated measures and Newman–Keuls as necessary.

Pre-treatment measures

Descriptive and generalization measures

1. Standard Progressive Matrices: No significant group differences were observed. The mean score for the five group was 38.48 (Standard Deviation 11.89).
2. The Mill Hill Vocabulary Scale: No significant group differences were noted. The mean score for the five groups was 48.63 (Standard Deviation 10.61).
3. The Agoraphobia Questionnaire (excluding Sections 36 and 39): Results for subjects in both Experiments I and II are detailed in Appendix III.
4. The 16 Personality Factor Test: No significant group differences were observed on any of the sixteen Factors. The mean scores and Standard Deviations of the 16 P.F. factors for the five groups are given in Table 6.3.
5. The Social Avoidance and Distress Scale: There were no significant group differences.
6. Fear of Negative Evaluation Scale: No significant initial group differences were noted.
7. The Eysenck Personality Inventory: No significant group differences were observed on the Neuroticism, Extraversion and Lie Scales. The Mean and

Table 6.3. Sixteen personality factor test—mean scores and standard deviations of the five groups of agoraphobics (N = 40)

	Mean	SD		Mean	SD
Factor A	10.58	2.40	Factor L	8.85	3.68
Factor B	6.78	1.94	Factor M	11.10	3.89
Factor C	9.78	4.05	Factor N	11.43	3.08
Factor E	9.73	4.01	Factor O	15.33	4.38
Factor F	11.08	5.11	Factor Q1	9.15	2.47
Factor G	11.78	2.90	Factor Q2	11.65	3.19
Factor H	8.73	5.23	Factor Q3	9.88	3.08
Factor I	13.18	2.67	Factor Q4	18.03	4.09

Standard Deviation for Neuroticism and Extraversion for the five groups are: Neuroticism, mean 18.05, SD 3.59; Extraversion, mean 10.37, SD 4.10.

Self-report and behavioural measures

1. Agoraphobic Questionnaire

   (a) Section 36: No significant initial group differences were noted.
   (b) Section 39: Pre-treatment group differences were non-significant.

2. Behavioural Test—unaccompanied walk: none of the measures showed significant initial group disparity.

Outcome measures

Generalization measures

1. Social Avoidance and Distress Scale: a general improvement over time was noted, there being no significant effects due to treatment (F (2,60) = 20.72, $P < 0.001$)
2. Fear of Negative Evaluation: on this measure there was a general improvement over time, there being no significant group effects (F (2,60) = 6.09, $P < 0.001$).
3. Eysenck Personality Inventory.

   (a) Neuroticism Scale (N): N scores decreased significantly over time (F (2,60) = 15.28, $P < 0.001$). There was also a significant interaction between treatment and trials (F (8,60) = 4.98, $P < 0.001$).
   (b) Extraversion Scale (e): There was a significant increase in E scores as a function of time (F (2,60) = 10.76, $P < 0.001$), not due to differential treatment effects.
   (c) Lie Scale (L): There was a significant increase in the L scores as a function of time (F (2,60) = 7.91, $P < 0.001$).

4. The 16 Personality Factor Test: The following significant results were obtained.

Factor C:	There was a significant general increase in emotional stability (F (1,30) = 7.10, $P < 0.025$), not associated with differential treatment effects.
Factor F:	Severely handicapped agoraphobics scored significantly higher on the 'surgency' factor (F (1,30) = 4.73), $P < 0.05$). An interaction effect (Treatment × Severity) is observed (F (4,30) = 7.47, $P < 0.01$).
Factor G:	A Significant Treatment × Trials Interaction is noted (F (4,30) = 3.81, $P < 0.025$).
Factor I:	A Significant Treatment × Severity Interaction is noted (F (4,30) = 3.59, $P < 0.025$).
Factor M:	Two interaction effects are observed; Treatment × Severity (F (4,30) = 3.24, $P < 0.05$), Treatment × Trials (F (4,30) = 2.75, $P < 0.05$).
Factor O:	There was a significant decrease in Guilt Proneness (apprehension, etc.) over time (F (1,30) = 4.34, $P < 0.05$), but it was not associated with differential treatment effects.
Factor Q3:	A significant increase in Self-Concept Control over time was observed (F (1,30) = 14.14, $P < 0.001$), but, again, this was not associated with differential treatment effects.

Self report and behavioural measures

1. Agoraphobia Questionnaire
   (a) Section 36: The results show a significant improvement over time (F (2,60) = 9.12, $P < 0.001$), not due to differential treatment effects. There is a significant interaction effect (Treatment × Severity) (F (4,30) = 3.55, $P < 0.025$).
   (b) Section 39: There is no significant difference, due to treatment, between the five groups from pre- to post-treatment. All groups showed general improvement as a function of time (F (2,60 = 45.12, $P < 0.001$). Severely handicapped agoraphobics scored significantly higher than non-severe subjects (F (1,30) = 7.76, $P < 0.001$).
2. Behavioural Tests—unaccompanied walk
   (a) Distance: Subjects progressed further from pre- to post-treatment (F (2,60) = 12.92, $P < 0.001$), but this was not associated with differential treatment effects. Severe subjects walked a significantly shorter distance that non-severe subjects (F (1,30 = 64.88, $P < 0.001$). There was an interaction effect (Severity × Trials) (F (2,60) = 4.81, $P < 0.025$).
   (b) Time: There was a significant difference in the amount of time the groups stayed out on the unaccompanied walk (F (4,30) = 3.19,

$P < 0.05$). On the Newman–Keuls' test inter-treatment group differences fell short of significance. The severe subjects remained on the walk a significantly shorter time than the non-severe subjects ($F\,(1,30) = 89.13$, $P < 0.001$). The overall scores of the groups showed a significant increase over time, ($F\,(2,60) = 23.45$, $P < 0.001$). There was a significant Treatment × Trials interaction ($F\,(8,60) = 2.17$, $P < 0.05$).

(c) Anxiety: No significant differences in anxiety ratings were noted.

Top three hierarchy items

The results show a clear difference between groups in response to treatment $F\,(4,35) = 499$, $P < 0.005$). A Newman–Keuls analysis showed that each of the four treatment groups accomplished more of the hierarchy ventures than did the waiting list group ($P < 0.01$).

DISCUSSION

Experiment I

Comparability of groups

In considering the results of Experiment I it is interesting to observe that, although the four groups were matched on only the Behavioural Walk Test—distance, there were no significant differences between the groups on a wide range of measures. The only significant difference to emerge between the groups related to Factor Q2 of the 16 Personality Factor Test where the probability was not less than, but was equal to, the 0.05 level; further analysis suggested that Group I showed a greater degree of self-sufficiency and resourcefulness than the other three groups. Thus, the evidence suggests that the four groups were very well matched before the commencement of treatment.

Representativeness of subjects

By making reference to the results of the National Survey of Agoraphobics ($N = 963$) evidence will be presented in the discussion of Experiment II which indicated that the subjects taking part in the research were very typical of agoraphobics as a whole.

Expectancy

Although there were no significant intergroup differences, subjects in all groups recorded significantly higher expectations of successful therapeutic outcome on the second presentation of this measure, the mean score for the four groups, on a seven-point rating scale, being 5.75. This higher expectancy presumably resulted from the subjects having, by the second assessment, a greater understanding of the therapeutic programme and the rationale for it.

Outcome measures

Trials effects

In Experiment I, in which all subjects received behavioural treatment on the many and varied assessment procedures which were used, including some generalization ones which do not directly measure agoraphobia, there is a general clinical improvement (Trials Effect).

Analysis of the continuous measure during treatment (the Benefit rating) shows that subjects recorded progressively greater benefit from treatment as the number of therapy sessions increased except for the last session, no. 16, where there was a very small decrease in the overall score.

Results from the Social Avoidance and Distress Scale indicates Trials Effect only, suggesting a general reduction of social anxiety over time. Closer inspection indicates that the social anxiety reduces progressively from pre-treatment to 3-month follow-up after which there is no further reduction. Results from the Fear of Negative Evaluation Scale also indicate a Trials Effect only suggesting a general reduction of social evaluative anxiety over time; subjects show cumulatively less social-evaluative anxiety from pre-treatment to the 12-month follow-up.

The Neuroticism Scale of the Eysenck Personality Inventory shows a progressive reduction in neuroticism over time from pre-treatment to 12-month follow-up, associated with differential treatment effects. There was a general increase in the extraversion score over time. However, all this increase occurred between pre- and mid-treatment. From mid-treatment to 12-month follow-up there was a very gradual decline in the 'E' score. There was a significant increase in the Lie scores as a function of time; however, the mean 'L' scores remained within normal limits for all groups.

On the 16 Personality Factor Test there were Trials Effects suggesting a general reduction of shyness (Factor H) and guilt proneness, apprehension and worrying (Factor O); Factor Q3 (Self-concept control) showed a general increase over time.

A Trials Effect is observed on Section 36 of the Agoraphobia Questionnaire and is indicative of a general improvement in the ability of the subjects from the four groups to handle difficult situations in the natural environment. Most of the improvement appeared to have been made from pre-treatment to mid-treatment; progress continued until 6-month follow-up when a slight deterioration was observed; this continued to 12-month follow-up.

A Trials Effect was also observed on Section 39 of the Agoraphobia Questionnaire and indicated a general reduction in self-reported anxiety in various situations. From 6-month follow-up there was a tendency for anxiety to increase. The extent of the general improvement may be judged from the fact that twenty-three of the thirty-two subjects obtained scores which placed them in the first quartile at post-treatment. Further analysis shows that three of the thirty-two subjects obtained scores at post-treatment which were higher (worse) than they obtained at pre-treatment; the three subjects came from Groups I, II and IV.

Analysis of the General Benefit Ratings (given at mid- and post-treatment) demonstrated a Trials Effect and indicated a general increase in reported benefit; this finding was in keeping with the continuous Benefit Ratings. Again, no intergroup (Treatment or Severity) differences were observed.

There were a number of significant results on the Unaccompanied Walk—distance. There was a Trials Effect indicating that subjects generally walked progressively further over the assessment sessions. Again, most of the progress was made during the pre- to mid-assessment interval; there was slight deterioration of performance during the 3-month and 6-month follow-up assessments but, at the 12-month assessment, performance improved to the highest level of the study. An indication of the extent of the improvement can be judged by the consideration that the performance of twenty-two of the thirty-two subjects on this test was sufficient to place them in the fourth quartile at the post-treatment assessment. However, three subjects (one each in Groups I, II, and IV), were unable to walk as far as they had at pre-treatment but the difference in the distance in each case was quite small.

There was a Trials Effect on the Unaccompanied Walk—time measure; as expected, subjects generally remained for longer periods of time on the Unaccompanied Walk over the assessment sessions; however, there was a slight deterioration in the amount of time subjects remained on the walk at the 3-month and 6-month follow-up assessments but performance improved at the 12-month assessment. These results, as anticipated, parallel those of the Unaccompanied Walk—distance measure.

There was only a Trials Effect on the Unaccompanied Walk—anxiety; a significant general reduction in anxiety was observed. On this measure the major drop in anxiety was at the 3-month follow-up with a slight progressive improvement until 12-month follow-up.

Consideration will now be given to three outcome measures which were given only at post-treatment and at 3-, 6-, and 12-month follow-ups. A Trials Effect is observed on the Clinician's Agoraphobic Ratings; a general improvement on ratings was noted from post-treatment to 6-month follow-up, with a slight deterioration at 12-month follow-up. The Clinician's converted ratings at post-treatment to follow-up (means 2.5 to 2.13) appear to be similar to the ratings of the main phobia reported by Gelder *et al*. (1967), Gillan and Rachman (1974), Mathews (1977a) etc. There were no significant Trials Effects on the Symptom Sign (PD) Scale. No significant results were observed on the Relative's Questionnaire. Thus, it would seem that relatives, over the follow-up period, did not see the subjects change significantly although the trend was in the direction of general improvement.

Severity effects

An interesting finding was that those subjects assessed as severe on the Unaccompanied Walk—distance measure were also assessed as being severe, in terms of the F-ratios, on other measures; specifically Section 39 of the Agoraphobia Questionnaire; Unaccompanied Walk—time and the Clinician's Agoraphobic Ratings after treatment. It will be noted that no such finding appertains to the subjects' anxiety ratings on the walk which suggests that subjective ratings of anxiety may not be good predictors of this kind of behavioural performance. The same conclusion may be drawn about Section 36 of the Agoraphobia Questionnaire and the behavioural measure; the items in the Section refer to factors which change the subjective feelings of the subjects for better or worse; these feelings may bear little relation to actual performance.

Severity × Trials Interactions

There is evidence that severe subjects respond differentially from non-severe subjects. For example, on the Eysenck Personality Inventory Extraversion Scale, there was a significant Severity × Trials interaction. A plot of this interaction shows a clear cross over of the groups between the 3- and 6-month follow-ups; the severe group at 6 and 12 months had E scores just above the mean of the normal population whereas the scores of the non-severe group had a tendency to become depressed at these follow-up intervals.

On the Q1 Factor of the 16 Personality Factor Test there was a significant Severity × Trials interaction. The scores of the severe subjects on conservatism remained virtually the same from pre- to post-treatment; however, the scores of non-severe subjects increased during this interval in the radicalism direction. On Factor Q3 severe subjects score lower at pre-treatment and then show a greater increase on self-concept control at post-treatment than non-severe subjects. In Factor Q4 severe subjects had reduced scores after treatment suggesting a more relaxed and tranquil state; on the other hand, the scores of the non-severe subjects remained virtually the same.

There was a Severity × Trials interaction on the Unaccompanied Walk—distance. However, due to a ceiling effect, this result can be largely discounted.

Treatment effects

Analysis of the continuous Benefit Rating shows that subjects in Group IV rated themselves as having obtained significantly greater benefit than those in the other groups. The greater benefit rating could be a function of the number of standard behavioural techniques being applied to the subjects in the group. It should be borne in mind that subjects were specifically requested not to discuss treatment procedures with other subjects in the research project; thus subjects should not have been aware of the procedures being used in the different groups. However, although the subjects in Group IV rated themselves as having derived greater benefit than those in other groups, there is little objective evidence from the various outcome measures to show that they did, indeed, make better progress.

There is a significant difference between treatment groups on the Neuroticism Scale of the Eysenck Personality Inventory; Group II shows significantly lower scores than the other three groups; although the 'N' scores of Group III did not show improvement reaching statistical significance, by the end of the 12-month follow-up period, these scores were within normal limits (using general population norms).

A significant Treatment Effect is observed in Factor Q2 (Self-Sufficiency) on the 16 Personality Factor Test; however, a Newman–Keuls analysis failed to identify a treatment group difference; the groups were not initially matched on this factor.

Treatment × trials interaction

The only significant Treatment × Trials interaction is seen on Factor M of the 16 Personality Factor Test. Analysis indicated that Group I had reduced scores at post-treatment assessment (indicating practicalness regulated by external reality) whereas Groups II, III and IV obtained increased scores on this Factor.

Post-treatment measures—hierarchy items and Arndale visit

Two assessment procedures were used at post-treatment.

1. Top three hierarchy items: No significant treatment group differences were found. Subjects reported that they had success in attempting fifty-seven out of a possible ninety-six items from their hierarchies.
2. The visit to the Arndale Centre, Middleton—time and anxiety: No significant differences were found on either measure. Subjects remain in the Centre 85.52 per cent of the total time allowed. The overall mean anxiety rating was 1.37 (SD = 0.93) suggesting the presence of only slight anxiety.

Therapist effects

On a wide range of measures there was evidence to show that the therapists were not conspicuously different. Thus, no significant differential therapist effects were found on the Social and Avoidance Scale, the Extraversion and Neuroticism Scales of the Eysenck Personality Inventory, the Agoraphobia Questionnaire—Sections 36 and 39, the Unaccompanied Walk—distance, time and anxiety, and the Benefit Ratings. However, a significant Therapist × Treatment interaction was observed on the Fear of Negative Evaluation Scale. Subjects in Groups I and III showed a greater reduction in FNE scores with therapist I (Dr L. E. Burns) whilst subjects in Group II and

IV showed a greater reduction in FNE scores with therapist II (Dr G. L. Thorpe). It would not, of course, be possible to predict a subject's improvement having regard to the therapist.

Most studies do not appear to show differential therapist effects; for example, Gelder *et al*. (1973): in one study (Mathews *et al*., 1976) some measures (therapist ratings of the phobic severity and depression; total phobic anxiety score and self-rating on mood scales) suggested the presence of outcome differences associated with therapist identity; the precise cause for these effects are unclear.

Experiment II

Experiment II was a more limited study and was planned after it became evident that the four groups in Experiment I showed few differential responses to treatment.

Comparability of groups

There were no significant differences between the five groups on the following Generalization, Self-Report, and Behavioural Measures: The Standard Progressive Matrices; The Mill Hill Vocabulary Scale; the 16 Personality Factor Test; the Social Avoidance and Distress Scale; the Fear of Negative Evaluation Scale; the Eysenck Personality Inventory; Sections 36 and 39 of the Agoraphobia Questionnaire and the Unaccompanied Walk (distance, time and anxiety). Thus, the five groups were extremely well matched at the time of the initial assessments.

Characteristics of the groups

The mean score of the five groups on the Standard Progressive matrices was 38.48. This is the equivalent to an IQ of approximately 99. The mean score on the Mill Hill Vocabulary Scale (Form 1 Senior) was 48.63; this is equivalent to a verbal IQ of 92.

Thus, these findings support the view that agoraphobics are not unusual with respect to intelligence (Gelder *et al*., 1967; Gillan and Rachman, 1974; Marks, 1969). With a mean score of 18.05 on the 'N' Scale of the Eysenck Personality Inventory, the score is nearly two standard deviations above the mean of the normal population suggesting a very high level of neurotic reactivity. The Extraversion and Lie scores are within the normal limits. The most significant feature of the 16 Personality Factor Test results is that the three factors which are the most important components of neuroticism are the ones which are outside normal limits. The means and standard deviations in brackets refer to the General Population (female) norms based on a mean age of 35 years. Thus, on Factor C (emotional stability) the mean score for the five groups is 9.78, SD 4.05 (mean 16.03, SD 4.17); Factor O (guilt proneness—apprehension, worrying, etc.) mean 15.33, SD 4.38 (mean 10.70, SD 3.84); Factor Q4 (tension), mean 18.03, SD 4.09; (mean 12.92, SD 4.96). The mean score for the Social Avoidance and Distress Scale was just outside normal limits indicating that the subjects felt they tended to avoid social interactions, were less confident with social relationships, etc. However, the mean score on the Fear of Negative Evaluation Scale was within normal limits suggesting that the subjects were less concerned about evaluative situations.

Representativeness of the subjects

It is clear from a comparison of data from the National Survey of Agoraphobics ($N = 963$) with the data from the subjects in the five groups ($N = 40$) that there are some striking similarities between the two populations (see Appendix III). The sex ratio of the five groups (87.50 per cent female) is very close to that expected (88.16 per cent); there is nothing unusual about the marital status of the sample; the mean age at treatment was 35.37 years which is in keeping with the data supplied by Marks (1969) and others. The mean age of onset (26.97 years) was similar to the result obtained from the National Survey. The forty subjects obtained very similar results to those of the National Survey subjects on characteristics such as religious affiliation, age of finishing school and further educational opportunities, age of marriage and age of spouse, percentage having children, the professional people they consulted about their agoraphobia and fears concerning panic attacks, etc. However, a somewhat higher percentage of the subjects in the five groups had a job outside their home (40.0 per cent as opposed to 28.6 per cent from the National Survey) but a larger percentage felt that the agoraphobia 'often' hindered their work (42.1 per cent versus 24.0 per cent).

In both studies, of those not working 83 per cent claimed they would obtain a job if it were not for their agoraphobia. A greater percentage of the subjects in the treatment research than in the National Survey felt that the agoraphobia was putting 'a lot' of strain on their marriage (35.0 per cent versus 22.01 per cent). Overall, however, it may be argued with a good degree of confidence that the sample of agoraphobics which took part in the present research was typical of agoraphobics as a whole.

Outcome measures

It needs to be remembered that, as the subjects in Group V were assessed only at the pre-, mid- and post-treatment equivalent time periods, the results from Group V will be considered with those from Groups I–IV at the same assessment periods.

Results from the Social Avoidance Distress Scale and the Fear of Negative Evaluation Scale indicate a Trials Effect only (reference is made in Experiment II to *Trials* Effect(s) although, perhaps, it should be defined more accurately as Occasion Effect(s)) suggesting a general reduction in social and evaluation anxiety over time; thus, it is apparent that, on these measures, waiting-list controls improve as much as subjects in Groups I–IV.

Gelder *et al*. (1967) report no change in social anxiety scores using check lists derived from the Tavistock Self-Assessment Inventory (Dixon *et al*., 1957a,b) and expectation that behavioural treatments might lead to change in social anxiety as measured by the Social Anxiety Scale (SAS) (Watson and Friend, 1969), was not confirmed in two studies by Emmelkamp *et al*. (1974, 1975).

Analysis of the Neuroticism scores of the Eysenck Personality Inventory suggests that the five groups respond differentially. Subjects in Group II show a progressive improvement from pre- to post-treatment when compared to those in Groups I, III, IV and V; these latter groups change little during the same period. Indeed, the mean score at post-treatment for Group II subjects is within normal limits. The Extraversion score of all five groups increased significantly from pre-treatment to post-treatment (Trials Effect); at post-treatment the group means remained within normal limits. Thus, waiting list controls changed in the same direction as the subjects of the four treatment groups. Similar findings appertain to the Lie score; the mean score for each group remained within normal limits.

Similar findings concerning the 'N' and 'E' scores of the EPI were reported by Evans and Kellam (1973); in this study subjects showed a significant decrease in neuroticism and a significant increase in extraversion by the end of treatment; these changes were maintained at follow-up. It was noted that the neuroticism and extraversion results were not related to type of treatment. However, in the study by Gillan and Rachman (1974) there were no significant changes in neuroticism and extraversion at post-treatment although, at 3-month follow-up, 'N' scores had significantly decreased. In the research by Gelder *et al*. (1967) the 'N' score had fallen significantly by the end of treatment in the behaviour therapy (systematic desensitization) group; a significant increase in the 'E' score was observed only in the psychotherapy group.

The most significant results obtained on the 16 Personality Factor Test appear to be those which indicated increases in emotional stability (Factor C) and self-concept control (Factor Q3) and significant decreases in guilt proneness (Factor O) not associated with differential treatment group effects. Few researchers report on the use of the 16 Personality Factor Test as an outcome measure in the behavioural treatment of agoraphobia; those that do indicate few treatment effects. In the study by Gelder *et al*. (1973) the only significant findings were that flooding patients had higher scores on Factor G (conscientiousness) than desensitization patients; flooding patients were lower than control patients on Factor O (apprehension). Mathews *et al*. (1976) felt that Factor C was a predictor of good therapeutic outcome but only at the 5 per cent level of confidence.

A significant general improvement over time as assessed on Section 36 of the Agoraphobia Questionnaire is observed. There is a significant improvement in the ability of subjects in the five groups to handle difficult environmental situations. However, whereas in Experiment I most of the progress appeared to have been made in the pre- to mid-treatment period, subjects in Group V made most of the progress during the mid- to post-treatment period.

A Trials Effect is again observed in Section 39 of the Agoraphobia Questionnaire suggesting that the five groups showed a general reduction in self-reported anxiety in various situations from pre- to post-treatment. Groups I–IV showed the major portion of the improvement during the pre- to mid-treatment period, whereas, with Group V, the major portion of the improvement occurred during the mid- to post-treatment period. Appendix XIII shows the means and standard deviations for all five groups for Section 39 of the Agoraphobic Questionnaire.

On the Unaccompanied Walk—distance, the Trials Effect indicates that subjects walk progressively further as a function of time. In Experiment I, most of the gains were made in the pre- to mid-treatment period. However, the gains in Group V were made in the mid- to post-treatment period (See Appendix XIII). The Severity Effect is, of course, expected. The Severity × Trials interaction is informative; severe and non-severe subjects differ in terms of their improvement. It appears that severe subjects improve more than non-severe subjects; however, it seems highly likely that this result is due to the ceiling effect of the assessment procedure.

There was a significant difference in the amount of time the five groups remained out on the Unaccompanied Walk but, on the Newman–Keuls Test, inter-treatment group differences fell short of significance. Severe subjects remained on the walk for a significantly shorter period of time than non-severe subjects. The overall scores of the five groups showed a significant increase over time. A significant Treatment × Severity × Trials interaction was observed; for the severe subjects a general increase in time spent on the walk was observed, regardless of the treatment group. For each of the severe groups the time score cumulatively increased from pre- to mid-treatment and from mid- to post-treatment. For non-severe subjects progress was related to treatment group. Subjects in Groups I and V spent slightly less time on the walks at the post-treatment than at pre-treatment, although Group I subjects made an initial gain from pre-treatment to mid-treatment. Subjects in Groups II, III and IV, on the other hand, spent more time on the walk after treatment although the performance of Group II subjects deteriorated slightly from mid- to post-treatment.

No significant differences were observed on the anxiety ratings made by subjects during the Unaccompanied Walk. Although some decrease in anxiety was observed in all groups, except Group IV, from pre- to mid-treatment, at post-treatment only Group III continued to improve. Groups I, II and IV deteriorated and Group V remained the same. It will be recalled that, in Experiment I, there was a significant ($P < 0.001$) reduction in anxiety over time; it appears that this was largely accounted for by the dramatic fall in anxiety which occurred at the 3-month follow-up period with continuing decreases until 12-month follow-up.

It is difficult to compare the results on the Unaccompanied Walk assessment with those of other researchers as the behavioural avoidance tests used were somewhat different. A number of studies report on the use of measured routes (Agras *et al.*, 1968; Crowe *et al.*, 1972; Leitenberg *et al.*, 1970; Watson *et al.*, 1973) but, clearly, the idiosyncratic responses to a particular route present problems. In many of the studies reported by the Dutch group (Emmelkamp, 1974; Emmelkamp and Wessels, 1975; and Everaerd *et al.*, 1973) a measured route is not used; the subject is merely instructed to go into the street and remain there until a feeling of discomfort or tension is experienced; thus, time away from the clinic was the measure under consideration. Gillan and Rachman (1974) used a similar procedure.

With regard to the top three hierarchy items test, there was a significant difference between the five groups in response to treatment. It will be recalled that, in Experiment I, no significant differences were found between the four treatment groups; these groups successfully completed, at post-treatment, nearly 60 per cent of the hierarchy items, whereas only 12.5 per cent of the items were completed by the waiting-list controls.

Prognostic variables

Earlier researchers have correlated pre-treatment scores on various measures (often general self-report inventories) with post-treatment and follow-up scores on major outcome measures (Emmelkamp and Kuipers, 1979; Mathews *et al.*, 1976; Mathews *et al.*, 1974). High correlations allow prognostic statements to be made from scores on the pre-treatment measure. Mathews *et al.* (1974) found EPI 'extraversion' and 16 PF Factor A ('outgoing') were correlated with beneficial outcome post-treatment and at follow-up ($P < 0.01$). In a later study, Mathews *et al.* (1976) showed that pre-treatment 16 PF Factor C ('emotional stability') scores correlated significantly with outcome on a composite measure, as did a 'total expectancy' score. No relationship was found between EPI scores and outcome. Emmelkamp and Kuipers (1979) found no clear relationship between pre-treatment inventories (including the SAD and FNE) and outcome at 4-year follow-up of patients from several studies.

Table 6.4 shows Pearson product-moment correlation co-efficients between pre-treatment self-report inventories and post-treatment and follow-up outcome measures in the present study. Factor C of the 16 PF showed a pre-treatment to post-treatment reliability of 0.71 ($P < 0.005$).

Eysenck Personality Inventory 'N' and the FNE are negatively related to post-treatment behavioural performance ('top three items'); 16 PF Factor C and the SAD are related to self-reported anxiety on a post-treatment behavioural test (Arndale Centre) and to self-reported agoraphobic difficulties (Agoraphobic Questionnaire, Section 39)—the 16 PF Factor C showed

Table 6.4. Prognostic variables. Pearson product-moment correlation coefficients between certain pre-treatment measures and outcome criteria

Pre-treatment questionnaire measures	Outcome measures: Behavioural test				Arndale centre		Agoraphobic Questionnaire Section 39		Top three items
	Distance		Anxiety		Time	Anxiety			
	Post	FU[1]	Post	FU[1]	Post	Post	Post	FU[1]	Post
EPI N	−0.04	−0.02	−0.34*[a]	−0.19	0.21	0.18	0.15	0.17	−0.46§
EPI E	−0.06	0.20	0.35†[b]	−0.19	0.05	−0.04	−0.32*	0.28	0.04
SAD	−0.05	−0.14	−0.26	0.16	−0.22	0.31*	0.25	0.36†	−0.02
FNE	0.05	0.06	−0.23	0.09	0.02	0.05	0.12	0.00	−0.31*
16PF C	0.15	0.18	0.09	−0.23	0.26	−0.40‡	−0.42‡	−0.48§	0.26

FU[1] refers to the 12-month follow-up assessment
* $P < 0.05$ (one-tailed)
† $P < 0.025$ (one tailed)
‡ $P < 0.01$ (one-tailed)
§ $P < 0.005$ (one-tailed)
[a]Since this result is not in the predicted direction, the two-tailed test is appropriate, giving $P < 0.10$
[b]The appropriate two-tailed test gives $P < 0.05$

this post-treatment and at 12-month follow-up, the SAD only at follow-up; EPI 'E' is associated with low scores after treatment on the Agoraphobic Questionnaire; and both EPI 'E' and 'E' are correlated with anxiety (post-treatment) on the behavioural test walk, but the direction of the relationships is paradoxical. Because the direction of this relationship was not predicted, it is not appropriate to use the one-tailed test. The two-tailed test shows statistical significance ($P < 0.05$) for EPI 'E' but not for 'N'. It is possible that patients high on pre-treatment 'N' placed themselves in a position to receive notably less anxiety than their counterparts low on neuroticism. Similarly, it appears that the more extroverted patients brought on more anxiety in that situation than the less extraverted. Therefore, EPI 'E' and 'N', the SAD and FNE, and the 16 PF Factor C may be helpful clinically in making prognostic statements about patients with extreme scores. It is not possible to recommend one behavioural treatment over and above another on the basis of these results.

Finally, change scores from pre- to post-treatment on the 16 PF Factor C were examined and correlated with pre-post change scores on 'distance walked' on the behavioural test. The obtained correlation of 0.40 ($P < 0.025$, one-tailed) does show an association between improvement in emotional stability and improvement in counter-phobic approach behaviour, in the predicted direction. This result does not allow any conclusions to be made about the process that may underlie the relationship, of course.

Hypotheses

The research findings allow us to make some comments on the hypotheses (see page 109).

Experiment I

Hypothesis 1	The results generally do not support the hypothesis.
Hypothesis 2	This hypothesis is disconfirmed.
Hypothesis 3	The findings generally confirm this hypothesis.
Hypothesis 4	This hypothesis is not confirmed as subjects in Group I continued to maintain gains of the same order as the other groups at the follow-up assessments.
Hypothesis 5	This hypothesis is confirmed.

Experiment II

Hypothesis 1. This hypothesis is not confirmed on most outcome measures.

Psychological assessment of therapeutic outcome

Many problems are recognized in the assessment of the effects of psychological treatment. Important issues are raised by baseline data and the improvement interval. Although the majority of subjects in the present research had suffered from agoraphobia for several years (the mean age of onset being 26.97 years while the mean age at the commencement of treatment was 35.37 years), it is well established that the condition can fluctuate, in many cases quite markedly; thus, it is possible that subjects volunteered, or were referred for treatment, at a time when their condition had deteriorated. Again, performance on pre-treatment tests could have been influenced by the desire to take part in the research programme. Thus, it needs to be borne in mind that the degree of change of pre- and post-test scores may, to some extent, be a function of the extreme value of the initial score. Wilder (1957), in referring to the 'Law of Initial Values', notes that the most 'severe' subjects on the basis of certain criteria will tend to show the most improvement over time regardless of the treatment procedure; the change may be erroneously credited to the procedure.

In the present study it may be noted that 'severe' subjects, on several measures, made greater progress than 'non-severe' subjects (although in the case of the Unaccompanied Walk—distance test a ceiling effect was present).

In the treatment groups most of the progress was made in the first half of therapy. This finding confirms those of Evans and Kellam (1973) and Teasdale *et al.* (1977) who noted that most improvement occurred as an immediate response to treatment. Marks *et al.* (1971) remark that both flooding and desensitization treatments had superior effects when given first rather than second. However, it is interesting to record that, whereas subjects in Group V appeared to have made, at the post-treatment period, as good progress on many measures as the subjects in the treatment groups, on several measures (Sections 36 and 39 of the Agoraphobic Questionnaire and Unaccompanied Walk—distance) the major portion of that improvement took place during the mid- to post-treatment period. It could be argued that non-specific factors in waiting list controls may take longer to operate than the immediate, intense treatment procedures.

Follow-up studies can present methodological problems involving differential drop out of subjects (which, fortunately, was not an important factor in the present research), unreliability of subjects' recall of events transpiring since the previous assessment and instrument error, etc. The longer the intervening time between post-treatment and the follow-up assessments the greater the influence of intercurrent life experiences in relation to the influence of therapeutic procedures. As Frank (1975) points out, follow-up studies may reveal more about the natural history of the disorder for which patients receive treatment than about the effectiveness of that treatment.

In view of the intricate nature of the agoraphobic syndrome, multi-assessment procedures were used in the present research. (Physiological measures were not used due to lack of facilities.) Gottman *et al.* (1974) argue for the concept of converging operational definitions which suggests that the most convincing measurement evidence comes from the convergence of several different measurement operations used in conjunction.

Although there is evidence that generalized response dispositions do not predict behaviour well (Mischel, 1968) and that there is a good deal of situation specificity to human behaviour suggesting that prediction is best from one situation to behaviour in similar situations (Bandura, 1969), several outcome studies report the use of generalization measures and it was felt useful, for comparative purposes, to include such measures in the study.

Self-report measures were also used even though behaviourists, as we have seen in Chapter 4, have attacked these at both empirical and theoretical levels since studies have shown poor correlations between such measures and data obtained by behavioural and physiological assessment (Hersen *et al*., 1973; Lang, 1969; Rutner, 1973). However, an advantage in using self-report measures is that it is a flexible procedure which can evaluate cognitive, behavioural and physiological indices of anxiety. In those studies which show low concordance between behavioural and self-report indices of fears, subjects are usually asked to assess their anxiety while performing target behaviours or to rate their anxiety before contact with a particular stimulus; thus, there may be poor correlations between anxiety and overt fearful behaviour even if the self-report procedure is a valid measure of anxiety. Particular attention was paid in the study to devising adequate measures (e.g. Section 39 of the Agoraphobia Questionnaire) which were appropriate to the problem and which allowed for self-reports of easily discriminable behavioural phenomena and the actual behaviours themselves; there is evidence from Twentyman and McFall (1975) that, under these conditions, good concordance can be obtained. The questionnaire items were selected after an extensive survey of the kinds of problematic situations which agoraphobics encounter in the natural environment. Thus, it was decided not to use, for example, fear survey schedules in view of the ambiguity of the verbal stimuli and the lack of appropriate fear arousing situations which agoraphobics may come into contact with in their everyday life.

Another objection which might be raised in relation to the use of self-report measures concerns the possibility that, under certain conditions (for example, if the subject has a very high level of anxiety), inaccuracy may result. However, it seems that the same arguments can be applied to nearly all behavioural observation, since it is frequently based on behaviour which, to a greater or lesser extent, is under voluntary control. At the present time very little is known about the biases associated with self-report measures in clinical populations; it remains to be demonstrated that these are greater than with other types of behavioural data.

An important perspective, from the agoraphobic's point of view, is the reduction of anxiety produced by contact with fearful stimuli, even though it is recognized that changes in behavioural and physiological functioning are of considerable importance. Hence the use of anxiety rating scales which were designed to reflect change in clinically relevant fear behaviour on the Unaccompanied Walk, Visit to the Arndale Centre, etc.

In order to obtain different perspectives on the functioning of the subjects, ratings were obtained from an informant (usually the spouse) and from a clinician. It was felt the former assessment would provide useful data on the day-to-day progress that had been made; however, the data must be subject to various biases. In order to obtain as meaningful a quantification as possible of the degree of agoraphobia by the clinician four standard questions were asked of each patient. It can be argued that the basic data being rated are the subjects' verbal self-report; however, the use of an experienced clinician may reduce some of the biases of the subjects. Unfortunately, it is easy to find published records of clinical progress that are based almost entirely upon ratings. As direct assessment methods improve and develop, rating scales completed by subjects/clinicians may ultimately be replaced.

The behavioural assessment of a subject in the presence of fear eliciting stimuli is the hallmark of the behavioural approach to assessment. As we mentioned in Chapter 4, it needs to be borne in mind that objective behavioural avoidance test data may be biased by demand characteristics in that subjects may exaggerate, (a) the extent of the disturbance at the pre-test assessment, and (b) the amount of improvement at the post-test assessment. The demand for good performance in the test situation may not exist in the natural environment. Feist and Rosenthal (1973) and Smith *et al*. (1974) have shown that performance on behavioural avoidance tests is modifiable, admittedly within limits, by instructional and contextual variables. The extent of this bias at the present time is unknown.

Another reason for exercising caution in the use of behavioural avoidance tests concerns the range of fear-eliciting stimuli and the secure environment within which they usually take place. However, it is felt that these concerns are of less importance in the present study than in some studies reported in the literature. Subjects were involved in several behavioural tests covering a wide range of stimuli. The Unaccompanied Walk involved crossing a wide dual carriageway, open areas, ramps, built-up commercial areas and going to the rear of a large departmental store. The Arndale Centre involved remaining within a large shopping complex with dozens of shops on three levels. The test involving the top three hierarchy items provided a further range of fear-provoking stimuli directly related to the subject's problematic behaviour.

With regard to the second concern—that the subject operated within a secure environment—a number of issues are raised. Only in the case of the Arndale Centre test were the therapists relatively near to the subjects. In the case of the Unaccompanied Walk, the subject, assuming completion of the task, was nearly 1 mile away from the clinic although it is recognized that the subjects were told not to leave the route and that this could have affected performance. However, in the case of the top three hierarchy items no such 'support' was apparent from the therapists although support from other sources could have been available. Another consideration here is that the subject approaches the fear-arousing situation in a step-wise direction and can usually escape from the situation by stopping the test. Thus, a self-controlled 'panic button' is available and this may increase the feeling of security. The presence of the experimenter, albeit from a distance, and the general context (known route, etc.), may influence the subject's performance on certain behavioural tests.

Other considerations are important. The subject may find that a behavioural test attempted from home may, because of past aversive experiences, be much more difficult than one attempted from the clinic. Clearly, subjects may be expected to show more approach behaviour on a familiar route; in exposure treatments the route should, as far as possible, not be covered during treatment. (The Reinforced Graded Practice sessions involved items as dissimilar from the Unaccompanied Walk Test as possible—visiting a local shop not on route, travelling in bus, etc., although, because the route extended to the main commercial centre, some overlap occurred.) As Watson *et al.* (1973) point out, it is hard to avoid practice effects and idiosyncratic responses to a particular course (e.g. passing a cemetery).

Demand characteristics

One of the important findings of the present study is that the subjects in Group V (waiting list controls) showed, on nearly all outcome measures, as much change as the subjects in the treatment groups. It may be argued that non-specific effects are largely responsible for this change.

Although these results were unexpected there is the suggestion (e.g. Frank, 1973; Shapiro *et al.*, 1978), that demand characteristics alone may bring about substantial and often permanent improvement in behavioural and physical problems.

There are now several studies which show that demand characteristics can reliably and significantly influence the degree of fear displayed by analogue subjects particularly during repeated behavioural avoidance tests. There is some suggestion that high fear subjects may be affected less by demand characteristics (Evans, 1972; and Nietzel, 1973).

Mathews (1977a) has argued, with reference to the Gelder *et al.* (1973) study, which showed that flooding and systematic desensitization were more effective than a control treatment which was convincing to the patients, that non-specific factors were unlikely to account for all the changes seen in the clinical phobias; thus, pseudo-treatments appear to be more effective with specific fears than with agoraphobia. The present study would cast some doubt on this conclusion.

Reference has been made in the previous section to some of the demand characteristics which could have affected the results; procedural and situational cues are clearly of importance. Thus, the context within which the assessments were made no doubt provided cues for the subjects; they were fully aware they were attending a specialized research unit for the purpose of treatment designed to modify their phobic behaviour. Mention has been made of problems related to the screening procedures; improvement at post-treatment may be, in part, a function of changes in demand characteristics preceding and/or accompanying repeated tests (Nietzel and Bernstein, 1975, had demonstrated that untreated subjects' approach behaviours can be increased as a function of the number of behaviour avoidance tests); thus, the assessment procedures in the study may, to some extent, have been reactive and could have altered the behaviour they were designed to measure.

Further implications and developing trends

The research programme has raised a number of important issues. There is a very real need for researchers in the field of agoraphobia to agree on adequate outcome measures. This would allow for the direct comparison of results from one centre to another; for economic reasons alone, bearing in mind that a well-controlled clinical trial takes 2 years at least to complete, each research centre cannot afford the luxury of using assessment procedures without reference to procedures being used at other centres. Fortunately there is a gradual movement toward standardization of measures (Marks, 1981d).

There is, however, still an urgent need to develop comprehensive questionnaires which will tap the cognitive, behavioural and physiological response systems of agoraphobics. There is still little doubt that the validity of self-report measures is likely to be enhanced if greater use were to be made of the 'behaviour analytic model' (Goldfried and D'Zurilla, 1969); emphasis should be placed on determining a comprehensive range of problematic situations in which agoraphobics experience particular difficulties in a given environment.

Another urgent need is to develop a daily written record of appropriate discriminable behaviours; it could possibly include cognitive and physiological manifestations of anxiety. This matter raises the problem of training the subject to monitor certain discriminable and pre-determined behaviours. It also raises the twin problems of reliability and reactivity; there seems little doubt now that self-monitoring can have a therapeutic effect (Emmelkemp, 1974; Leitenberg *et al*., 1975).

There is little doubt that behaviour therapy has gained recognition as an important method in helping patients overcome behavioural problems (Burns and Worsley, 1970); this is particularly true in the field of phobic disorders. Psychologists, by virtue of their training and skills in the scientific investigation of human behaviours, have made significant contributions to the development of behaviour therapy (Burns, 1982b). However, the question arises as to who should administer the treatment. As Marks (1981d) points out, behavioural treatment need not always be given by highly trained psychiatrists or clinical psychologists. In the present study, a nurse therapist provided competent assistance in the administration of the procedures. This is a trend which is likely to develop in the future (Gosling, 1980). Even general practitioners with minimal training may be able to teach their patients adaptive ways of coping with problems such as agoraphobia (Burns, 1981a).

Former phobics have been used in the treatment of agoraphobia (Ross, 1979).

Some of the problems related to behavioural tests have already been discussed. A major assumption is that agoraphobics want to have modified their reactions to a particular population of anxiety eliciting stimuli in the natural environment; subjects do not seek therapy to change their responses to restricted behavioural tests (or to questionnaires for that matter). Thus, the behavioural tests will be of little value unless they correlate highly with the patients' reactions to the problematic situations encountered in the environment. It is perhaps true that too much research in the past has tended to employ statistical definitions of treatment effectiveness (Lick, 1973) and outcome criteria which have little demonstrable treatment effectiveness; it has frequently been pointed out that 'statistical significance does not imply clinical utility'. Hence the use of behavioural assessment procedures based on the hierarchial problematic behaviours of the subject may be of considerable value; there is a strong argument for using outcome measures which are closely tied to the *in vivo* behaviours which the subject wishes to change.

Therapist observations of the subject in the natural environment is time consuming and presents other problems; however, confidence in behavioural outcome data will be increased when there is convergent agreement between the subject and an observer about the existence of improved functioning.

It is clear that a fundamental problem of behaviour research is a need to disentangle the confounding effects of demand characteristics from the effects of the treatment procedures; most of the studies have failed to rule out these differential effects (Kazdin and Wilcoxon, 1976) and, indeed, it has been argued that the benefits derived from the behavioural treatments may be due mainly to such characteristics (Fix and Haffke, 1976; Kazdin and Wilcoxon, 1976). Bearing in mind these views and the results from the present study future investigations need to identify specific sources of demand characteristics which may affect the various parameters of behaviour and to ascertain ways in which they may be controlled.

APPENDIX I: DEFINITION OF AGORAPHOBIA

In confirming the diagnosis of agoraphobia, which had usually been made by a psychiatrist or a general practitioner, considerable emphasis was placed on the current *functioning* of the patient. For example, potential subjects were asked about their ability to go, unaided, for short walks; to use public transport; to queue in supermarkets; to walk around the nearest, largest shopping centre; to attend places of public entertainment; etc. Thus, if the potential subject was unable to attempt the above or similar items because of high levels of anxiety or was unable to do so only under conditions of considerable anxiety (either alone or accompanied), the diagnosis of agoraphobia was strengthened. Potential subjects were required to complete the Agoraphobia Questionnaire which was used in the National Survey of Agoraphobics; their responses to the questionnaire were also taken into consideration when confirming the diagnosis. The behavioural tests provided further confirmation of their condition.

APPENDIX II: PSYCHOLOGICAL TREATMENT RESEARCH UNIT. AGORAPHOBIC RESEARCH—THE CONTRACT

A considerable sum of money has been allocated to this research project by the Manchester Regional Hospital Board and Birch Hill Hospital, Rochdale. In view of the cost, not only in monetary terms but in terms of the therapists' time, only patients who conscientiously agree to be co-operative in the research programme will be selected. To be selected the following conditions must be met:

1. Patients must conscientiously attend all treatment sessions. (In the event of emergencies such as illness, additional sessions will have to be arranged.)
2. Patients must conscientiously carry out instructions, given during treatment, as far as possible; you will not, of course, be asked to do anything unreasonable bearing in mind your condition.
3. Patients must not discuss with other participants details of his/her individual treatment programme until the research programme has been completed. *This is very important.*

I wish to participate in the Agoraphobic Research Treatment programme. I have read the above conditions and hereby agree to abide by the same.

.... Signed

.... Witness

.... Date

(Copy to be handed to each participant)

APPENDIX III: CHARACTERISTICS OF SUBJECTS IN EXPERIMENTS I AND II COMPARED TO THE CHARACTERISTICS OF SUBJECTS IN THE NATIONAL SURVEY OF AGORAPHOBICS

	Subjects in projects (N = 40)	National Survey subjects (N = 963)
Sex		
Female	87.50%	88.16%
Male	12.50%	11.48%
Marital status		
Single	5.0%	10.8%
Married	77.5%	71.0%
Separated	2.5%	2.4%
Divorced	2.5%	2.8%
Remarried	12.5%	6.1%
Engaged	—	0.5%
Widowed	—	6.3%
Age		
Mean	35.37 years	43.6 years
SD	9.67 years	11.0 years
Religious affiliation		
C of E	60.0%	62.0%
Roman Catholic	10.0%	11.0%
Methodist	2.0%	5.0%
None	18.0%	11.0%
Other	10.0%	11.0%
Age of finishing school		
Mean	14.8 years	15.0 years
SD	0.7 years	1.1 years
Percentage taking advantage of further education (e.g. college, night school, etc.)	35.0%	41.0%
Percentage having job outside of home	40.0%	28.6%
Percentage reporting that agoraphobia hinders their work		
Never	10.5%	9.0%
Seldom	21.1%	15.0%
Sometimes	26.3%	52.0%
Often	42.1%	24.0%
Percentage that would take work if it were not for the agoraphobia	83.0%	83.2%
Percentage having part-time work at home	12.5%	15.9%
Age at marriage		
Mean	21.9 years	22.6 years
SD	4.41 years	4.30 years

	Subjects in projects (N = 40)	National Survey subjects (N = 963)
Age of spouse		
Mean	38.3 years	44.8 years
SD	12.1 years	11.2 years
Percentage having children	89.0%	87.0%
Percentage of female subjects having one or more miscarriages	30.0%	25.0%
Strain agoraphobia is putting on marriage		
None	3.0%	15.0%
A little	35.0%	36.0%
Fair amount	27.0%	27.0%
A lot	35.0%	22.0%
Age of onset		
Mean	26.97 years	28.02 years
SD	8.81 years	10.35 years
Whom the subjects have consulted about their agoraphobia		
GP	100.0%	95.8%
Psychiatrist	72.5%	76.6%
Religious/spiritual healer	5.0%	16.41%
Hypnotherapist	10.0%	9.2%
Psychologist	2.5%	3.5%
Percentage not receiving adequate help for their agoraphobia	85.0%	73.8%
Percentage reporting fluctuations in their agoraphobia for no apparent reason	87.5%	90.0%
Percentage reporting a gradual onset (3 months or more) of their agoraphobia	60.0%	57.1%
Percentage of worst fears of what might happen during a panic		
Death	10.5%	13.2%
Fainting/collapsing	44.8%	37.9%
Heart attack	2.6%	4.1%
Losing memory	2.6%	0.3%
Becoming mentally ill	2.6%	5.8%
Causing a scene	2.6%	6.2%
Inability to get home/place of safety	8.0%	5.9%
Losing control	13.2%	7.4%
Other personal illness	10.5%	10.4%
Other	—	8.6%

APPENDIX IV: AGORAPHOBIA QUESTIONNAIRE, SECTION 36

Do the following situations make you feel worse or better or no different? Please give a tick to each situation under the heading that best describes your feelings.

	Makes me feel very much worse	Makes me feel moderately worse	Makes me feel mildly worse	Makes no difference	Makes me feel mildly better	Makes me feel moderately better	Makes me feel very much better
(a) Having a definite appointment (e.g. dentist)	( )	( )	( )	( )	( )	( )	( )
(b) Feeling trapped (e.g. when at hairdressers, etc.)	( )	( )	( )	( )	( )	( )	( )
(c) Having to queue (e.g. at shop etc.)	( )	( )	( )	( )	( )	( )	( )
(d) Particular places in the neighbourhood	( )	( )	( )	( )	( )	( )	( )
(e) Increase of distance away from home	( )	( )	( )	( )	( )	( )	( )
(f) Being accompanied by a friend	( )	( )	( )	( )	( )	( )	( )
(g) Domestic arguments and stress	( )	( )	( )	( )	( )	( )	( )
(h) Having to cross a main road	( )	( )	( )	( )	( )	( )	( )
(i) Bright, clear weather	( )	( )	( )	( )	( )	( )	( )
(j) Sitting near door in a restaurant, hall, etc.	( )	( )	( )	( )	( )	( )	( )

(k) Talking my problems over with a friend	( )	( )	( )	( )	( )	( )	( )
(l) Talking my problems over with my doctor	( )	( )	( )	( )	( )	( )	( )
(m) Thinking about my problems	( )	( )	( )	( )	( )	( )	( )
(n) Darkness	( )	( )	( )	( )	( )	( )	( )
(o) Being by myself	( )	( )	( )	( )	( )	( )	( )
(p) Cloudy, depressing weather	( )	( )	( )	( )	( )	( )	( )
(q) Wearing sunglasses	( )	( )	( )	( )	( )	( )	( )
(r) When out for a walk, taking perambulator, dog, etc.	( )	( )	( )	( )	( )	( )	( )
(s) When out, having a way open for a quick return home	( )	( )	( )	( )	( )	( )	( )
(t) Talking 'sense' to myself (e.g. reassuring myself)	( )	( )	( )	( )	( )	( )	( )
(u) Focusing my mind on something else	( )	( )	( )	( )	( )	( )	( )
(v) Being accompanied by husband/wife	( )	( )	( )	( )	( )	( )	( )

Scoring: 1 = Makes me feel very much worse
2 = Makes me feel moderately worse
3 = Makes me feel mildly worse
4 = Makes no difference
5 = Makes me feel mildly better
6 = Makes me feel moderately better
7 = Makes me feel very much better

APPENDIX V: AGORAPHOBIA QUESTIONNAIRE, SECTION 39

Listed below are a number of fears you may have: please tick every item to indicate the severity of the fear.

	Virtually no fear never avoid	Mild fear; seldom avoid	Moderate fear; sometimes avoid	Very fearful; often avoid	Extremely fearful; always avoid
(a) Travelling on a bus by yourself (5 min journey)	( )	( )	( )	( )	( )
(b) Travelling on a bus by yourself (10 min journey)	( )	( )	( )	( )	( )
(c) Travelling on a bus by yourself (Longer than 15 min)	( )	( )	( )	( )	( )
(d) Walking away from home by yourself (5 min walk)	( )	( )	( )	( )	( )
(e) Walking away from home by yourself (10 min walk)	( )	( )	( )	( )	( )
(f) Walking away from home by yourself (Longer than 15 min)	( )	( )	( )	( )	( )
(g) Sitting in hairdressers	( )	( )	( )	( )	( )
(h) Going to the doctors	( )	( )	( )	( )	( )
(i) Travelling by train	( )	( )	( )	( )	( )
(j) Going to local shop	( )	( )	( )	( )	( )
(k) Walking round the nearest large shopping centre	( )	( )	( )	( )	( )

(l) Crossing a main road	( )	( )	( )	( )	( )
(m) Being in crowds	( )	( )	( )	( )	( )
(n) Sitting in cinema/theatre	( )	( )	( )	( )	( )
(o) Having a meal in a restaurant	( )	( )	( )	( )	( )
(p) Going to visit a friend's home	( )	( )	( )	( )	( )
(q) Talking to a neighbour in the street	( )	( )	( )	( )	( )
(r) Answering the door bell	( )	( )	( )	( )	( )
(s) Being at the dentists	( )	( )	( )	( )	( )
(t) Going to a party	( )	( )	( )	( )	( )
(u) Going into tunnels	( )	( )	( )	( )	( )
(v) Travelling in lifts	( )	( )	( )	( )	( )
(w) Travelling in a car	( )	( )	( )	( )	( )
(x) Sitting in a hall	( )	( )	( )	( )	( )
(y) On holiday	( )	( )	( )	( )	( )

Scoring: 1 = Virtually no fear, never avoid
2 = Mild fear, seldom avoid
3 = Moderate fear, sometimes avoid
4 = Very fearful, often avoid
5 = Extremely fearful, always avoid

APPENDIX VI: QUESTIONNAIRE USED FOR INDEPENDENT ASSESSMENT. AGORAPHOBIC RESEARCH—INDEPENDENT ASSESSMENT QUESTIONS

Name: ______________________________

1. (Following the course of treatment just completed . . . .)
   What do you feel you can do now (in terms of agoraphobic difficulties) that you could not do before?
2. What things can you still not do or have great difficulty in doing?
3. Has there been improvement in other areas (e.g. depression, self-confidence, getting a job, etc.)?
4. Has there been any deterioration in your agoraphobic difficulties or in other areas?

Degree of agoraphobia (rated by clinician).

0	1	2	3	4
Absent	Mild	Moderate	Severe	Very severe

APPENDIX VII: QUESTIONNAIRE SENT TO THE SPOUSES/RELATIVES OF THE SUBJECTS

Psychological Treatment Research Unit,
ROCHDALE

Agoraphobic Research Programme

Your wife/husband/friend has completed a course of treatment; we would be glad to have *your* views on what progress has been made. Please complete the questionnaire below and return it as soon as possible in the enclosed stamped addressed envelope.

L. E. BURNS
G. L. THORPE

QUESTIONNAIRE

Please give a tick to each item under the heading that best describes your feelings.
Is your wife/husband/friend better, worse or no different with regard to the following items?

	Very much better	Moderately better	Mildly better	No change	Mildly worse	Moderately worse	Very much worse
(a) Visiting relatives/friends	( )	( )	( )	( )	( )	( )	( )
(b) Queuing at a shop	( )	( )	( )	( )	( )	( )	( )
(c) Visiting nearest town centre	( )	( )	( )	( )	( )	( )	( )
(d) Getting out more	( )	( )	( )	( )	( )	( )	( )
(e) Visiting the hairdressers	( )	( )	( )	( )	( )	( )	( )
(f) Travelling on a bus	( )	( )	( )	( )	( )	( )	( )
(g) Visiting a local shop	( )	( )	( )	( )	( )	( )	( )
(h) Travelling in a car	( )	( )	( )	( )	( )	( )	( )
(i) Crossing a main road	( )	( )	( )	( )	( )	( )	( )
(j) Being left alone in the home	( )	( )	( )	( )	( )	( )	( )
(k) Tension	( )	( )	( )	( )	( )	( )	( )

APPENDIX VII: *(continued)*

	Very much better	Moderately better	Mildly better	No change	Mildly worse	Moderately worse	Very much worse
(l) Depression	( )	( )	( )	( )	( )	( )	( )
(m) Tiredness	( )	( )	( )	( )	( )	( )	( )
(n) Confidence	( )	( )	( )	( )	( )	( )	( )
(o) Cheerfulness	( )	( )	( )	( )	( )	( )	( )
(p) Panic attack	( )	( )	( )	( )	( )	( )	( )
(q) ____________	( )	( )	( )	( )	( )	( )	( )
(r) ____________	( )	( )	( )	( )	( )	( )	( )
(s) ____________	( )	( )	( )	( )	( )	( )	( )
(t) ____________	( )	( )	( )	( )	( )	( )	( )

In what other ways do you feel your wife/husband/friend has improved?

In what other ways has no improvement been made or ways in which your wife/husband/friend has got worse?

Has it been possible to reduce medication (tablets, etc.) during treatment? YES/NO

Any other comments

APPENDIX VIII: SCHEDULING OF ASSESSMENT AND THERAPEUTIC SESSIONS

	Experiment I		Experiment II
Experimental Session	Assessment	Treatment	Assessment
1. PRE A	SPM/MHV: 16PF: BT Walk	—	SPM/MHV: 16PF; BT Walk
2. PRE B	EPI; SAD/FNE; Agoraphobia Questionnaire; BT Walk	—	EPI: SAD/FNE; Agoraphobia Questionnaire; BT Walk
3. TR A	Expectancy Rating	Therapy programme and rationale described. Contract signed. Construction of anxiety hierarchies begun. Training begun in relaxation, visualisation (neutral scene), stress inoculation, as appropriate	Anxiety hierarchies constructed
4. TR B	Expectancy Rating	Further information on treatment programme provided as required. Construction of anxiety hierarchies completed. Further training in therapeutic procedures	—
5. TR 1	Benefit Rating	Treatment Programme	—
6. TR 2	Benefit Rating	Treatment Programme	—
7. TR 3	Benefit Rating	Treatment Programme	—
8. TR 4	Benefit Rating	Treatment Programme	—
9. TR 5	Benefit Rating	Treatment Programme	—
10. TR 6	Benefit Rating	Treatment Programme	—

APPENDIX VIII: (*continued*)

	Experiment I		Experiment II
Experimental Session	Assessment	Treatment	Assessment
11. TR 7	Benefit Rating	Treatment Programme	—
12. TR 8	Benefit Rating	Treatment Programme	—
13. MID	EPI: SAD/FNE; Agoraphobia Questionnaire—Sections 36 and 39; General Benefit Rating; BT Walk	—	EPI; SAD/FNE; Agoraphobia Questionnaire—Sections 36 and 39; BT Walk
14. TR 9	Benefit Rating	Treatment Programme	—
15. TR 10	Benefit Rating	Treatment Programme	—
16. TR 11	Benefit Rating	Treatment Programme	—
17. TR 12	Benefit Rating	Treatment Programme	—
18. TR 13	Benefit Rating	Treatment Programme	—
19. TR 14	Benefit Rating	Treatment Programme	—

20.	TR 15	Benefit Rating	Treatment Programme	—
21.	TR 16	Benefit Rating	Treatment Programme	—
22.	Post A	EPI; SAD/FNE; General Benefit Rating; BT Walk; Spouse Rating Questionnaire given; top three hierarchy items to be attempted by Session 24	—	EPI; SAD/FNE; BT Walk; top three hierarchy items to be attempted within 1.5 weeks
23.	Post B	16PF; Agoraphobia Questionnaire—Sections 36 and 39	—	16PF; Agoraphobia Questionnaire—Sections 36 and 39
24.	Post C	BT; Arndale Shopping Centre; Report on attempts at top three hierarchy items; Independent assessment by psychologist	—	Report on attempts at top three hierarchy items
25.	FU, 3 months	EPI; SAD/FNE; Agoraphobia Questionnaire—Sections 36 and 39; Spouse Rating; BT Walk	—	—
26.	FU, 6 months	EPI; SAD/FNE; Agoraphobia Questionnaire—Sections 36 and 39; Spouse Rating; BT Walk	—	—
27.	FU, 12 months	EPI; SAD/FNE; Agoraphobia Questionnaire—Sections 36 and 39; Spouse Rating; BT Walk	—	—

APPENDIX IX: THERAPIST'S MANUAL

Modified behavioural counselling

The aim of this treatment method, either in isolation or in combination with other techniques, is to provide the subject with a good knowledge and comprehension of the basic principles of learning (respondent and operant behaviour, positive and negative reinforcement, self and covert reinforcement, operant and classical conditioning, generalization, extinction, modelling, etc.).

Treatment is aimed at doing a thorough behavioural analysis, in helping the subject to achieve understanding and comprehension of her condition (in terms of learning theory) and is non-directive in so far as no specific recommendations are made.

The following material is read to the patient:

'Your treatment' (i.e. for Group I subjects; for others 'This part of your treatment') 'is aimed at helping you gain understanding into your anxiety problems and by the use of modern experimental psychology (particularly learning principles) to enable you to arrive at ways of changing your reactions and behaviour. The relaxation exercises will have a general impact on your anxieties because relaxation inhibits anxiety responses. On top of that though I am going to go over your everyday experiences in detail in these sessions so that you can get the benefit of modern psychological thinking. We will do three main things:

1. Assess in detail your own, individual experiences and those of other agoraphobic sufferers.
2. Discuss these experiences in terms of known principles of conditioning and learning.
3. See if you can use these principles and the conclusions we arrive at to manage and control your own anxieties.'

Each counselling session will include the above three strategies. That is, about a third of the time will be spent on detailed questioning regarding the previous few days experiences (the behavioural analytic approach, using the daily record). The subject is encouraged to talk as much as possible. The next third of the time will be spent on explaining the principles of learning as outlined above. Give as much detail as necessary, relevant clinical applications, etc. Then for the last third, the subject will be asked to think of ways the concepts can be used to effect change. Make no specific recommendations; let the subject do the deciding ('What you *you* really feel?' etc.). Simply encourage the subject to think about the problem and the principles and to try to use this understanding to help combat her anxiety.

Be very business-like in sticking to the three procedures; it will be necessary to monitor this technique very closely, e.g. frequent discussions, exchange of tapes, nurse therapist to sit in both therapists' sessions and provide feedback, etc.

APPENDIX X: THERAPIST'S MANUAL

Systematic desensitization

Say to the subject:

'In this part of your treatment we are going to use a method called systematic desensitization. This method helps to eliminate the anxiety which is attached to the various feared situations, which you have described, through the use of deep relaxation; relaxation is incompatible with anxiety for you cannot be relaxed and tense at the same time. Systematic desensitization consists of two parts: teaching you to relax and the construction of an anxiety hierarchy; this is a list of items associated with your fears; these items are ranked according to how much anxiety they evoke in you; that is, the least-anxiety producing item is at the top of the list and the most-anxiety producing item at the bottom. Between these two extremes there are many other items. When you are deeply relaxed you will be asked to imagine an item from the list; if you find yourself becoming tense or anxious whilst you are imagining an item you must let me know by raising a finger a few inches. You will then be asked to stop imagining the item and to concentrate on relaxation again. Thus we will work our way over the list deconditioning/eliminating the anxiety associated with each item.'

Each anxiety hierarchy is to be of a standard size and consist of sixteen items. For each subject the items will be obtained by means of interview and with reference to the agoraphobia questionnaire. The items will be arranged by the subject from the least anxiety provoking (no. 1) to the most anxiety provoking (no. 16).

During the pre-treatment sessions (TR A and TR B) practice will be given to the subject in visualization; the subject will be asked to imagine on four occasions a neutral stimulus (flower) for 15 s followed by an intertrial interval (relaxation) of 30 s.

During the administration of items from the hierarchy similar timings will be used; two items will be presented per day; e.g. day 1, items 1 and 2; day 2, items 2 and 3, etc. On day 16, item no. 16 will be presented four times. Should the subject signal anxiety, the subject should be asked to stop imagining the item and 2–3 min should be spent on giving relaxation instructions; the item should then be represented; the subject should visualize an item, without experiencing anxiety, on four consecutive occasions before proceeding to the next item.

APPENDIX XI: THERAPIST'S MANUAL

Reinforced graded practice

Say to the subject:

'As part of your treatment you will be asked to do various exercises from the clinic; for example, you may be asked to go for a short walk by yourself or to purchase something in a local shop, etc. You will not be asked to do anything unreasonable. We find that practice in situations which cause some anxiety often leads to good progress being made.'

The exercises for practice will be obtained by means of interview and reference to the results on the behavioural test (walk) and the agoraphobia questionnaire. On satisfactory completion of the exercise the subject will receive ample social reinforcement by the therapists. If the subject fails to complete the exercise this fact will simply be recorded in the notes and no comment made by the therapists.

APPENDIX XII: THERAPIST'S MANUAL

Stress inoculation training

The aims of this treatment technique are (1) to educate the subject about the nature of fearful or anxiety reactions, basing the rationale on the theory of Schachter (1966); (2) to have the subject rehearse certain coping behaviours, i.e. immediate muscle relaxation and self-instructional training, and (3) to provide a form of conditioning in which the subject practises the coping skills package in response to imaginal representations of aversive scenes relevant to agoraphobia; specifically in response to the scenes from the subject's systematic desensitization hierarchy.

(1) Educational phase

This aspect of stress inoculation is implemented by presenting the treatment rationale to the subject:

'In this part of your treatment I am going to give you a technique for *coping with* the anxieties you feel when you are out and about. While we are *reducing* your anxieties by the other treatment techniques you are receiving, this additional technique will help you further by giving you skills for coping with any anxieties that may remain. Taken together the treatments will do a thorough job in solving the problems of the agoraphobia.

Your anxiety reactions have two main parts. First, the *bodily* symptoms of agoraphobia—dizziness, sweaty hands, heart racing, etc.,—and, second, the *thoughts* and *images* you experience which can make you even more anxious. These thoughts may go like this: "I can't cope; I knew this would happen";

"What if I faint?"; "I *have* to get home". Thoughts like these can make you anxious; in a way by telling you to become anxious. If you are thinking to your self, "I can't cope", well, no matter whether you can cope or not, you will believe yourself and get very anxious.

So, in this part of your treatment, I am going to teach you to cope with both parts of the anxiety. The bodily part by getting you to use a quick form of the relaxation you have already learnt and the "thinking" part by teaching you to think more positively about things. I am going to get you to use these "coping" tactics whilst you are imagining fearful situations.'

(2) **Coping behaviour**

In the first pre-treatment sessions (TR A and TR B) the subject is to practise the package of coping behaviours. In future sessions the subject practises them whilst imagining SD hierarchy items.

The coping behaviours consist of *relaxation*; the subject induces this by inhaling deeply, tensing the arms and hands, pausing and exhaling slowly while consciously slackening the muscles; and a form of self-instructional training which proceeds through four stages, each to be carried out whilst concentrating on the SD item for the day: preparing for onset of anxiety; handling the anxiety; possibly being overwhelmed by anxiety and self-reinforcement after handling it successfully.

The subject goes through the immediate relaxation exercise, then *says aloud* the coping self-instruction; each of the four types of situation is used in the context of the SD item of the day.

In the first two pre-treatment sessions, say to the subject:

'Let's begin to practise this technique. For today just close your eyes and imagine a peaceful situation, watching TV at home, for example. Now I want you to breathe right in, tensing your hands and arms, hold your breath, now relax, slackening your muscles, breathing out in a controlled sigh. Now say aloud, "If I were to become anxious right now, I could think of a calm way of handling it" Fine. That's a way of preparing yourself for anxiety. Now, do the "immediate relaxation" exercise again. Now, let's suppose you feel a little anxious for some reason. Say aloud, "Relax, I'm in control. I can handle this". Fine.'

For these two practice sessions proceed with self-instruction for being overwhelmed and for having handled the anxiety (see Meichenbaum's (1973) examples of coping self-statements below):

EXAMPLES OF COPING SELF STATEMENTS.
(MEICHENBAUM, 1973).
Stage of Preparing for a Stressor.
What is it I have to do?
No negative self-statement; just think rationally.

I can develop a plan to deal with it.

Stage of Confronting and Handling a Stressor.
One step at a time. I can handle the situation.
Relax; I'm in control. Take a slow, deep breath. Ah good.

Stage of Coping with the Feeling of Being Overwhelmed.
When the fear comes just pause.
It will be over shortly.
Its not the worst thing that can happen.

Stage of Reinforcing Self-Statements.
It worked; I was able to do it.
It wasn't as bad as I expected.
I'm really pleased with the progress I'm making.

(3) **Conditioning**

The subject goes through this procedure (i.e. in sessions 5 onwards) whilst imagining the SD scene for the day. Subjects begin at scene no. 9 (i.e. halfway down the anxiety hierarchy, all of which consist of sixteen items); each scene is presented at two consecutive treatment sessions. In the context of the scene the subject uses self-instructions—preparing for the anxiety, handling the anxiety, being overwhelmed by the anxiety and self-reinforcement. The subject repeats twice each of the four components of self-instruction, i.e. the subject uses the scene and self-instructions twice before proceeding to the next step, handling the anxiety, etc.

It was decided to commence at scene no. 9 of the hierarchy in view of possible incompatibility with the systematic desensitization approach; stress inoculation deliberately seeks to evoke anxiety, whereas desensitization aims to evoke a minimal amount of anxiety; it was felt inadvisable to use the same hierarchy item on the same day for both stress inoculation and desensitization, although this occurred during the final two treatment sessions. Thus, on Treatment Day 1 item 9 of the hierarchy was used in the stress inoculation method and items 1 and 2 in systematic desensitization; on Day 2 item 9 (SI) and items 2 and 3 (SD); on Day 3 item 10 (SI) and items 3 and 4 (SD), etc.

APPENDIX XIII: SUMMARY TABLE OF DATA FROM CONTROLLED TRIAL

1. Behavioural Test; Distance Walked as a percentage of the total possible Distance (4240 feet)

Assessment stages	Pre		Mid		Post		3 months		6 months		12 months	
	$\bar{X}$	SD	$\bar{X}$	SD	$\bar{X}$	SD	$\bar{X}$	SD	$\bar{X}$	SD	$\bar{X}$	SD
Group 1	53.15	30.96	76.92	33.51	83.53	27.26	86.72	31.10	78.36	37.51	97.14	7.57
Group 2	49.46	40.40	45.53	39.29	84.76	30.80	98.35	4.04	85.32	30.97	82.67	32.48
Group 3	52.56	39.86	66.54	43.75	64.83	45.72	75.53	41.74	73.41	41.03	63.72	46.86
Group 4	49.93	38.32	71.45	38.52	84.55	28.92	65.23	36.63	72.79	37.56	86.88	17.46
Group 5	47.44	34.43	46.32	29.43	51.98	17.18	—	—	—	—	—	—

2. Scores on Section 39, Agoraphobic Questionnaire

Assessment stages	Pre		Mid		Post		3 months		6 months		12 months	
	$\bar{X}$	SD	$\bar{X}$	SD	$\bar{X}$	SD	$\bar{X}$	SD	$\bar{X}$	SD	$\bar{X}$	SD
Group 1	79.75	10.15	67.25	14.29	62.50	11.09	60.25	9.87	52.25	9.87	58.50	16.86
Group 2	74.25	26.97	55.38	23.16	46.00	23.21	46.25	27.60	45.13	27.60	55.25	33.07
Group 3	80.50	21.29	66.38	21.99	52.38	23.00	56.88	27.55	56.50	27.55	59.63	30.73
Group 4	88.13	21.13	64.88	15.85	52.25	11.37	55.50	18.27	55.63	18.27	58.50	13.61
Group 5	78.63	14.54	74.00	15.26	66.63	13.97	—	—	—	—	—	—

CHAPTER 7

Behavioural Concepts of Aetiology and Treatment Effectiveness

Having reviewed the results of reported research, and presented some of our own findings, we now turn to the challenging theoretical problems of explaining the aetiology and the successful treatment of agoraphobia. As we have noted earlier, the division of aetiological issues into two discussions is somewhat arbitrary, but we hope to give a clearer account by progressing from general issues of personality and the social context (Chapter 3) to specific learning theory concepts in understanding acquired fear and its treatment.

First, we discuss the advantages and limitations of particular learning paradigms (classical conditioning, negative reinforcement, etc.) that have been offered to explain the development and maintenance of phobias. Agoraphobia poses a special challenge, because two phenomena—anticipatory fear of certain environments, and apparently spontaneous panic attacks—have to be explained. In this discussion we ignore historical sequence; for example, Wolpe's (1958) early contributions are discussed under 'conflict', later in this section, rather than at the onset.

Second, we discuss some of the theories of treatment effectiveness. There is a clear link here with theories of aetiology, because each view of the acquisition of a phobia implies a treatment approach; it would seem that the theory underlying the most successful treatment would automatically be the most promising aetiological formulation. However, successful treatment procedures for agoraphobia are consistent with several theories of aetiology, and accordingly the advocates of any particular acquisition paradigm are likely to point to the relevance of a successful treatment to the favoured theory. We discuss treatment mechanisms separately, then, for three reasons. First, the success of a treatment does not logically validate its original rationale. Second, some theories of treatment efficacy have no clear aetiological understructure (the multimodal approach, for example, and Marks' (1981a, b) clinical paradigm for exposure treatment), and therefore have to be discussed separately from aetiology. Finally, some hypotheses transcend specific therapeutic procedures and aetiological formulations (for example, self-efficacy theory, and the argument that treatments operate by means of pervasive, 'non-specific' influences).

THEORIES OF THE ACQUISITION OF PHOBIAS

Two-factor theory

The most influential pre-1970 formulation of phobias in learning theory terms is two-process or two-factor theory (Eysenck and Rachman, 1965; Mowrer, 1947, 1960; Rescorla and Solomon, 1967), in which the two 'factors' involved are classical and instrumental conditioning procedures. Central to two-factor theory is the claim that avoidance behaviour is acquired and maintained 'by the intermediation of fear' (Mowrer, 1960, p. 25).

The classical conditioning component

In classical conditioning terms, the phobic situation (or, more accurately, the environment in which phobic behaviour is manifested) has acquired the potential to evoke anxiety, a conditioned response (CR), through pairing with a noxious (usually unspecified) unconditioned stimulus (UCS). Reiss (1980) summarizes the concepts in this way:

> Initially neutral stimuli become conditioned elicitors of fear when experienced in temporal contiguity with such aversive events as conflict, trauma, pain, and confinement. A phobic stimulus is regarded as a conditioned stimulus (CS), acquired fear is regarded as a conditioned response (CR), and aversive events are regarded as reinforcing stimuli and as unconditioned stimuli (USs). (p. 381)

Candidates for the unconditioned stimuli producing fear could include the onset of a mild physical illness, unfamiliar sensations produced by fatigue or general stress, or actually threatening events such as witnessing an accident or being taken violently ill. Thus, for a pre-agoraphobic individual who becomes dizzy and faint because of the onset of influenza while shopping in a crowded shopping centre, the environment could become a CS for anxiety (that is, CRs similar to those UCRs produced by the illness). The strength of this conditioned fear would be proportional to the number of pairings of CS and UCS (supermarket and illness), the intensity of the initial fear response, and the degree of physical confinement (Rachman, 1977).

However, after these hypothesized initial conditioning (or acquisition) experiences, conditioned fear in the phobic situation would be expected to decline rapidly because of the phenomenon of *extinction*. Because the situation is regarded as a CS, and because the UCS is assumed no longer to obtain, conditioned fear—the CR—is assumed to be under experimental extinction, and accordingly any further contact with the surroundings in which the UCS was originally presented would tend to produce the extinction effect.

The most striking clinical aspect of phobias, however, is their persistence. Phobic anxiety and behaviour are perpetuated even for those patients who occasionally confront their feared surroundings, although the usual observation is that those individuals often beat a hasty retreat at the first sign of anxiety. Classical conditioning procedures alone, at any rate, seem inadequate to explain phobias, because the predicted rapid extinction of conditioned fear does not seem to occur.

The instrumental learning component

The addition of an instrumental learning procedure to the hypothesized classical conditioning of fear is vital to the two-factor formulation. *Escaping* the CS, or phobic situation, is negatively reinforced by anxiety-reduction. Because of this, escaping becomes established as a habitual response to the phobic surroundings, and—more important—the escape behaviour curtails exposure to the CS. Brief exposure to the CS is likely to be insufficient to promote extinction of the CR, and, furthermore, anxiety-reduction becomes correlated with new environments that may assume the connotation of safety. *Avoidance* of the CS in the first place, another prominent feature of phobic behaviour, equally protects the CR from extinction (Seligman, 1971; Wilson, 1973). Sidman (1966) summarizes the sequence of events as follows:

> The literature on avoidance behavior consists largely of a series of variations on a single theme: The subject is first made anxious through a process of Pavlovian conditioning; his avoidance behavior is reinforced when it terminates or reduces the conditioned anxiety state. (p. 448)

The escape or avoidance response is theoretically subject to two possible extinction procedures (Hineline, 1977). In one, responses would be *ineffective* in escaping the CS or avoiding the UCS, which would therefore occur despite the response. This paradigm has not been extensively studied, although it has been used clinically in aversion therapy by Feldman and MacCulloch (1971; see also Thorpe, 1972). In the other procedure, commonly used in laboratory paradigms, the UCS does not occur whether or not the response is emitted. It is well known that the extinction of avoidance behaviour under this extinction procedure can be an extremely protracted process (Sidman, 1966; Hineline, 1977). In either of these extinction procedures, behaviour is irrelevant to the presentation of the UCS. The second procedure (UCS omission regardless of responding) is of course assumed to prevail for phobic patients in the natural environment.

Two-factor theory, then, provides an explanation for the persistence of phobias despite the fact that classically conditioned fear and the escape and avoidance behaviours are under procedural extinction. Classical conditioning procedures explain how the phobic situation comes to elicit fear; the patient may reduce the fear by escaping or avoiding the situation. The instrumental escape response is strengthened by drive-reduction (Mowrer, 1960) or, in modern terminology, by negative reinforcement, and accordingly it persists, automatically curtailing exposure to the CS and thereby protecting the CR from extinction. Behavioural treatment consistent with two-factor theory would make the extinction procedures explicit for the patient, or would involve the provision of additional procedures to facilitate the otherwise intractable extinction process.

Behavioural treatment of agoraphobia has been consistent with two-factor theory. In systematic desensitization (SD; Wolpe, 1958), imaginal exposure to situations related to the CS seems to constitute a procedure for experimental extinction: the CS is presented for substantial periods of time throughout treatment, presumably without any aversive UCS ensuing. Studies demonstrating that muscle relaxation may be redundant to the SD procedure for phobic patients (Gillan and Rachman, 1974) do not, of course, contradict this view. Similarly, graded practice, imaginal flooding, and *in vivo* flooding all emphasize direct exposure to phobic stimuli, and clearly allow procedurally for classical extinction to take place. Flooding procedures seem particularly relevant to two-factor theory because exposure is prolonged and escape responses are, as far as possible, prohibited, allowing for behaviours other than escape to become correlated with fear-reduction.

That behavioural treatments that have been found to be helpful are *consistent with* two-factor theory does not, of course, validate that theory. The point just made about flooding—that new behaviours may occur contiguously with the diminution of anxiety—is also consistent with the discrimination theory of avoidance extinction, for example; the 'discrimination' hypothesis is that avoidance behaviour will extinguish when experimental extinction is detected by the subject (D'Amato, 1970; Wilson, 1973). Similarly, it would appear that the Hullian concepts invoked by Wolpe (1958) to provide part of the rationale for his reciprocal inhibition theory (see below) could also give an account of flooding. Hence, prolonged exposure to the CS with maximal evocation of the CR could generate reactive inhibition (Ir) which could then provide the basis for conditioned inhibition (sIr) of the CR in that situation (Hull, 1952).

Criticisms of two-factor theory

Challenges to two-factor theory focus on the credibility of classical conditioning as a basis for phobic anxiety (its acquisition and maintenance) and on the explanatory power of avoidance behaviour in protecting conditioned fear from extinction.

Acceptability of the classical conditioning model

Evidence taken to support classical conditioning as a model for phobias in general is derived from experiments with laboratory animals, clinical observations of some phobic patients (Rachman, 1977), and experimental demonstrations with children, notably the historic case of Albert B. (Watson and Rayner, 1920). Studies of classical conditioning with mildly aversive shock in non-clinical volunteers have also been cited recently (e.g. Öhman *et al.*, 1978).

The relevance of any of these sources of evidence to phobias may be questioned. Phobic patients often show intense, multiple, and generalized fears, and may be operating within adverse interpersonal environments, quite unlike analogue research volunteers (Marks, 1969; Mathews, 1978). Differences between phobias and laboratory demonstrations of classical conditioning include the persistence of fear despite the fact of experimental extinction in phobic patients (Eysenck, 1976), the 'non-cognitive' nature of phobias (Öhman *et al.*, 1978), and the fact that, whereas in the laboratory many pairings of CS and UCS are required to demonstrate conditioning, phobic patients seem to acquire severe and lasting anxiety in one trial—or less! (Emmelkamp, 1979; Rachman, 1977). The demonstration of fear-induction in little Albert (Watson and Rayner, 1920), theoretically based on classical conditioning principles, has not been reliably replicated and in any case the unconditioned stimuli listed by Watson and Rayner in their theoretical passages seem arbitary and irrelevant to clinical phobias (Emmelkamp, 1979; Eysenck, 1976). (It is, however, important to acknowledge that several of the replication attempts were themselves inadequate procedurally and conceptually (Delprato, 1980).) Despite popular accounts to the contrary, it is doubtful that Albert became truly phobic, there is no evidence of any great resistance to extinction, operant and classical procedures were confounded, and stimulus generalization was limited (Harris, 1979).

A classical conditioning account of phobias seems to require a concept of equipotentiality (Seligman and Hager, 1972): that is, that *any* stimulus coinciding with the elicitation of fear could become a CS. Seligman (1971) illustrates quite clearly that phobias are distinctly non-arbitrary, and he proposes that phobic stimuli are 'biologically prepared' for rapid learning. This view is taken up again in a later section.

A further difficulty with the classical conditioning account is that it does not convincingly explain phobias of gradual onset without an identifiable original traumatic event (Emmelkamp, 1979; Franks and Wilson, 1978; Marks, 1969; Rachman, 1977). The argument that a series of 'sub-traumatic' UCSs can substitute for a single traumatic one poses problems of verification and is generally unappealing (Eysenck, 1976).

Adequacy of the escape/avoidance formulation

Despite these challenges to classical conditioning as a model for phobias, two-factor theorists would argue that the addition of the second factor—negative reinforcement of operant escape behaviour—resolves at least some difficulties by showing how the CR, once acquired, is protected from extinction. Unfortunately, this argument has weaknesses also. Conditioned autonomic reactions could still extinguish rapidly despite the persistence of escape or avoidance behaviour (Eysenck, 1976; Franks and Wilson, 1978), so the mere fact of continued escape is insufficient to explain the persistence of a classically-conditioned fear.

Important dissimilarities between conditioned avoidance responses and phobias have been noted by Costello (1970). First, laboratory-induced avoidance responses are adaptive, whereas phobias are not; and second, in the laboratory, avoidance responses do not conflict with approach tendencies, as do phobias (otherwise, phobic patients would not seek therapeutic help).

Furthermore, the idea that escape/avoidance responses protect the CR from extinction by preventing exposure to the 'full CS' may be an overgeneralization from the laboratory studies. Suppose that, in acquisition trials, the CS is followed by the aversive UCS 10 s later. Operant responses that successfully avoid the UCS also prevent exposure to the full training CS; that is, the signal plus 10 s. Blocking of the avoidance response permits exposure to that full CS situation (Wilson, 1973; Wilson and Davison, 1971), and therefore behavioural extinction can ensue. It is possible, however, to quibble with the hypothesis that something analogous happens when agoraphobics confront crowded shopping centres for more than a few minutes, because it seems unlikely that, during acquisition of the phobia, aversive unconditioned stimuli were routinely delivered to the agoraphobic individual a given time interval after he or she entered those surroundings.

It can be shown that avoidance behaviour *may* occur without any apparent classical conditioning of fear, and demonstrations to this effect challenge the universality of two-factor theory in explaining avoidance behaviour. Similarly, the results of several experiments suggest that stimuli correlated with aversive events do not necessarily become aversive (Hendry, 1969). Dinsmoor *et al*. (1969) noted that subjects were not at all reluctant to 'observe' a stimulus correlated with punishment, whereas a prediction might have been that such a stimulus would become aversive; Field and Boren (1963) devised an adjusting avoidance procedure in which temporal 'steps' away from shock were indicated by distinctive light-sound combinations, and subjects accepted a stimulus combination indicating imminent shock for most of the time, as opposed to escaping this stimulus which had been paired with shock; and Findley *et al*. (1966) found that under certain conditions monkeys on a three-component multiple schedule would not escape a stimulus that could initiate an avoidance component.

Avoidance paradigms in which specific, exteroceptive stimuli are not presented preceding the aversive stimulus seem to create an additional problem for two-factor theory. In free-operant or Sidman avoidance (Sidman, 1953) rats may postpone shocks by responding in the absence of a signal, and to say that the avoidance behaviour is based upon anxiety requires the identification of a suitable eliciting or discriminative stimulus. Anger (1963) finds a suitable 'stimulus' in the fixed, temporal relationship between responses and shocks; he concludes that the stimuli which acquire the role of anxiety-elicitors are the conditioned aversive temporal stimuli (CATS), which increase in similarity to the CS (the point on the stimulus-trace immediately preceding scheduled shock) as the time after the last shock or response increases. There seems to be no way of disproving this hypothesis, since classical and operant procedures are almost inevitably confounded in avoidance techniques, and thus there is always a CS, whether it be light-onset or passage of time, to take the function of the anxiety-elicitor. A dispute between Brown (1967) and Keehn (1966) over the functions of stimuli in discriminated avoidance was doomed to be unresolved until a design to unconfound the classical and operant procedures could be devised; Brown argued that the signal in avoidance paradigms acquires classically-conditioned aversiveness, which is escaped by the avoidance response, while Keehn held that the stimuli were solely discriminative in function.

The universality of two-factor theory has been clearly limited by demonstrations by Herrnstein (1969) and Herrnstein and Hineline (1966; see also Hineline, 1977) that avoidance behaviour can be acquired and maintained with no classical conditioning procedure involved in the experimental paradigm. In their avoidance situation, a randomly-occurring series of shocks was programmed in the absence of avoidance responding, and no other stimuli were provided. The effect of the designated response was to shift to another series of random shocks, at a lower overall density, for a specified duration. Rats acquired the response, and up to 20 000 responses to extinction were recorded. There was no explicit discriminative stimulus in the situation, and no correlation of shocks with time. Thus the only variable in the situation was the shock-frequency reduction itself, which was sufficient for avoidance to be acquired and maintained. The impact of this is to demonstrate that avoidance behaviour can occur without an explicit anxiety-eliciting stimulus.

Whereas these studies are extremely valuable in showing that classical conditioning is not *necessary* to the acquisition of avoidance, they do not, of course, allow us to conclude that it *never* plays a part in generating anxiety or avoidance. Granted that the mere presence of avoidance behaviour does not allow one to conclude that anxiety is present (provided, of course, that anxiety is not *defined* in terms of avoidance behaviour), and allowing that it does not presuppose that classical conditioning has taken place either, there are situations in which anxiety is undeniably present. Agoraphobic patients clearly do complain of anxiety and panic, for example, and in this clinical context two-factor theory remains a strong contender as an aetiological theory. Hence, although avoidance behaviour *may* occur without classical conditioning of fear, avoidance and fear clearly coexist in phobic patients. Two-factor theory therefore remains potentially relevant in understanding the aetiology of these phobias.

Counter-arguments in favour of two-factor theory

Criticisms of the instrumental component of two-factor theory have succeeded in limiting its generality; escape and avoidance behaviour does not necessarily require prior classical conditioning of fear. These criticisms, however, have been shown to be irrelevant to the status of two-factor theory in describing the aetiology of phobias. More to the point are the criticisms of the classical conditioning component of the theory. Here, too, a modified classical conditioning account of phobias may be retained if we invoke hypotheses that certain CS-UCS combinations are pre-programmed for strong conditioning under less than optimal conditions, that classically-conditioned fear responses may 'incubate' under certain circumstances, and that expectancy effects are particularly important in fear conditioning in humans.

The preparedness hypothesis

It could be argued that people quite commonly develop conditioned fear reactions to situations contiguous with aversive events, and that the conditioned fear, as predicted by theory, quickly extinguishes when the conditioned stimuli are confronted without the UCS. Such people, of course, never become clinically phobic, and do not come to professional attention. On the other hand, those people that *do* present with clinical phobias may have been exposed to unusual acquisition experiences in which the stimuli involved are particularly likely to produce a CR even under less than optimal conditions: unfavourable interstimulus intervals, for example. Whereas the traditional account of aversive classical conditioning relies upon the concept of equipotentiality—*any* stimulus contiguous with the elicitation of fear could become a CS (Seligman and Hager, 1972)—phobic conditioned stimuli are distinctly non-arbitrary, and may have been 'biologically prepared' for rapid learning (Seligman, 1971). Patients rarely present with phobias of electricity, for example, despite the likelihood that electrical appliances, wires, outlets, and so on will occasionally be present contiguously with that 'aversive stimulus' *par excellence*, electric shock. However, insects, small animals, and groups of people are strongly represented in the list of fears presented by phobics. De Silva *et al*. (1977) have recently shown that in a sample of 151 phobic and obsessive patients whose case records were examined by independent raters, there was a 'marked preponderance' of 'highly prepared' feared stimuli. The researchers distinguished between prepared phobic or obsessional *content* and prepared neurotic *behaviour*. In terms of this evolutionary theory of preparedness, the most highly prepared neurosis involves a feared situation that would *probably* and *not uncommonly* have been dangerous for pre-technological humans. Similarly, the defensive behaviour involved in the neurosis would *probably* and *usually* have been successful in minimizing threat for our pre-historic ancestors. The results of the De Silva *et al*. (1977) study are consistent with the preparedness theory of the aetiology of neuroses. Experiments by Öhman *et al*. (1978) seem to confirm that, for volunteers, certain stimuli are more readily conditioned than others, but it is premature to draw firm conclusions because inconsistent results have been reported (see Emmelkamp, 1979; Franks and Wilson, 1978; for reviews of this area). In this context Delprato (1980) offers some important criticisms of the 'preparedness' hypothesis. First, research on human classical conditioning by Öhman and associates (e.g. Öhman *et al*., 1978) have tended to show similar *acquisition* patterns with 'prepared' and 'non-prepared' stimuli, but different *extinction* phenomena; for example, conditioned responses to 'spiders' wane more slowly than CRs for 'houses'. However, the preparedness theory would in fact predict quicker acquisition of CRs to prepared stimuli. Second, 'houses' and 'faces' would be likely to have been correlated with neutral or positive experiences (by contrast with 'snakes') in an individual's *own* developmental history; such stimuli, therefore, do not permit an unconfounded test of the *evolutional* aspect of the theory.

Of course, the preparedness hypothesis does not invalidate two-factor theory but merely places limits on the kind of stimuli involved in phobias, and consequently a slight modification salvages the two-factor view (Rachman, 1977). In any event, there are two conceptual criticisms of the preparedness theory quite aside from the conflicting empirical data: first, without independent confirmation that certain stimuli are 'prepared'—confirmation, for example, by means of continued research on the differential conditionability of different stimuli—preparedness can become a circular definition and therefore non-explanatory. Second, preparedness potentially explains why people in general are more likely to fear rats than electric sockets, but it does not immediately show how only *some* people, not all, become phobic.

In summary, the preparedness hypothesis posits enhanced acquisition processes in accounting for the idiosyncracy of human phobias in learning theory terms. As it happens, Marks (1981a) has recently argued that another view is just as consistent with observation and may be more helpful; the question of 'failure of extinction'. Of course, enhanced acquisition and failure of extinction are not incompatible as theories of the aetiology of phobias, and both are consistent with preparedness despite the greater emphasis given to acquisition in preparedness theory as currently formulated.

The 'Garcia' effect

The apparently high resistance to extinction (if, indeed, extinction is the appropriate concept) of phobias as compared with laboratory illustrations of classical conditioning can be addressed by the argument that phobic objects or situations are in important respects like the kind of CS studied by Garcia and his associates (Garcia *et al*., 1966; Garcia and Koelling, 1966). In these studies, the 'laws of conditioning' were apparently violated by demonstrations of conditioned taste aversion in which interstimulus intervals of several hours did not prevent strong conditioning. For phobic objects to be credibly regarded as conditioned stimuli, we would have to assume not only that they are non-arbitrary as stimuli, but that they can become conditioned in one trial while 'disobeying' the laws that predict effective conditioning only with ultra-short interstimulus intervals. The 'Garcia effect' seems to provide the needed precedent. Difficulties here are that independent evidence is required that in phobias, stimuli like those studied by Garcia are involved. The essential aspect of those stimuli was the relevance of the sense modality stimulated to the later aversive stimulus, i.e. taste (CS) and physical illness (UCS); and it is not immediately clear where to look for appropriate unconditioned stimuli in agoraphobia.

Furthermore, Delprato (1980) cites studies that seem to undermine the argument that Garcia's extinction-resistant and unusually-acquired conditioned reflexes are biologically pre-programmed. Flavoured water would be more *novel* (and therefore more salient) to the experimental animal than the lights and sounds commonly used; relatedness of cue to consequence does not demand an 'evolutionary' explanation; and the subject's *individual* developmental history may lead to a certain preparation or sensitivity to certain CS-UCS combinations, not necessarily an *evolutionary* connection.

'Incubation' and classical conditioning

Eysenck (1968, 1976) calls attention to the 'Napalkov phenomenon' in an attempt to defend a classical conditioning view of phobia-acquisition. The phenomenon refers to a paradoxical enhancement of the CR during experimental extinction when an aversive UCS was used during conditioning. As Eysenck (1976) points out, conventional views of classical conditioning are that CRs are usually weaker and of lesser amplitude than the UCR produced in the conditioning trials. However, a 'neurotic breakdown', as a CR, would seem to involve more anxiety than any UCR we could reasonably postulate; hence, some form of 'incubation' of the CR must be involved.

Eysenck finds the needed laboratory analogue in data from Napalkov (1963). In experiments with dogs, Napalkov observed that the sound of a pistol shot (UCS) initially produced, among other responses, an increase in blood pressure (UCR); however, after twenty-five trials the UCR had habituated completely. When a neutral stimulus was paired with the pistol shot once, and once only, subsequent presentations of this CS alone elicited CRs that progressively increased in amplitude to a value several times that of the initial UCR. If phobic reactions 'incubate' in this way, then they could still exemplify classically conditioned CRs. This view could account for the gradual onset of some phobias and their resistance to extinction. Eysenck argues that those CSs that produce drives will follow the law of enhancement or incubation, because the CRs produced, after conditioning, by the CS are in fact identical to the UCR. This argument questions the common assumption that the phobic patient's CR is under experimental extinction. The stimulus that maintains the conditioned reflex is the CS, because it is functionally equivalent to the UCS. The phenomenon is more likely to occur in neurotic introverts (Eysenck, 1976).

Difficulties with the theory include the lack, to date, of substantial experimental evidence bearing on the issue (Emmelkamp, 1979; Franks and Wilson, 1978).

'Expectancy' and classical conditioning

Rachman (1977) has detailed several criticisms of early conditioning theories of fear-acquisition, including the observation that fears in humans can be acquired indirectly, contrary to the tenets of conditioning theory. He concludes that there are three avenues to acquiring fear: conditioning, vicarious experience, and instruction (or, receiving information). Recently, Reiss (1980) has discussed an 'expectancy' model of Pavlovian conditioning in application to human fear, and thereby provides a rationale for accommodating Rachman's criticisms by means of a revised conditioning theory.

Reiss argues that *actual* pairing of CS and UCS seems unnecessary in humans; many phobics have never encountered their 'phobic situation' in real life. Such individuals have, of course, had symbolic and imaginal exposure to CS and UCS equivalents. If these covert 'conditioning trials' are admissible as constituting conditioning, then conditioning theory, thus modified, survives the challenge. Nevertheless, difficulties remain in accounting for individual differences in the kind of covert conditioning sequences experienced. Reiss goes on to recommend the informational model of Pavlovian conditioning proposed by Wagner and Rescorla (1972) as potentially helpful in understanding human fear acquisition. This theory is offered to contrast with the problematic contiguity model. Essentially, the informational model focusses on the degree to which conditioned stimuli are informative in predicting what will happen next; for example, adding a new stimulus or dimension to a preconditioned CS is redundant to the predictive power of that CS, and hence responses to the new component or additional stimulus will not be acquired. The theory is consistent with observations such as the following: whereas contiguity theory predicts no learning from an explicit unpairing procedure, informational theory predicts that the unpaired CS would acquire informational value ('no UCS is forthcoming') and hence will become inhibitory; the latter is consistent with laboratory findings (Wagner and Rescorla, 1972). The expectancy model proposed by Reiss takes account of these difficulties with the contiguity model of classical conditioning.

Assumptions of the expectancy model are that, (a) classical conditioning is a form of stimulus-expectancy learning; what is expected is a reinforcing stimulus, and (b) the laws governing the acquisition of expectancies and CRs are essentially the same. There are, then, four processes in the acquisition of a phobia:

1. The acquisition of 'danger' expectancies via conditioning, instruction, etc. (cf. Bandura, 1977; Rachman, 1977).

2. The acquisition of 'anxiety' expectancies through *in vivo* or covert experience.
3. Initial avoidance, which at least sometimes occurs via negative reinforcement.
4. The persistence of avoidance by means of self-regulatory processes (e.g. 'safety signals' may be generated by one's own avoidance behaviour).

The model also accounts for the operation of SD and flooding; danger expectancies are weakened by CS exposure, and anxiety expectancies weaken if 'surprising' information is imparted, for example by the fatigue of anxiety CRs if exposure is prolonged.

This model provides a rationale for defending conditioning explanations of phobias against some of its criticisms; we will return to the issue of the mechanisms in successful treatment in a later discussion of self-efficacy theory.

Alternative aetiological concepts

Punishment

Some criticisms of two-factor theory suggest that classical conditioning processes cannot explain avoidance behaviour (Herrnstein, 1969). Others find classical conditioning inadequate to account for acquired fears in humans because of the quick extinction of CRs that would be predicted from non-reinforcement (Wilson, 1973; Wilson and Davison, 1971). Yet *some* aversiveness must prevail in the phobic situation, or the patient would not report fear, anxiety, or panic. If the aversiveness derives from an exogenous stimulus, there are two candidates from a classical conditioning perspective: the CS and the UCS. Granted that the stimuli correlated with the UCS do not *necessarily* become aversive themselves, it is conceivable that phobic environments are discriminative rather than aversive. That leaves the UCS as the prime candidate for the aversive element in the phobic situation. This view, similarly to Eysenck's (1976), challenges the assumption that there is no longer a UCS and that the patient's phobia is under experimental extinction.

Agoraphobics report both anticipatory anxiety and relatively unpredictable panic attacks. The 'fear of the fear' component of agoraphobia (Goldstein and Chambless, 1978; Marks, 1970) can be translated as 'fear of the panic attack'. Zitrin *et al*. (1976) argue that behavioural treatments like SD are helpful in reducing anticipatory anxiety, but do not bring lasting relief because panic attacks in real life bring the anticipatory anxiety to the fore again. The panic attack, then, could potentially be regarded as a UCS, thus explaining the maintenance of anticipatory anxiety and avoidance behaviour. To approach a CS that predicts an aversive UCS is to emit behaviour that produces punishment, and accordingly the agoraphobic sufferer continues to operate under an 'acquisition', rather than an 'extinction', paradigm. Watson and Marks (1971), significantly, reserve judgment on whether or not agoraphobia is 'conditioned' initially, and use the term 'habituation' as a possible account of the learning process operating in successful treatment.

In any event, the treatment approach predicted by this 'punishment' view would not be hastening or facilitating the extinction process, because experimental extinction does not prevail. Instead, treatment would involve helping the patient *cope with*, or in some way reduce the impact of, the aversive UCS, the panic attack. Treatment may well be effective to the extent that it satiates the patient to the UCS, or that it leads to habituation of the UCR. Flooding could provide the optimal conditions for both, especially when anxiety is experienced during treatment (Chambless, 1978). Even when anxiety does not occur within treatment, there is the possibility that anticipatory anxiety may be experienced beforehand, and this may provide for a form of satiation akin to inoculation. Watson and Marks (1971) found that chronic phobics improved equally when flooded with relevant and irrelevant fantasies, but the mechanisms of treatment appeared to be different: outcome to irrelevant fear correlated positively with anxiety shown during treatment, whereas outcome to relevant flooding did not. A possible interpretation is that irrelevant fear cues elicited responses that subsequently habituated, and that relevant cues produced stimulus satiation.

Indications that patients learn to *cope with* panic attacks in successful therapy are given in some clinical reports. A patient who had received flooding treatment said: 'I still get the panics, but I can cope with them now and don't need to run away during them' (Marks, 1972b, p. 134). Similarly, Emmelkamp *et al*. (1978) note that a number of their patients 'reported spontaneously that their "thoughts" had undergone a much greater change during prolonged exposure *in vivo* than during cognitive restructuring' (Emmelkamp *et al*., 1978, p. 40). These 'thoughts' may have taken the form of coping self-statements, such as 'there you are, nothing will go wrong with me' (Emmelkamp *et al*., 1978, p. 40). The authors observe that it is possible that 'a more effective cognitive modification takes place through prolonged exposure *in vivo* than through a procedure which is focused directly on such a change' (p. 40). Marks *et al*. (1971) quote some remarkably similar observations on the part of their patients who were treated by flooding; for example: 'if I suddenly thought I was going to have a fit I could talk myself out of the feeling—I suppose because the imagined scenes (during flooding) were so horrific that I rejected my own small panics' (Marks *et al*., 1971, p. 368). These comments seem less consistent with an 'extinction' view of therapeutic change than with the idea that these patients achieved a sense of being able to cope.

A difficulty with our argument that it may be helpful to view panic attacks as primary UCSs is that we have not specified how the panic attack comes about in the first place. Mathews *et al*. (1981), commenting on this view that panic may be a traumatic conditioning stimulus, acknowledge that panic may derive from sources other than the immediate environment. It is possible that agoraphobia is similar to a somatoform or dissociative disorder in which panic attacks represent an indirect response to conflict from a source removed from the phobic situation (Chambless, 1978). This 'conflict' view will be taken up next.

Conflict

Early in their discussion of the acquisition of phobias, Eysenck and Rachman (1965) note that anxiety may be produced *either* by noxious stimulation *or* by conflict. With respect to conflict, these authors referred to early studies of experimental neurosis (Pavlov, 1927), especially those in which mild noxious stimulation with physical confinement (Liddell, 1944) or approach/avoidance conflicts (Miller, 1944) were involved. These demonstrations, together with the 'neurosis' produced in dogs by certain difficult discriminations without explicit aversive stimulation (see, for example, Shenger-Krestovnikova—cited by Pavlov, 1927), seem to be potentially helpful analogues of certain human neuroses. However, behaviour therapists have subsequently given 'conflict' relatively little attention, focussing almost exclusively upon the two-factor formulation and its modifications in recent years. Two decades ago Yates (1962) lamented this same neglect.

As it happens, the 'conflict' issue has been revived recently in a reformulation of agoraphobia by Goldstein and Chambless (1978) and, similarly, Mineka and Kihlstrom (1978) have called attention anew to the early experimental neurosis studies. The context for our discussion is provided by the pioneering formulations of Wolpe (1958).

(1) Wolpe's formulation

Wolpe's (1958) original theory of phobias developed from his experiments with 'neurotic' cats, experiments which derived in turn from Masserman's (1943) studies of conflict (Patterson, 1980). Adopting a largely Hullian theoretical perspective, Wolpe reasoned that the extinction of autonomic fear reactions (a necessary precursor of the elimination of avoidance behaviours) takes place by means of conditioned inhibition of those fear responses. Fear responses generate reactive inhibition, a negative drive which leads to the cessation of the response which produces it, and which diminishes with inactivity. The cessation of activity is strengthened by drive-reduction (i.e. the reduction of reactive inhibition). 'Conditioned inhibition' refers to the conditioning of a resting response to the stimuli in the learning situation (Kimble, 1961, p. 305). However, because autonomic 'anxiety' produces little reactive inhibition, a response *incompatible with* anxiety needs to be elicited so as to operate counter to those anxiety responses. This *reciprocal inhibition* creates enough of an aversive drive to provide the basis for the conditioned inhibition of anxiety.

The reciprocal inhibition formulation of the extinction of fear responses has since been seriously called into question. Wolpe (1958) omitted crucial control procedures in his early experiments, procedures which could have shown anxiety-antagonistic responses unnecessary to his treatment techniques (Wilson and Davison, 1971). Non-reinforced exposure to the full CS—the feared situation confronted for enough time to replicate the situation obtaining in the acquisition trials at the point at which the UCS was presented—has proved sufficient to extinguish avoidance behaviour, the technique being simply that of blocking of the escape/avoidance response, or response-prevention (Wilson, 1973).

Because 'conflict' was involved in Wolpe's procedures for establishing the anxiety response initially in his experimental cats, and because reciprocal inhibition involves conflicting response tendencies, Wolpe's theoretical formulation can be said to rely on concepts of conflict. We now turn to a specific formulation of agoraphobia in terms of conflict.

(2) The Goldstein and Chambless formulation

Goldstein and Chambless (1978) distinguish between 'simple' and 'complex' agoraphobia. In simple agoraphobia, the patient fears streets and public places, *per se*, often as a secondary effect of hypoglycaemia, for example. Complex agoraphobia, by far the more common, is assumed to occur in conjunction with certain personality characteristics: the patient lacks a sense of self-sufficiency, and tends to misunderstand the source of emotional responses to conflict. 'Symptoms' begin in a climate of notable conflict, generally interpersonal in nature. The authors explain the agoraphobic panic attacks as a response to the interpersonal conflict, misattributed by the patient to exogenous situations such as crowded shops. The paradigm case suggested as typical by Goldstein and Chambless is the woman who feels trapped in an unsuccessful marriage, is sufficiently lacking in self-confidence that to contemplate leaving the marriage is not a realistic option, and who develops agoraphobia as an indirect resolution of the conflict. This rationale is similar to that commonly provided to account for the somatoform or dissociative (previously called 'hysterical') disorders (Davison and Neale, 1978). This theory by Goldstein and Chambless that emotional effects of interpersonal conflict are misattributed to external stimuli is consistent with the several reports that implicate marital dysfunction in agoraphobia (see Chapter 3).

A major difficulty with the Goldstein and Chambless formulation is that the theory is practically irrefutable. 'Conflict' is essential to the definition and the explanation of agoraphobia, a classic example of a circular definition. Patients whose problems do not arise in a climate of conflict are not labelled complex agoraphobics. Similary, the self-assured, assertive agoraphobic who would pose problems for the theory is not a complex agoraphobic by definition. Clinical experience does not confirm that self-reliant or apparently conflict-free agoraphobics can only suffer from simple fears of specific situations. The attempt by Goldstein and Chambless to validate these points empirically has been criticized by Emmelkamp (1979), who calls attention to the *post hoc* nature of their retrospective study of case records and their compilation of the 'recollections' of clinicians. Despite these criticisms, it is of course quite conceivable that interpersonal conflict provides a necessary condition for developing agoraphobia in some people. In fact, the concept of the panic attack as an emotional consequence of conflict fits neatly with the view that the panic attack functions similarly to an unconditioned aversive stimulus.

The implication of conflict in the development of a neurotic disorder like agoraphobia is anticipated by early studies of experimental neurosis. Key elements here are confinement and conflict: conflict as represented by difficult discriminations in classical conditioning, or uncontrollable and/or unpredictable events (Mineka and Kihlstrom, 1978). It is notable that Costello (1970) finds laboratory studies of avoidance irrelevant to phobias precisely because the laboratory analogues involve no conflict between approach and avoidance tendencies. After reviewing the historical accounts of experimental neurosis, Mineka and Kihlstrom hypothesize that the crucial variable is that 'environmental events of vital importance to the organism become unpredictable, uncontrollable, or both' (Mineka and Kihlstrom, 1978, p. 257). (This view leads immediately to the hypothesis that perceptions of self-efficacy could be destroyed by such removal of predictability and control — see below.) These authors note two independent parameters in conditioning situations:

1. The probability of occurrence of the UCS, given the CS (this is manipulated in studies of partial reinforcement).
2. The probability of occurrence of the UCS, granted the *absence* of the CS.

The latter variable has hardly been studied at all, which is unfortunate because unpredictability of the UCS seems very relevant to agoraphobia. Clinical observation confirms that crowded, confined places do not invariably produce panic attacks in agoraphobics, for example. In the 'punishment' view presented above, the rush-hour bus is the CS, and the panic attack is the UCS. In this case, the CS does not reliably predict the UCS, and therefore a form of partial reinforcement is in effect. The absence of the CS, conversely, does not guarantee that no panic attack will occur, because many agoraphobics experience panics while alone at home. If Goldstein and Chambless (1978) are correct, interpersonal conflict could produce the panic attack initially, and this would be misunderstood by the patient and attributed to a phobia of the surroundings or of 'being away from help'. The panic attack then forms a UCS which is neither reliably predicted by any one CS, nor easily controllable by the patient. A form of 'experimental neurosis' could well ensue.

It is interesting to note that physical restraint, or confinement, is a feature of the paradigm cases of experimental neurosis, and such confinement seems prominent in the fears of agoraphobics, both literally (e.g. feeling trapped in a lift or in a queue at the supermarket checkout) and, perhaps, symbolically (e.g. feeling trapped in a difficult interpersonal relationship).

When the subject has no *control* over events (operant paradigm), then the probability of reinforcement, given the response, and the probability of reinforcement, given *no* response, are equal. With this kind of paradigm, 'learned helplessness' or depression can ensue (Overmier and Seligman, 1967; Seligman, 1975). It could be parsimonious to formulate the depression often reported by agoraphobics in these terms. Hence, if we assume the presence of marital or other interpersonal conflict that the patient does not attempt to resolve directly and forthrightly, panic attacks could result and then serve as aversive and unconditioned stimuli which seem relatively unpredictable and uncontrollable. This state of affairs could produce something akin to experimental neurosis. As Masserman (1971) puts it,

> the various forms of 'conflict' . . . may be subsumed under a broader etiological rubric: namely, that in each instance, the organism apprehends a failure to predict and control events important to its welfare. (p. 9—referenced by Mineka and Kihlstrom, 1978)

There is an apparent difficulty with the 'interpersonal conflict' view of agoraphobic panic attacks. If panic attacks in the supermarket occur as an unrecognized response to a household argument earlier in the day, how is it that behavioural tests arranged by researcher/clinicians are relevant at all? It would seem that a patient would only experience panic in the behavioural test situation if there had, by chance, been a marital dispute at home a couple of hours earlier! This objection may, of course, be countered by the argument that supermarkets have become conditioned stimuli for anxiety by means of earlier intermittent pairing with panic attacks.

Positive reinforcement

Goldstein and Chambless (1978) note briefly that agoraphobics may be rewarded for their passive, phobic behaviour. In this formulation, the focus is on the 'secondary gain', or the benefits indirectly derived by the patient for phobic behaviour. In some cases, the solicitous attentions of a spouse may be exclusively responsible for maintaining the patient's phobic orientation and behaviour. Studies of treatments which emphasize social reinforcement of approach behaviour (cf. Agras *et al.*, 1968—see Chapter 5) are consistent with this argument, but it is important to note that therapeutic encouragement of approach behaviour is also consistent with an avoidance model of the maintenance of the phobia. It is to some extent implausible to attribute agoraphobia solely to secondary gain, if only because this would require the notion that autonomic responses (increased heart rate, skin conductance, and so forth) are readily reinforced in this way. Generally, successful treatments seem compatible with avoidance, punishment, and positive reinforcement formulations, whereas the 'conflict' theory would predict that treatments reviewed in Chapter 5 would be found incomplete.

A plausible view which is unfortunately difficult to test is that women develop phobias because, traditionally, society has reinforced passive, dependent, and phobic behaviours on their part (Fodor, 1974, 1978). A major treatment implication here is the addition of assertiveness training to the therapeutic regimen, and this is also quite consistent with the Goldstein and Chambless (1978) formulation. However, social phobia is equally represented in the sexes, unlike agoraphobia, and it has to be explained why women are not in the majority in social phobia samples.

Expectancy learning

Bandura's (1977) view of the maintenance of phobic behaviour is that noxious events (experienced directly or vicariously) induce expectations of harm—expectations that produce anxiety and avoidance behaviour. However, anxiety does not mediate avoidance; anxiety and avoidance are correlated co-effects of the expectations, so that modifying autonomic anxiety will not necessarily produce changes in avoidance behaviour, nor *vice versa*. This view subsumes the notion that avoidance behaviour may occur (or even persist protractedly) without 'anxiety', a point strongly supported by the laboratory literature (Field and Boren, 1963; Hendry, 1969; Herrnstein, 1969; Hineline, 1977; see above). A correlational study by Bandura and Adams (1977), while not producing unequivocal cause-effect conclusions, gives results consistent with the theory as applied to the success of SD with snake-phobics.

Hence, avoidance behaviour is maintained to the extent that it reduces aversive events, and reducing anxiety (or physiological arousal) obviates avoidance not because an activating drive is eliminated, but because expectations of self-efficacy are encouraged. Research findings that relaxation training seems irrelevant to clinical SD (Gillan and Rachman, 1974) fit this context well. Research summarized by Bandura (1977) produces results consistent with the hypothesis that self-efficacy expectations are more important than anxiety-reduction in promoting behaviour change.

An integrated model

The most recent aetiological formulation of agoraphobia has been presented by Mathews *et al.* (1981). It is similar to the Goldstein and Chambless (1978) account of 'complex agoraphobia' in assuming that anxiety reactions are not, initially at least, elicited by the immediate surroundings in which most phobic anxiety is experienced. According to Mathews *et al.* (1981), there may be three general 'vulnerability' factors that, if operative, increase the likelihood that the individual will develop agoraphobia: over- or under-protection in the early family environment (see also Chapter 1), high levels of trait anxiety, and general background stress. An increased level of general anxiety results from the combination of trait anxiety and stress, setting the scene for a panic attack to occur more or less haphazardly. If the panic attack first appears when the individual is out of doors, then agoraphobia could develop. The sufferer may attribute the panic to external stimuli, and may begin to rely more and more on dependent and avoidant behaviour patterns (particularly if the individual has previously displayed this kind of defensive behaviour). Finally, certain aversive influences (e.g. conditioned fear of public places; anticipatory anxiety about the prospect of a panic attack) discourage patients from tackling their fear, and other positive experiences (e.g. sympathy and attention from other people; being given less responsibility in the household) reinforce staying at home.

This model is consistent with results of questionnaire surveys which show agoraphobics to score high on trait anxiety; with results of many of the available studies on the childhood background of agoraphobics; with the high percentage of women in self-referred samples of agoraphobics, in that historically a dependent social role has been expected of women (Fodor, 1978); and, finally, with the finding that agoraphobics tend to sense an external locus of control, which has a bearing on the issue of misattribution of emotional reactions (Mathews *et al*., 1981, pp. 46–49).

Unfortunately, some of the limitations (discussed earlier) of the Goldstein and Chambless theory apply equally to that of Mathews *et al*. (1981). Both theories are helpful clinically in calling attention to important features of agoraphobia: background stress and interpersonal conflict, misattribution of emotional reactions arising from outside the immediate surroundings, and the possible reinforcement of dependent and phobic behaviour. On the other hand, neither theory is directly testable because some of the presumed aetiological factors are difficult, at best, to ascertain, and because of the possibility of conceptual (or definitional) issues being intertwined with the empirical. These failings are likely to be involved in any comprehensive formulation of this complex disorder.

THEORIES OF TREATMENT EFFECTIVENESS

Presumably, treatments are likely to bring benefit to the extent that their rationales match corresponding theories about the maintenance of phobic anxiety and behaviour. Thus, for a treatment to be found effective is sometimes taken as evidence to validate its theoretical foundation. Not only is the success of a procedure said to confirm the accuracy of its theoretical underpinnings, but it is further held to indicate that mechanisms based on these underlying concepts are responsible for treatment effectiveness. The logic here is invalid: treatments may be helpful because of, regardless of, or despite their theoretical context (cf. Lazarus, 1976). (An example, discussed above, is Wolpe's (1958) reciprocal inhibition theory.) Additionally, a successful treatment may have a *modus operandi* consistent with more than one theory.

Despite these conceptual problems, it remains entirely possible that theories (notably extinction) originally put forward to design treatments, and to explain their effectiveness, are in fact correct. Revisions of conditioning accounts of the aetiology of phobias, discussed earlier, leave extinction a strong candidate for the crucial therapeutic process. Because we have already discussed extinction hypotheses in some detail, we will now examine attempts to explain the mechanisms of treatment in terms of habituation, acclimatization through exposure, expectancy (self-efficacy theory), the adoption of broad-ranging problem-oriented techniques (multimodal therapy), and the operation of crucial 'non-specific' factors.

Habituation

A hypothesis basic to the views discussed so far is that phobic patients have received some form of conditioning, and that treatment is successful to the extent that it promotes extinction of conditioned fear and avoidance behaviour. As Marks (1975) notes, it is usually an unproved assumption that phobic patients acquire their fears by conditioning, and he suggests that adaptation and habituation are rivals to extinction in explaining the effectiveness of treatment. Adaptation and habituation are more theoretically neutral concepts than extinction, in that they do not necessarily imply that conditioning has taken place. Because behavioural treatments of obsessions and phobias involve some form of exposure to problem situations, Marks contends that some form of acclimatization of the patient to feared situations is the key fear-reduction process. His cautious stance in not committing himself to any single theory of aetiology has drawn criticism from Wolpe (1976), who describes Marks as a behaviour therapy 'malcontent'.

Difficulties with habituation as a postulated process in phobia removal include empirical findings that response decrement to phobic stimuli is *directly* proportional to stimulus intensity, whereas in habituation, response decrement would normally be *inversely* proportional to the strength of the stimulus (Marks, 1975, p. 67). It might also be supposed that anxiety has to be elicited before it can habituate, but empirical findings are mixed: Marks *et al*. (1971) and Mathews and Shaw (1973) have failed to show that the arousal of anxiety in exposure treatment facilitates improvement, whereas Chambless (1978) provides conflicting evidence. The waters are further muddied by results of a study by Watson and Marks (1971), cited earlier, who observed that the induction of 'irrelevant fear' (e.g. imagery of being savaged by a tiger) was as effective as imaginal exposure to phobia-relevant fear in treating phobias. Watson and Marks argue that different processes may be operative for relevant versus irrelevant fear: extinction applies to the former, and habituation to the latter. A further difficulty is that habituation (as usually defined) of an unlearned response would be only a transitory phenomenon (Thompson and Spencer, 1966).

Caution is therefore necessary in the use of the term 'habituation' as an explanatory concept. Marks (1981b), commenting on this, is careful to use habituation as a description rather than as an explanation, which would involve circular reasoning. He goes on to list several labels (adaptation, habituation, extinction, inhibition, satiation, exhaustion, and boredom) which may be defined distinctly in terms of length of stimulation, recovery time, nature of the stimulus, and behavioural effect, but which all refer essentially to procedures producing (in atheoretical terminology) 'response decrement' (Marks, 1981b, p. 229).

A clinical paradigm

Consistent with his aetiological caution, Marks (1981a, 1981b) has proposed a clinical paradigm for exposure treatment. Because the familiar conditioning terminology assumes an unverified theoretical explanation of the acquisition of phobias, it may be rejected in favour of a theory-neutral notation. An evoking stimulus (ES) is one that triggers phobic reactions, or evoked responses (ERs). This simple formulation is useful clinically because it clarifies the therapeutic task: identify the relevant evoking stimuli, and have the patient confront them until the ERs subside. Empirical and theoretical problems are to identify differences between sensitizing and therapeutic exposure procedures. Important parameters identified to date include massing of practice (Foa *et al*., 1980) and protracted, versus brief, exposure within sessions (Marks, 1972b; Stern and Marks, 1973a; see also Reiss, 1980). Marks' delineation of these and other important, testable parameters of exposure treatment has been commended by Wilson (1981a), who, however, is dubious about the advantages offered by the proposed terminological changes from the language of conditioning theory to an aetiologically-neutral vocabulary.

Self-efficacy

The theory of self-efficacy advanced by Bandura (1977) calls attention to an important process that could well be central to a variety of treatment strategies: the acquisition by the patient of a sense of confidence that he or she will be able to cope adequately with the problematic situation. This process is potentially activated by therapeutic satiation of feared stimuli, extinction or habituation of fear responses, modification of expectancies, and so forth, although performance-based methods are predicted to be most successful. The theory seems to fit agoraphobia very well, at least at the level of clinical anecdote and plausible speculation. For example, Emmelkamp (1979) states 'self-observation of "improvement" seems to be an important factor' (p. 110). Describing how imaginal exposure and cognitive factors could interact, he goes on to say:

> Self-observation of imagining phobic stimuli no longer arousing anxiety, combined with the strong therapeutic suggestion that he has 'improved', enables the patient to venture in the phobic situation *in vivo*. Habituation *in vivo* is eventually affected [sic]. A reappraisal of his performance in real-life situations may lead to further cognitive changes. (Emmelkamp, 1979, p. 111).

Quotations from patients of Marks (1972b) and Emmelkamp *et al*. (1978) make similar points (see 'Punishment', above).

Self-efficacy theory provides an explanation for findings that are difficult to accommodate by two-factor theory. For example, fear-arousal is unnecessary during therapeutic exposure to phobic situations, despite the prediction by two-factor theorists that anxiety has to be aroused and then extinguished (Franks and Wilson, 1978). Another tenet of two-factor theory is that to retreat from the feared situation before anxiety subsides is to reinforce the patient's escape and avoidance behaviour, but Hand *et al*. (1974) note that 'cognitive set' is more important than this procedural detail. A parsimonious prediction is that the right 'set' would be a strong self-efficacy expectation (Franks and Wilson, 1978).

It is important to note in this context the contrast between therapeutic procedure and theoretical process (Wilson, 1981b). In self-efficacy theory, alterations in patients' expectations in the direction of greater confidence in their ability to enact the relevant behaviours constitute the crucial process in fear reduction. The optimal procedures for effecting these changes are, as far as we know at present, behavioural—the patient is asked to *do* something (confront feared situations) rather than to alter his or her thinking. The previously discussed comparison of *in vivo* exposure with cognitive restructuring reported by Emmelkamp *et al*. (1978) makes this point clearly; cognitive restructuring had a distinctly weaker therapeutic effect than exposure, although 'exposure' patients reported changes in their attitudes consonant with self-efficacy theory as a result of treatment. In any event, Wilson (1981b) argues that cognitive restructuring *procedures* may yet form a vital component of exposure treatment in agoraphobia. In asking patients to confront feared environments with a willingness to relax and let anxiety arise if it will, in discouraging defeatism in response to momentary setbacks, and in stressing coping mechanisms for dealing with panic, Mathews *et al*. (1981) have clearly incorporated cognitive-behavioural treatment procedures into their successful home-based practice regimen.

Evidence is available from clinical trials with agoraphobics that performance-based treatment has an advantage over symbolic treatments (see Chapter 5), and that self-efficacy expectations predict favourable response to treatment. Mathews *et al*. (1976) failed to show differences between imaginal and *in vivo* exposure to phobic situations, but did show the predicted difference in self-efficacy expectations—despite the fact that this study was conducted before Bandura's (1977) theory had been articulated. Only *in vivo* patients showed significant positive changes in their ratings of hierarchy items to be attempted next, ratings that seem to parallel the kind of assessment used by Bandura and his associates (e.g. Bandura *et al*., 1980). These results are reported in a separate paper on the within-treatment data of the Mathews *et al*. (1976) study (Johnston *et al*., 1976). Furthermore, a composite of expectancy ratings about future performance on the phobic hierarchy was predictive of favourable response to treatment in terms of other measures (Mathews *et al*., 1976), as would be clearly predicted by self-efficacy theory. In connection with the general argument that successful anxiety-reduction therapy essentially modifies expectancies, Reiss (1980) illustrates a possible resolution of the apparent paradox that SD and flooding may both be helpful therapeutic procedures (see also Wilkins, 1973).

Reiss calls attention to the crucial importance of CS duration, CS intensity, and their interaction in determining level of fear and, hence, anxiety expectancies thereafter. In general, the shorter the CS duration, and the greater its intensity, the greater the fear. However, relatively short CS durations may be therapeutically beneficial provided that CS intensity is kept low, as in SD. High CS intensity may also lead to fear-reduction, provided that CS duration is prolonged, as in flooding. In each case, anxiety expectancies may be weakened, because by the time the CS is terminated anxiety is declining through either minimal elicitation in the first place (SD) or exhaustion (flooding). It has to be noted that Reiss' formulation has been criticized by Burgess (1981), who regrets the implied circumvention of an operant analysis (cf. Skinner, 1966).

Multimodality

The agoraphobic syndrome is multifaceted, with manifestations in behavioural, affective, cognitive, and interpersonal modalities of functioning. Interactions between events in these different modalities complicate things further. For example, studies by Hafner and his associates (Hafner, 1976, 1977a, b; Milton and Hafner, 1979) seem to show several patterns of interactions: reducing agoraphobic avoidance behaviour may be followed by the development of a sexual problem in the patient; by an exacerbation of marital difficulties; or by the onset of any of a variety of disorders in the patient's spouse. Such disorders have included depression, paranoia, and psychophysiological complaints (Thorpe *et al*., 1982). Conversely, successful treatment of a sexual disorder may be followed by the development of agoraphobia (Hand and Lamontagne, 1976).

It is tempting to conclude from such clinical reports that one modality may be more fundamental than another, and that events in one domain are therefore 'symptomatic' of events in the more fundamental one. The data do not permit such straightforward conclusions to be drawn. An alternative to this kind of speculation is to perform a comprehensive assessment, and then to address the various problems that emerge in an integrated, but multifaceted, treatment programme. Lazarus' (1976) multimodal behaviour therapy conceptualizations provide the logical framework. His prediction is that if all relevant modalities are addressed in assessment and treatment (e.g. phobic avoidance behaviour, depressed affect, troubled interpersonal relationships, and psychophysiological problems), then treatment will be comprehensive, effective, and lastingly beneficial. The multimodal approach easily accommodates the variety of procedures that seem indicated for many agoraphobics: assertiveness training (Chambless, 1978), marital counselling (Hafner, 1977b), and group *in vivo* exposure to feared surroundings (Emmelkamp *et al*., 1978).

Although the multimodal formulation poses some problems of verification by research, it nevertheless offers a clinically useful framework for guaranteeing thorough assessment and treatment. Perhaps the most important attribute of a helpful theory is its ability to promote an effective and comprehensive sequence of treatment interventions.

Non-specific factors

Finally, it has to be noted that 'non-specific factors'—a phrase justifiably criticized by Wilkins (1979) as having no conceptual or operational definition—could be responsible for treatment effectiveness. One such factor is 'expectancy'.

Expectancy of benefit

On this argument, therapy is effective to the extent that it successfully mobilizes in the patient a high degree of faith in treatment, and in its eventual effectiveness, by means of the influence of some general features of the therapeutic situation: having the concern of a therapist, engaging in conversation about issues relevant to the presenting complaints, and, generally, perceiving that the whole enterprise is designed to bring benefit.

As it happens, whereas non-specific factors of this kind are potentially difficult confounding variables that bedevil much psychotherapy research in general, their influence on the improvement of agoraphobic patients seems minimal (Mathews, 1978). Important evidence for this is provided by Gelder *et al*. (1973), who found that agoraphobics, by contrast with 'specific' and social phobics, were particularly immune to the effects of a 'free-association' comparison treatment designed to control for non-specific influences of treatment. It is important to distinguish this kind of 'expectancy'—i.e. general faith in treatment or in the powers of the therapist—from Bandura's self-efficacy formulation in terms of efficacy and outcome expectations: or, expectations about one's *ability* to carry out the behaviour, and expectations about the subsequent *effect* of performing the behaviour.

Reactivity of behavioural assessment

It is important to note that 'expectancy' is not the only non-specific factor in treatment. One general feature of agoraphobia research is the behavioural test situation (see Chapter 4). Because *in vivo* exposure to the feared situation seems the most important ingredient of successful treatment (Mathews, 1977b, 1978), then the behavioural assessment—in which the patient enters feared situations—is treatment in itself! This feature of treatment, common to all treatment conditions in many controlled trials, qualifies as the kind of non-specific factor that may be responsible for general improvement in agoraphobics. This effect will predictably be more pronounced, the more behavioural tests are given (Emmelkamp, 1979). The reactive effects of repeated behavioural assessment could well have masked some differential effects of the treatments in the study reported in Chapter 6.

CONCLUDING REMARKS

As yet, no all-encompassing theory of the aetiology and treatment of agoraphobia has been offered, although the formulation of complex agoraphobia by Goldstein and Chambless (1978) and the integrated model of Mathews, Gelder, and Johnston (1981) seem the most promising attempts to date to integrate many disparate observations relating to aetiology. More data on the possible interaction of interpersonal conflict and agoraphobic behaviour are required.

Two-factor theory may be criticized in several ways, perhaps most obviously in terms of the nature of the presumed aversive UCS that is required by the classical conditioning formulation. Such a UCS could be highly 'prepared' biologically; it is equally possible that 'conflict' and its autonomic aftermath could serve as the UCS/UCR combination. Conditioned responses could 'incubate', and thus prove resistant to prevailing extinction procedures and contingencies. Nevertheless, despite the observation that agoraphobics behave *as if* their behaviour is being negatively reinforced, it is difficult to prove that straightforward conditioning paradigms are involved. An alternative possibility is that agoraphobic behaviour continues to be reinforced under experimental *acquisition*, rather than *extinction*, contingencies. This concept poses problems of verification, but leads to the conclusion that therapeutic change could involve coping or habituation mechanisms rather than extinction. Marks' (1981a, b) atheoretical treatment prescriptions derive explicitly from this general dissatisfaction with a conditioning view of aetiology.

The origins of agoraphobics' panic attacks are puzzling to theoreticians as well as to patients. It is easy to criticize the conditioning view that panic attacks are a form of conditioned response, but the alternative view that they derive from sources unrelated to the immediate surroundings poses further problems of verification. Nevertheless, the idea that anxiety can be produced by confinement and conflict is not new in behavioural circles (as witnessed by early studies of experimental neurosis in the Pavlovian laboratory, and the importance accorded to conflict by Eysenck and Rachman (1965) and Yates (1962)). Discussion of interpersonal conflict in the household as precipitant of panic in the supermarket does not, of course, logically entail the view that the operation of a 'dynamic unconscious' is the chief causal mechanism. Despite this, the behavioural clinician is often perhaps unnecessarily reluctant to make this kind of aetiological assumption. Goldstein and Chambless (1978) have made a helpful contribution in calling attention to the clinical utility of positing interpersonal conflict as an important aspect of agoraphobia in at least some patients.

In practical terms, the clinical paradigm described by Marks (1981a, b) and the self-efficacy theory of Bandura (1977) hold great promise in advancing our understanding of the processes and procedures involved in successful treatment. Continuing research into the complicating confounds and concomitants of agoraphobia—before, during, and after treatment—will likely enough prompt further development of behavioural theories of aetiology and treatment mechanisms.

CHAPTER 8

Clinical and Ethical Issues

We are fortunate in being able to draw upon a considerable research literature in selecting tried and tested treatments for agoraphobia. In applying these treatments to patients seen in clinical practice, there are some special considerations not always addressed directly in the research reports. For example, *in vivo* exposure in groups has fared extremely well in research trials, but an individual agoraphobic may reject this approach and make good progress with desensitization. Furthermore, many agoraphobics have problems in addition to, or intertwined with, their specific phobic sensitivities; such problems include depression, alcoholism, marital strife, and physical disorders. Clinical guidelines for addressing multiple problems like these would be invaluable, but are seldom found in the research literature. Finally, there are some important ethical issues particularly relevant to agoraphobia treatment. These include the potentially arduous nature of exposure treatment for some patients, and the possibility that successful removal of phobic sensitivity may 'rock the boat' in other areas of the patient's life. This chapter is mainly devoted to a discussion of some of these important clinical and ethical issues, but first we will summarize relevant research findings from our review in Chapter 5.

INDICATIONS FROM THE RESEARCH LITERATURE

Systematic desensitization

Systematic desensitization (SD) would seem to have been supplanted by direct exposure methods as far as the outcomes from controlled clinical trials are concerned. However, to conclude that direct exposure is generally more helpful than SD for most participants in research studies does not logically indicate that the use of SD should be suspended. SD is a viable alternative treatment, at least initially, for the significant proportion of patients who refuse exposure treatment, and there is clear evidence that SD is effective when it is followed by *in vivo* exposure activities later in treatment (Gelder *et al.*, 1973). Occasionally a patient will improve markedly when SD forms the major component of treatment. There are some informal indications that SD treatment is particularly effective when the patient imagines not only typical phobic situations, but also the concomitant cognitive and affective reactions to them.

Imaginal flooding

Imaginal flooding has fewer potential advantages in agoraphobia treatment than SD, despite the fact that these two techniques usually produce comparable outcomes. The patient who refuses *in vivo* treatment will be just as likely to refuse imaginal flooding, because of the intensity of emotion that may be produced by the procedure. Researchers have observed that patients and therapists generally dislike the method. SD is a gentler method than imaginal flooding, and is apparently equally helpful.

Graded practice and prolonged *in vivo* exposure

The general instruction to a patient to progress into phobic surroundings until she feels anxious, and then to retreat, seems controversial theoretically, because it could encourage continued avoidance behaviour. However, treatment based on this principle produced encouraging results in a trial by Everaerd *et al.* (1973). In general, researchers have argued that it is the real-life practice aspect of treatment that counts, and have produced evidence that feedback and praise are particularly beneficial in graduated practice exploits (e.g. Leitenberg *et al.*, 1975). There are clear indications that graded practice *in vivo* is generally more helpful than SD or imaginal flooding (Crowe *et al.*, 1972). Apart from its superior efficacy, advantages of this method are found in its non-threatening nature in protecting the patient from high levels of anxiety, and the immediacy of feedback of progress in treatment. A disadvantage is that a patient may become discouraged if a panic attack suddenly arises, and this is certainly possible even if the patient progresses gradually from easier to more difficult environments: panic attacks are not as predictable as could be wished.

Another observation made by researchers studying the effects of praise and feedback on treatment by graded practice is that in 'reversal' stages, in which praise and feedback are withdrawn for experimental purposes, patients describe depressive episodes and tend to make self-defeating statements. These problems are alleviated when treatment proper is resumed.

Graduated *in vivo* exploits can be particularly beneficial when the patient participates in a carefully-planned home-based treatment programme with the assistance of the spouse (Mathews *et al.*, 1981), or when the patient joins forces with other sufferers who live in the same geographic area (Sinnott *et al.*, 1981).

The most successful outcomes in comparative treatment trials derive from direct exposure to phobic surroundings with or without benefit of a graduated hierarchy of assignments. Effects seem to be potentiated further by group excursions. There is evidence that *in vivo* treatment in general encourages patients' expectations of efficacy more successfully than imaginal flooding or SD (Johnston *et al*., 1976).

In vivo exposure treatment is optimally implemented with prolonged sessions (2 h or more) that are frequently spaced; more than one session per week is preferable.

Some researchers have noted from *post hoc* analyses of data that patients who are most depressed, have the most frequent panic attacks, and display high levels of general anxiety, tend to have a relatively poor prognosis with confrontive exposure. For these individuals graded practice may be more suitable.

Cognitive-behaviour modification

Research evidence is clear in indicating that techniques aimed at encouraging cognitive relabelling of fear reactions and promoting coping thoughts are less effective than performance-based methods. However, this kind of statement can be misleading because cognitive restructuring on the part of the patient is clearly implied in the whole rationale for exposure treatment, and in this sense cognitive and performance-based strategies are always used in combination when exposure to feared surroundings is a component of treatment. Usually it is only when exposure methods are omitted from treatment that outcomes tend to be disappointing.

The use of medication

Tranquillizing drugs may be helpful in encouraging the otherwise reluctant patient to initiate real-life ventures into phobic environments. The fear that a patient may attribute progress to the use of the drug, and thereby show disappointing or short-lived outcomes, seems to be unfounded. The routine use of tranquillizers as total clinical management has several disadvantages, including relatively disappointing outcomes and the symptomatic or palliative nature of such treatment.

The use of antidepressants has found favour recently, and they may play a role in diminishing the impact of the panic attack, but this conclusion is not well founded as yet. Again, relapse is usually associated with drug withdrawal.

Therapist characteristics

Rabavilas *et al*. (1979) conducted a retrospective study of patients' reactions to their therapists. Subjects were thirty-six neurotics (phobics and obsessive-compulsives) who had been treated by members of a group of five therapists about a year and a half earlier. Treatment had consisted of *in vivo* exposure to environments in which phobic or compulsive behaviour had been manifested. Therapist qualities correlated with successful outcomes included respect, understanding, and interest. Patients preferred the therapist to be encouraging, but appropriately demanding and ready to provide challenges. Poor outcomes and patient evaluations were associated with permissiveness, over-tolerance, neutrality, and over-protectiveness in the therapist.

In reporting a study of imaginal and *in vivo* exposure, Mathews *et al.* (1976) note that the least successful therapist was a relatively inexperienced male; the patients were all agoraphobic women.

Apart from these observations, there are few indications from research to help develop effective therapist attitudes or behaviours or specify desirable therapist characteristics.

THE CLINICAL MANAGEMENT OF AGORAPHOBIA

Research findings outlined above derive from studies that are in general of high quality methodologically. Not all questions have yet been answered by research studies, of course, and there is plenty of scope for clinical acumen in applying treatments to individual clients. In the controlled trials, it is understandable that researchers will 'screen out' potential participants who show a complex clinical picture in which disorders other than the phobia are present, or who are at the time of the study on regimens of psychoactive medication other than minor tranquillizers. Some potential subjects remove *themselves* from consideration because they are unimpressed or even alarmed by the nature of the treatment being offered. Finally, research methodology makes it difficult for treatment to be prescribed for individual patients on the basis of their unique clinical characteristics or pattern of problems. These factors can place limits on the generality of research findings to patients seen in clinical practice, and creativity on the part of the therapist is called for. We will now outline some general issues in clinical practice, starting with the broad assumption that *in vivo* exposure treatment will be the first strategy for phobia-removal recommended to the patient.

Educating the patient and spouse

Before treatment possibilities are discussed with the patient, the therapist will normally present the sufferer (and, ideally, the spouse or other close companion) with a clear description of agoraphobia and its typical features. Describing the agoraphobic syndrome accurately and openly can be extremely reassuring for patients, many of whom have tormented themselves with the view that they are alone in experiencing this puzzling constellation of symptoms. This erroneous belief, and the even more troubling fear that anxiety episodes and panic attacks signify the impending onset of severe mental illness, is unfortunately not restricted to those who are presenting for treatment for the first time. Several agoraphobics report previous professional contacts with therapists who have apparently not recognized the syndrome, and who have proceeded to meet the patient weekly over a period of months for unfocussed conversations about her life-history, or events in her daily life, without providing any concrete procedures for removing the phobia.

The patient may be reassured that fears of fainting, dying, losing control, or becoming psychotic are common features of the agoraphobic syndrome, and that episodes of depersonalization and the like do not necessarily betoken an impending 'nervous breakdown'. It is also helpful for the therapist to try to allay guilt about the effect of the sufferer's phobia on the children (Buglass *et al*., 1977).

Patients are often distressed by the recognition that their panic attacks arise suddenly, 'out of the blue', for no apparent reason. The theoretical points here can be rather subtle, and it is probably unwise to risk confusing the patient by going into all the abstruse niceties. For example, the therapist may believe that it is misleading and countertherapeutic for the patient to regard her anxieties as firmly attached to concrete situations, because this view could help her avoid examining possible interpersonal conflicts in the aetiology of the panic attacks. On the other hand, it could also be unhelpful to allow the patient to continue to be distressed by the idea that the panics are spontaneous and inexplicable; instead, it seems desirable to point out that, once the phobia has been established, certain surroundings can instantaneously trigger a panic attack because of the perfectly understandable operations of a conditioning process. The clinician can always explain to the patient that, admittedly, there is probably more to the phobia than a fear of shops and streets as such, but nevertheless some aspects of those environments certainly can spark off a panic rapidly enough that the process is impossible to detect.

Presenting the rationale for behavioural treatment

Clinic-based treatment approaches may vary widely from patient to patient, with SD treatment the first priority for one, group *in vivo* exposure for another, and so on. Despite this potential variety, one therapeutic procedure is common to all patients treated by a behavioural therapist: he or she will give the patient a rationale and protocol for tackling phobic surroundings in real life. This kind of advice is given whether or not *in vivo* methods are used in treatment proper, and whether or not the patient is specifically asked to practise between sessions, although patients are usually encouraged to do some practical 'homework' in any case. Indeed, in the successful treatment approach described by Mathews *et al*. (1977) the patient conducts the whole therapeutic programme in her local environment with the assistance of her husband. In this programme, patient and spouse are given specific manuals of procedure from which to work, and these manuals would be an invaluable addition to those treatment regimens based primarily on clinic sessions. Normally, however, the clinician spends much time in early treatment sessions in explaining a rationale for confronting feared surroundings.

The patient is usually given a rationale based theoretically on two-factor conditioning concepts. She is invited to consider the idea that the phobia persists because she has adopted a habit of avoiding feared surroundings, or of retreating when she feels a certain amount of anxiety. If she leaves a situation when anxious, it will continue to be associated with anxiety, and running away with relief. To break this habit, she needs to learn to alter her approach slightly, and to pause (rather than escape) when anxiety arises. Although it can certainly cause discomfort to stay put when anxiety is beginning to be noticeable, it will sooner or later fade, and then a breakthrough has been achieved: remaining in the situation becomes associated with anxiety dwindling rather than increasing. It can be helpful to express this by saying that the sufferer's 'bodily systems' need a chance to adapt to a new habit of not retreating or avoiding.

The patient can be advised that there are several ways of rearranging things so that feared surroundings are no longer coupled with fear reactions. She can be carefully desensitized in the clinic by having her imagine progressively more challenging exploits, comforted by pleasant sensations of relaxation and by the knowledge that she can terminate an imagined scene simply by signalling the therapist. She can be told that this approach is a little indirect, and is usually very time-consuming, but it is the gentlest way of dealing with at least the anticipatory anxiety; like the other treatments based on exposure to phobic stimuli, it gradually alters the damaging habit of shying away from perceived danger. It is likely, however, that desensitization alone will not suffice to deal with the most challenging aspect of the syndrome, the panic attack.

At the other extreme, the patient can tackle the most daunting situation right away—for example, being in a large shopping area in a city centre when it is most crowded—and this will work, too, provided she remains there for long enough for the fear to subside. Realistically, this could take a couple of hours or more per session. If the patient resists the heroics of this frontal attack on the phobia, she could tackle an easier situation first, following the principle of holding her ground until anxiety declines.

The message that anxiety *can* be withstood until it finally declines is implicit in all this, of course, and it is best to go into this notion very explicitly as well. A common objection raised by patients at this point is that they may experience a panic attack proper, despite the idealistic plan of proceeding to a point at which anxiety first appears; after all, the panics can arise suddenly and at full force, and if they could be forestalled by pausing at the first signs of increasing anxiety, then the phobia would probably not be disabling enough to warrant the effort of seeking professional help. The therapist is best advised to acknowledge this concern fully, because patients do in fact have panic attacks *in vivo* even in the presence of the trusted therapist. However, some reassuring points can be made. First, the success of treatment does not necessitate the deliberate induction of panic attacks, so progressing through a graded hierarchy of *in vivo* excursions and pausing to take stock when problems first appear do at least reduce the chances of panicking. Second, the patient has experienced panic attacks before, and, because she is here to tell the tale, has obviously survived them. Perhaps she could therefore contemplate having a few more panic attacks, if necessary, in treatment, comforted by the reasonable expectation of long-term relief. Finally, an important aspect of treatment is for the patient to alter her attitude to the panic attacks in any case. It would be pointless for treatment to protect her carefully from any chance of panicking, if this encourages the view that panics, indeed, are to be avoided for evermore at all costs; this would hardly be a counter-phobic attitude.

The patient can be asked to think through all the possible consequences of experiencing anxiety to the full—dying; having a fit of some kind; being dragged, screaming, to a psychiatric hospital by people in the proverbial white coats; and so on—and this can help expose unrealistic and exaggerated aspects of the fundamental fear. Attempts at cognitive restructuring by means of verbal persuasion are demonstrably less effective, in treatment proper, than the actual experience of mastery achieved by the patient in getting out and about and getting to grips with some anxiety, but in giving the patient the preliminary rationale of and philosophy behind treatment such attempts at altering attitudes seem indispensable (Wilson, 1981b). Just as an overweight patient starting a weight-reduction programme can be encouraged to seek out hunger pangs and welcome them as signals that he or she is working at the cutting edge of the treatment effort, so the agoraphobic can be persuaded to take a less avoidant attitude to the discomforts entailed by dealing directly with phobic situations.

Consistent with this rationale, the therapist can reassure the patient about early failures to follow treatment protocol. It is not necessarily a therapeutic setback even if she retreats prematurely when anxiety is mounting. As long as she can mobilize a long-run optimism about treatment, and is prepared to confront that situation again as soon as possible, all will be well.

Some practitioners will pursue this attitude-change rationale to the full by using paradoxical therapy, or 'prescribing the symptom'. The kind of directive given would be 'Make yourself as anxious as possible! Let's see those legs really wobble! If you're going to feel some anxiety anyway, let's see a full-blown panic!' (cf. Chambless and Goldstein, 1980). If the therapist is reluctant to apply paradoxical treatment proper (and it does require a certain *panache* on the part of the therapist), he or she could still tell the patient that even if she chose to exaggerate the anxiety deliberately, this could be very therapeutic indeed, but such extremes are not necessary as long as she will contemplate dealing with whatever anxiety she does experience in the normal course of events.

Patients can be encouraged to relax when beginning to feel anxious. This may sound trite if expressed halfheartedly or mechanically, but can be most helpful and extremely credible if they are given relaxation training and are asked to let go and loosen tense muscles in the neck, shoulders, and abdomen actively and deliberately when in centre stage *in vivo*. It is not helpful in the long run to ask the patient to try and stay in control, or distract herself from the most feared aspects of the surroundings, because this encourages a form of avoidance. Instead, in addition to relaxing and releasing her control, she can be advised to walk slowly, again in the spirit of deliberately courting some anxiety-provoking stimuli. She can try to breathe as naturally as possible, as opposed to controlling her respiration by breathing too shallowly or deeply; all one has to do is to leave respiration on 'automatic pilot'. Finally, she is advised to hold her head erect and take in her surroundings to the full by looking unabashedly around her.

When a patient continues to be dubious about exposure treatment because of her fear that 'the worst will happen', the therapist can (judiciously, of course) give a carefully disguised anecdote about another patient who successfully overcame similar concerns. For example, one middle-aged woman who had avoided shops totally for almost 20 years because of her dread of vomiting in public actually *did* vomit in a shop early in her phobia treatment. As a result of this experience she became neither defeated nor discouraged but pronounced herself well on the way to recovery. Obliging shop assistants had comforted her, sympathetically murmured that there was a lot of 'tummy trouble' about, and had given her a glass of water and a chair to sit in to rest while they cleaned up the mess. When the fuss had died down, the patient found herself perfectly at ease, and still in the middle of a large shop. She proceeded to spend a further half-hour in relaxed perusal of the shelves of merchandize, alarmed only by the ubiquitous evidence of the ravages of inflation!

Agreeing on a treatment plan

It is an important tenet of behaviour therapy that the therapist will inform the patient quite openly about the advantages and disadvantages of treatment being offered, and that therapist and patient agree on therapeutic tactics after the merits and demerits of each potential method have been discussed. It is quite acceptable for therapists to let patients know what the research literature suggests, provided that the promise of a technique that has fared well in research trials is not exaggerated. The patient can be told that the general rationale for exposure treatment (outlined above) is consistent with several therapeutic techniques. Group *in vivo* exposure to situations graduated in difficulty can be recommended quite confidently, but a clinician in some settings may find it difficult to form a group, and some patients will prefer individual attention. Similarly, home-based treatment with the active involvement of a close companion can be suggested with enthusiasm, but the patient may be operating within an adverse interpersonal climate and this approach may be unrealistic.

Alternative procedures at this point are graduated or confrontive practice from the clinic, with the therapist present during initial ventures; if the sufferer is home-bound, the therapist will need to make home visits in the early stages of treatment. If the patient cannot agree to tackling the phobia *in vivo* under any circumstances, SD can be offered to reduce anticipatory anxiety about tasks involved in therapist-assisted practice. If there are problems in implementing SD (for example, because the patient cannot imagine phobic material sufficiently clearly), then cognitive restructuring methods can be brought in early.

Ideally, patient and therapist will agree on a plan of action in which the whole course of treatment is anticipated. For example, the treatment plan may go as follows: first, three sessions on relaxation training, hierarchy-construction, and rationale-giving; next, eight sessions of SD, with the patient attempting non-threatening *in vivo* homework assignments between sessions; then, graduated exposure (eight sessions) to early items of the hierarchy with the therapist present; finally, clinic-based exposure ventures in a small group, facilitated by the therapist (six sessions). In many cases the treatment plan will have to be renegotiated after a few sessions to take account of how things are going, and sometimes it is unnecessary to agree on a long-term plan at the outset; the limited goal of being in a position to contemplate therapist-assisted exposure may be the first one for the patient.

The patient may present problems aside from the phobic sensitivity *per se*. One patient seen recently showed features of agoraphobia and social phobia, and she was troubled by social evaluation and recognized a clear difficulty with assertiveness. She was given the choice of working on the assertive problem first and then entering treatment for the agoraphobia, or deferring the assertion training until after the agoraphobia treatment had been pursued. The patient decided on the latter because a group for *in vivo* exposure was being formed at that point.

Although it is often unrealistic to formulate a complete plan of action at the outset, the general idea of following an agreed treatment plan which can be modified at any point is invaluable; the patient always knows what to expect, what is the idea behind each treatment component, and what can be done if the particular treatment method being pursued at any point produces disappointing results.

The role of the spouse or companion

In most cases the agoraphobic sufferer has a spouse or other close companion, and often this significant other person will be willing to help in treatment. He or she can attend a session or two with the patient so as to learn the rationale and methods of treatment, and—with luck—can offer sympathetic encouragement and support. In most cases the companion is a husband, and he can play an important role in home-based practice, accompanying the patient at first, and then gradually withdrawing his support according to a systematic programme. For example, when shopping, he can agree with his wife to remain out of sight for a few minutes by shopping in a different aisle of the supermarket, and the duration of this absence can be gradually extended. When walking in the street or in a shopping arcade or centre, the partners can agree to walk a few yards apart at first, and then to extend this distance progressively. Sufferer and spouse need to be advised that, because the phobic sensitivity fluctuates from day to day, they need to be prepared to repeat steps previously accomplished from time to time, and that this does not represent a therapeutic setback.

Self-monitoring

It is very helpful for the patient to keep a daily record of counterphobic activities. This record includes details of specific ventures in terms of location, distance, and duration, and may include the feelings and thoughts associated with each one. Records like this can provide feedback of progress to the patient (particularly over relatively long periods—when progress is gradual, it can be difficult to detect without a written record), and can enable the therapist to give praise and encouragement for progress. He or she can also use the record for analysing the patient's potential problems in following appropriate exposure principles. Ideally the patient has a list of specific assignments each week, and treatment sessions with the therapist can begin with a routine perusal of the record and discussion of the past week's homework.

Relaxation and cognitive techniques

As we have already noted, the possibility of beneficial cognitive restructuring in treatment is implied in the rationale usually given for exposure homework. The patient can be given a general explanation of the principles of rational-emotive therapy (RET; Ellis, 1962) and can be shown that her negative cognitive reactions to challenging environments can be seen as a part of the problem; if she can alter her view that anxiety or panic are potentially disastrous and cannot be withstood, she will be likely to make swifter progress in exposure treatment. Cognitive 'acceptance' is a central feature of the apparently successful programme of Weekes (1978).

RET, positive self-instruction, and acceptance are consistent with the exposure rationale we have discussed earlier. Relaxation is also recommended. The patient can work on the principle that fear can be tolerated by simply letting go, relaxing, and allowing it to 'do its worst', as opposed to attempting to control her reactions by stiffening, avoiding, and trying to distract herself from her surroundings. Consistent with this it is probably unhelpful for the therapist to use thought-stopping or cognitive distraction methods, in which the patient is shown how to cut off anxiety-provoking thoughts, as methods of dealing with situational anxiety. These techniques do have a place, however, in helping the patient who is troubled by obsessional ruminations about phobic themes before or after exposure sessions.

Giving an account of the development of the phobia in attributional terms can sometimes be extremely helpful. One patient was treated successfully in fourteen sessions within a 10-week period; 'cognitive relabelling' was an important component of treatment.

Alan (we have altered the names of actual patients discussed for illustrative purposes), a married man in his twenties, referred himself to a mental health clinic in Maine about 3 months after the onset of 'anxiety attacks' in shops, at work, and in public places in general. He had received marital counselling at the same clinic, with a different therapist, 2 years previously. He reported that his anxieties began during a holiday weekend, when he had driven about 200 miles to see some long-lost friends. He had been exhausted by the drive but stayed up late that night and drank a considerable amount of alcohol. He awoke the next morning after only a few hours of sleep, still tired, with a hangover, and in the unfamiliar surroundings of his friends' home. During breakfast he experienced a 'funny feeling' which greatly alarmed him. He reports having had an immediate train of thought similar to the following: 'What's wrong with me? Is it a heart attack? A nervous breakdown? Whatever can be wrong!' and pondered the episode long and hard while driving home a day later. Later in that week he experienced the same 'feeling' in a small shop, and again became very worried as to the meaning of his strange sensation. The feelings became progressively more frequent, and an increasing range of environments came to elicit them.

Treatment consisted partly of systematic desensitization to specific locations in which he experienced anxiety, but a significant proportion of treatment time was devoted to extensive discussion of the importance of attribution effects in the development of his phobia. A possible explanation similar to the following was suggested to him. He had been tired, hungover, and in unfamiliar surroundings with people he had not seen for years. He understandably felt a little below par, and experienced what was presumably a reaction to his long drive and enthusiastic partying the day before. If only he had been able to say to himself 'I am feeling peculiar this morning. Hardly surprising, considering the day I had yesterday!' he would probably not have become so obsessed with his strange 'symptom', nor would it have developed and spread. He received this account enthusiastically, and proceeded to practise reattributing his anxieties to benign sources whenever he became fearful in public. He pronounced himself recovered at the fourteenth session, and in a telephone call almost 5 years later reported that he was functioning well, and only occasionally had a twinge of anticipatory anxiety when planning to go to an unfamiliar place. This was not at all disabling, and he never avoided any situation for reasons of anxiety. He had required no further professional contact after the initial treatment had been terminated.

This patient, of course, had a good prognosis from the outset. The phobia had only been developing for 3 months when he was first seen, and it began under fairly clear-cut and understandable circumstances. Alan had few of the characteristics of the 'complex agoraphobic' described by Goldstein and Chambless (1978). Nevertheless, the case does serve to illustrate the kind of account in attributional terms that can be offered even to the most challenging patient as part of the treatment battery.

Self-help groups

Finally, the patient can be encouraged to contact a local phobics' self-help group if one is available. This form of support is potentially very helpful to agoraphobics who are motivated to resolve their phobias (and those agoraphobics who consult therapists clearly have some degree of motivation for change). Some members of a self-help group may continue to avoid dealing with the phobia directly, of course, and may regard their attendance at meetings as their sole concession to treatment, and as a device for avoiding confronting the challenges imposed by other outside exploits; but, as far as we can determine without the benefit of controlled evaluations, self-help groups are potentially an excellent resource for the agoraphobic.

ETHICAL ISSUES

Responsibilities of the therapist

To increase the accountability of therapist to patient (and vice versa), a written treatment contract in which the responsibilities of therapist and patient are listed (including homework exercises, the daily record, availability of the therapist, treatment plan, length of treatment before review, etc.) is highly desirable.

Evaluation of progress

Therapist and patient will ideally agree on what to take as evidence that progress is being made. Not only does this keep the therapist focussed on the objectives of treatment, but it also helps the patient keep track of progress. Some patients become discouraged easily, and fail to recognize (or minimize the significance of) behavioural and emotional gains. Agreeing on what to evaluate, when, and how often helps therapist and patient remain in tune with progress.

Comprehensiveness of treatment

Exposure methods to decrease phobic sensitivity may not be the only therapeutic techniques used with a patient. The clinician is best advised to look out for other potential problems that may be present at the outset (for example, as in the case of the patient who complained of having assertiveness difficulties) or that may emerge during the course of treatment (for example, resistance of treatment progress by the husband). It is good practice for the clinician to consider the possibility that factors unrecognized by the patient are playing a role in maintaining the phobia, or deserve clinical attention in their own right (cf. Goldstein, 1978).

Side-effects of behavioural treatment

No particular contra-indications for behavioural treatment for agoraphobia have been reported, although there are indications that patients who are particularly troubled by depression, frequent panic attacks, and high general anxiety may do better with graduated practice than with confrontive exposure. Some patients report depression and, occasionally, nightmares between sessions of confrontive exposure, but these problems are usually short-lived. Sometimes a patient undergoing exposure treatment will awaken at night in a panic at the realization of what she accomplished the day before, and disturb herself by dwelling on the immensity of the challenge she accepted. This short-term phenomenon is, ironically, a pitfall for patients who are making good progress in treatment. Ruminative, self-defeating thoughts like these can be very damaging if they occur during the night or early in the morning before the patient normally arises, because she is not in full conscious control of her thought-processes and is more likely to exaggerate her fears and preoccupations and, generally, dwell on irrational or unhelpful trains of thought. The patient is best advised to short-circuit such episodes by getting up and walking around so as to raise her arousal level to a point at which she can consider her preoccupations more objectively.

Other potential side-effects are more long-term and have to do with the patient's lifestyle. A maritally-troubled agoraphobic who successfully resolves the phobia may be in a position to leave the marriage, for example. The therapist's ethical responsibility here is to discuss the possible effects of treatment on the patient's life-style early in the therapy programme. If the patient is fully informed of such possibilities, she is in a better position to decide whether, or how, to proceed with treatment. The therapist can offer marital therapy at the outset, for example, and simply accept the patient's wishes in the matter. This kind of ethical difficulty for the therapist is illustrated in the brief case-history which follows.

Becky, a married woman in her late twenties, was almost completely housebound when she made the initial clinic contact. On a 'good' day she was able to take a few steps from her front door alone; she was able to drive short distances locally if her husband accompanied her. She was generally anxious when she was alone in the home. Treatment was conducted by two male therapists, and early sessions were conducted in the patient's home. Her husband was present during each session, but he made only a minimal contribution to the conversations.

Becky stated clearly at the outset that if she were free of her phobia, she would be faced with a conflict about leaving her husband. Her husband acknowledged her feelings about this, and said that, although he loved her and did not want her to leave, he would not stand in her way. The therapists attempted discussion of marital conflicts and offered marital therapy, but Becky resisted this and her husband expressed an attitude of resignation toward the possibility that she might leave him. The therapists decided to honour Becky's request for treatment of her agoraphobia. Thirty-three treatment sessions were given in a period of 9 months. Early sessions, in the patient's home, were devoted to SD; the anxiety hierarchy included items dealing with Becky's anxiety at having the therapists come to the house for treatment sessions. Later sessions centred upon graduated exposure to shops in the locality, short drives, and, eventually, the building in which the clinic was located. Before treatment was terminated, Becky was able to travel alone quite independently, but she had not resolved her phobia completely. She and her husband continued to resist marital therapy, but they continued to live together despite Becky's marked progress in terms of the phobia. The therapists speculated that neither Becky nor her husband were, at that point, ready to contemplate the possible dissolution of their marriage that could have been entailed by continued work on the phobia.

Four months later Becky re-referred herself because her relationship with her husband was deteriorating. Patient and husband were seen in therapy for several sessions, but the husband became discouraged and seemed to adopt a passive attitude thereafter, which persisted when Becky petitioned for divorce. When treatment terminated for the second time, Becky had been granted her divorce, and had made such progress in terms of her agoraphobia that she no longer considered herself handicapped by it. Twenty-five additional sessions had been held, and they had centred on Becky's emotional expressiveness, her dependency, and her unresolved feelings about losses and bereavements in the past.

This case illustration is more typical of outpatient practice than is the case of 'Alan' presented earlier. Becky had multiple concerns and treatment was protracted, consisting of fifty-eight sessions over 17 months (with a hiatus of 4 months). She presented difficulties not only with specific phobic sensitivities, but also with dependency, emotional expressiveness, and unresolved grief; her relationship with her husband deteriorated when her phobia improved, although she was clearly aware of marital problems when the phobia was most severe. In short, Becky would be classed as a 'complex agoraphobic' by Goldstein and Chambless (1978). (We are grateful to Philip J. Smith of the University of Maine for allowing us to use this illustration.)

The ethical problem posed by cases like this, in which it seems likely that the patient will divorce if treatment of agoraphobia is successful, is that the therapist can choose, in a sense, whether to facilitate a divorce by treating the phobia, or leave the phobia untreated so as to help preserve the marriage. If treatment is given, the patient's marriage ends, which could be seen by many as a negative outcome. If treatment for the phobia is withheld, the patient remains handicapped by it, and remains married because she has no reasonable alternative. Our view is that the patient, not the therapist, should make the decision about whether or not to proceed with treatment of the phobia in a case like this. Provided that the therapist has alerted the patient to possible pitfalls in treatment, has ensured that the possible impact of successful treatment on the patient's life-style has been carefully discussed, and has offered marital treatment (or suggested the possibility of an alternative referral), it would seem that he or she has accepted the appropriate ethical responsibilities.

CONCLUSIONS

Little more than two decades ago, agoraphobia was regarded by clinicians of many different theoretical persuasions as a poor-prognosis syndrome. Today, it can be said that agoraphobia may respond readily to treatment. Important caveats here are that assessment has to be broad-ranging, a battery of treatments may be required, and the most satisfactory resolution may take several more sessions than would normally be regarded as constituting 'short-term therapy'. Very few patients do not respond to treatment. When treatment is successful, the extended navigable environment of the former agoraphobic opens up a variety of social, occupational, and recreational opportunities. Powerful reinforcers for the therapist are found in a post-card from a former patient on holiday overseas; a letter from another who, formerly housebound, is now a travelling salesman; and a telephone conversation from a previous agoraphobic in which he reports having had five phobia-free years. Such events (and these are actual samples of communications we have had recently from our former patients) amply reward the behavioural practitioner who attempts to apply the theoretical, research, and treatment approaches to agoraphobia that we have summarized in this book.

References

Abraham, K. (1913). A constitutional basis of locomotor anxiety, in *Selected Papers*, Hogarth, London, 1948. (Cited by E. Weiss, 1964.)

Agras, W. S. (1967). Transfer during systematic desensitization therapy, *Behaviour Research and Therapy,* **5**, 193–199.

Agras, W. S., Leitenberg, H., Barlow, D. M., and Burlington, M. A. (1968). Social reinforcement in the modification of agoraphobia, *Archives of General Psychiatry,* **19**, 423–427.

Agras, S., Sylvester, D., and Oliveau, D. (1969). The epidemiology of common fears and phobia, *Comprehensive Psychiatry*, **10**, 2.

Agulnik, P. (1970). The spouse of the phobic patient, *British Journal of Psychiatry,* **117**, 59–67.

American Psychiatric Association (1980). *Diagnostic and Statistical Manual of Mental Disorders*, 3rd edn, The American Psychiatric Association, Washington, DC.

Anger, D. (1963). The role of temporal discriminations in the reinforcement of Sidman avoidance behavior, *Journal of the Experimental Analysis of Behavior*, **6**, 477–506.

Arrindell, W. A. (1980). Dimensional structure and psychopathology correlates of the fear survey schedule (FSS-111) in a phobic population: a factorial definition of agoraphobia, *Behaviour Research and Therapy*, **18**, 229–242.

Ascher, L. M. (1981). Employing paradoxical intention in the treatment of agoraphobia, *Behaviour Research and Therapy*, **19**, 533–542.

Asso, D. and Beech, H. R. (1975). Susceptibility to the acquisition of a conditioned response in relation to the menstrual cycle, *Journal of Psychosomatic Research*, **19**, 337–344.

Ayllon, T., Haughton, E., and Hughes, H. B. (1965). Interpretation of symptoms: Fact or fiction? *Behaviour Research and Therapy*, **3**, 1–8.

Bandura, A. (1969). *Principles of Behaviour Modification*, Holt, Rinehart and Winston, New York.

Bandura, A. (1977). Self-efficacy: Toward a unifying theory of behavior change, *Psychological Review*, **84**, 191–215.

Bandura, A. (1978). Self-efficacy: Toward a unifying theory of behavioral change, in *Annual Review of Behavior Therapy: Theory and Practice* (Eds. C. M. Francks and G. T. Wilson, Vol. 6). New York: Brunner/Mazel, 1978.

Bandura, A. and Adams, N. E. (1977). Analysis of self-efficacy theory of behavioral change, *Cognitive Therapy and Research,* **1**, 287–310.

Bandura, A., Adams, N. E., Hardy, A. B., and Howells, G. N. (1980). Tests of the generality of self-efficacy theory, *Cognitive Therapy and Research,* **4**, 39–66.

Barlow, D. H., Mavissakalian, M., and Hay, L. R. (1981). Couples treatment of agoraphobia: Changes in marital satisfaction, *Behaviour Research and Therapy,* **19**, 245–255.

Barlow, D. H., Mavissakalian, M. R., and Schofield, L. D. (1980). Patterns of desynchrony in agoraphobia: A preliminary report, *Behaviour Research and Therapy,* **18**, 441–448.

Beck, A. T. (1978). *Depression Inventory,* Center for Cognitive Therapy, Philadelphia.

Beech, H. R., Burns, L. E. and Sheffield, B. F. (1982). *A Behavioural Approach to the Management of Stress*, Wiley, Chichester.

Benedikt, V. (1870). Uber Platschwindel, *Allgemeine Wiener Medizinische Zeitung,* **15**, 488.

Benjamin, S., Marks, I. M., and Huson, J. (1972). Active muscular relaxation in desensitisation of phobic patients, *Psychological Medicine,* **2**, 381–390.

Berg, I., Marks, I., McGuire, R., and Lipsedge, M. (1974). School phobia and agoraphobia, *Psychological Medicine,* **4**, 4, 428–434.

Berg, I. (1976). School phobia in the children of agoraphobic women, *British Journal of Psychiatry,* **128**, 86–89.

Bernstein, D. A. and Nietzel, M. T. (1977). Demand characteristics in behaviour modification: A natural history of a 'nuisance', in *Progress in Behavior Modification* (Eds. M. Hersen, R. M. Eisler, and P. M. Miller) (Vol. 4), Academic Press, New York.

Biran, M. and Wilson, G. T. (1981). Treatment of phobic disorders using cognitive and exposure methods: A self-efficacy analysis. *Journal of Consulting and Clinical Psychology,* **49**, 886–899.

Blake, B. G. (1965). The application of behaviour therapy to treatment of alcoholism. *Behaviour Research and Therapy*, **3**, 75–85.

Bland, K. and Hallam, R. S. (1981). Relationship between response to graded exposure and marital satisfaction in agoraphobics, *Behaviour Research and Therapy,* **19**, 335–338.

Boulougouris, J. C. (1976). Personal communication.

Boulougouris, J. and Marks, I. M. (1969). Implosion (flooding): A new treatment for phobias, *British Medical Journal*, **2**, 721.

Boulougouris, J. C., Marks, I. M., and Marset, P. (1971). Superiority of flooding (implosion) to desensitisation for reducing pathological fear, *Behaviour Research and Therapy,* **9**, 7–16.

Bowen, R. C. and Kohout, J. (1979). The relationship between agoraphobia and primary affective disorders, *Canadian Journal of Psychiatry,* **24** (4) 317–322.

Bowlby, J. (1973). *Separation: Anxiety and Anger*, Basic Books, New York.

Brown, R. (1967). Indiscriminate operationism: A reply to Keehn on 'Avoidance responses as discriminated operants', *British Journal of Psychology,* **58**, 163–165.

Buglass, D., Clarke, J., Henderson, A. S., Kreitman, N., and Presley, A. S. (1977). A study of agoraphobic housewives, *Psychological Medicine,* **7**, 73–86.

Burgess, I. S. (1981). Some comments concerning Reiss' 'Pavlovian conditioning and human fear: An expectancy model', *The Behavior Therapist*, **4**, 9–12.

Burns, L. E. (1977) *An Investigation into the Additive Effects of Behavioural Techniques in the Treatment of agoraphobia.* Unpublished doctoral dissertation, University of Leeds.

Burns, L. E. (1980a). Survey of fears and phobias in the general population: a preliminary report, *Pharmaceutical Medicine*, **1**, 2, 1–9.

Burns, L. E. (1980b). The epidemiology of fears and phobias in general practice, *Journal of International Medical Research,* **8**, 3, 1–7.

Burns, L. E. (1981a). Teaching patients coping skills, *Psychiatry in Practice,* **1**, 2, 16–23.

Burns, L. E. (1981b). Relaxation in the management of stress, in *Coping with stress at work* (Eds. J. Marshall and C. L. Cooper) Gower, Aldershot.
Burns, L. E. (1982a). Fears and phobias—epidemiological and phenomenological aspects, *Psychiatry in Practice*, **1**, 8, 25–28.
Burns, L. E. (1982b). The role of the clinical psychologist in primary care, in *Clinical Psychology and Medicine: A Behavioural Approach* (Ed. C. J. Main) Plenum, New York.
Burns, L. E. and Thorpe, G. L. (1977a). Fears and clinical phobias: Epidemiological aspects and the National Survey of Agoraphobics, *The Journal of International Medical Research,* **5** (Supplement 1), 132–139.
Burns, L. E. and Thorpe, G. L. (1977b). The epidemiology of fears and phobias (with particular reference to the National Survey of Agoraphobics), *The Journal of International Medical Research,* **5** (Supplement 5), 1–7.
Burns, L. E. and Worsley, J. L. (1970). *Behaviour Therapy in the 1970s*, Wright, Bristol.
Burton, R. (1621). *The Anatomy of Melancholy*, 11th edn, 1813, Vol. 1. London.
Caine, T. M., Foulds, G. A., and Hope, K. (1967). *The Manual of the Hostility and Direction of Hostility Questionnaire (HDHQ)*, University of London Press, London.
Caine, T. M. and Hope, K. (1967). *The Manual of the Hysteroid-Obsessoid Questionnaire (HOQ),* University of London Press, London.
Cattell, R. B. (1946). *Description and Measurement of Personality,* World Book Co., New York.
Cattell, R. B. (1957). *Personality and Motivation: Structure and Measurement*. World Book Co., New York.
Chambless, D. L. (1978). *The Role of Anxiety in Flooding with Agoraphobic Clients*, Unpublished doctoral disseration, Temple University.
Chambless, D. L., Foa, E. B., Groves, G. A., and Goldstein, A. J. (1979). Flooding with brevital in the treatment of agoraphobia: Countereffective? *Behaviour Research and Therapy,* **17**, 243–251.
Chambless, D. L. and Goldstein, A. (1980). The treatment of agoraphobia, in *The handbook of Behavioral Interventions: A Clinical Guide* (Eds. A. Goldstein and E. Foa), Wiley, New York, pp. 322–415.
Cheshire, N. M. (1975). *The Nature of Psychodynamic Interpretation*, Wiley, London.
Cheshire, N. M. (1979). A big hand for Little Hans, *Bulletin of the British Psychological Society,* **32**, 320–323.
Cheshire, N. M. (1980). Hands off Little Hans (Correspondence), *Bulletin of the British Psychological Society,* **33**, 69–70.
Chiari, G. and Mosticone, R. (1979). The treatment of agoraphobia with biofeedback and systematic desensitization, *Journal of Behavior Therapy and Experimental Psychiatry,* **10**, 109–113.
Clapham, H. I., Freeman, N. T., and Sclare, E. B. (1956). Some clinical observations on phobic states, *Scottish Medical Journal,* **1**, 165–172.
Clevenger, S. W. (1890). Heart disease in insanity and a case of panphobia, *Alienist and Neurologist,* VII, 535–543.
Cobb, J. P., McDonald, R., Marks, I. M., and Stern, R. (1980). Marital versus exposure therapy: Psychological treatments of co-existing marital and phobic-obsessive problems, *European Journal of Behavioural Analysis and Modification*, **4**, 3–17.
Coleman, R. E. (1981). Cognitive-behavioral treatment of agoraphobia, in *New Directions in Cognitive Therapy: A Casebook*, (Eds. G. Emery, S. D. Hollon, and R. C. Bedrosian), The Guilford Press, New York.
Cone, J. D. (1979). Confounded comparisons in triple response mode assessment research, *Behavioral Assessment,* **1**, 85–95.

Cordes, E. (1871). Die Platzangst (Agoraphobie): Symptom einer Erschopfungsparese, *Archiv fur Psychiatrie und Nervenkran heiten,* **3**, 521–524.

Costello, C. G. (1970). Dissimilarities between conditioned avoidance responses and phobias, *Psychological Review*, **77**, 250–254.

Crowe, M. J. (1976). *Evaluation of Conjoint Marital Therapy*, Unpublished thesis, University of Oxford.

Crowe, M. J. (1978). Conjoint marital therapy: A controlled outcome study, *Psychological Medicine,* **8**, 623–636.

Crowe, M. J., Marks, I. M., Agras, W. S., and Leitenberg, H. (1972). Time-limited desensitization, implosion and shaping for phobic patients. A crossover study, *Behavior Research and Therapy,* **10**, 319–328.

Crown, S. and Crisp, A. H. (1966). A short clinical diagnostic self-rating scale for psychoneurotic patients, *British Journal of Psychiatry,* **112**, 917–923.

D'Amato, M. R. (1970). *Experimental psychology*, McGraw-Hill, New York.

Davidson, P. W. (1966). Depersonalisation, *Psychiatric Quarterly*, **40**, 702.

Davison, G. C. (1968). Systematic desensitization as a counterconditioning process. *Journal of Abnormal Psychology*, **73**, 91–99.

Davison, G. C. and Neale, J. M. (1978). *Abnormal Psychology: An Experimental Clinical Approach*, 2nd edn, Wiley, New York.

Delprato, D. J. (1980). Hereditary determinants of fears and phobias: A critical review, *Behavior Therapy,* **11**, 79–103.

De Silva, P., Rachman, S., and Seligman, M. E. P. (1977). Prepared phobias and obsessions: Therapeutic outcome, *Behaviour Research and Therapy,* **15**, 65–78.

DiLoreto, A. O. (1971). *Comparative Psychotherapy: An Experimental Analysis*. Aldine-Atherton, Chicago.

Dinsmoor, J. A., Flint, G. A., Smith, R. F., and Viemeister, N. F. (1969). Differential reinforcing effects of stimuli associated with the presence or absence of a schedule of punishment, in *Conditioned reinforcement* (Ed. D. P. Hendry), Dorsey, Homewood, Illinois.

Dixon, J. J., de Monchaux, C., and Sandler, J. (1957a). Patterns of anxiety: an analysis of social anxieties, *British Journal of Medical Psychology,* **30**, 107.

Dixon, J. J., de Monchaux, C., and Sandler, J. (1957b). Patterns of anxiety: the phobias, *British Journal of Medical Psychology,* **30**, 34–40.

Dugas, L. and Moutier, F. (1911). *La depersonnalisation,* Alcan, Paris.

Ellis, A. (1962). *Reason and Emotion in Psychotherapy*, Lyle Stuart, New York.

Ellis, A. and Harper, R. A. (1961). *Guide to Rational Living*, Lyle Stuart, New York.

Ellis, A. (1979). A note on the treatment of agoraphobics with cognitive modification versus prolonged exposure *in vivo, Behaviour Research and Therapy*, **17**, 162–164.

Emmelkamp, P. M. G. (1974). Self-observation versus flooding in the treatment of agoraphobia, *Behaviour Research and Therapy,* **12**, 229–237.

Emmelkamp, P. M. G. (1977). Comment to A. Mathews: Recent developments in the treatment of agoraphobia: A critical analysis, *Behavioural Analysis and Modification,* **2**, 76–79.

Emmelkamp, P. M. G. (1979). The behavioral study of clinical phobias, in *Progress in Behavior Modification* (Eds. M. Hersen, R. Eisler, and P. M. Miller) Vol. 8, Academic Press, New York.

Emmelkamp, P. M. G. (1980). Agoraphobics' interpersonal problems: Their role in the effects of exposure *in vivo* therapy, *Archives of General Psychiatry*, **37**, 1303–1306.

Emmelkamp, P. M. G. and Cohen-Kettenis, P. (1975). Relationship of locus of control to phobic anxiety and depression, *Psychological Reports,* **36**, 390.

Emmelkamp, P. M. G. and Emmelkamp-Benner, A. (1975). Effects of historically portrayed modelling and group treatment on self-observation: A comparison with agoraphobics, *Behaviour Research and Therapy*, **13**, 135–139.

Emmelkamp, P. M. G. and Kuipers, A. C. M. (1979). Agoraphobia: A follow-up study four years after treatment, *British Journal of Psychiatry,* **134**, 352–355.

Emmelkamp, P. M. G., Kuipers, A. C., and Eggeraat, J. B. (1978). Cognitive modification versus prolonged exposure *in vivo*: A comparison with agoraphobics as subjects, *Behaviour Research and Therapy,* **16**, 33–41.

Emmelkamp, P. M. G. and Ultee, K. A. (1974). A comparison of 'successive approximation' and 'self-observation' in the treatment of agoraphobia, *Behavior Therapy,* **5**, 605–613.

Emmelkamp, P. M. G. and Wessels, H. (1975). Flooding in imagination vs. flooding *in vivo*: A comparison with agoraphobics, *Behaviour Research and Therapy,* **13**, 7–15.

Errera, P. and Coleman, J. V. (1963). A long-term follow up study of neurotic phobic patients in a psychiatric clinic, *Journal of Nervous & Mental Diseases,* **136**, 267–271.

Evans, I. M. (1972). A conditioning model of a common neurotic pattern: Fear of fear, *Psychotherapy: Theory, Research, and Practice*, **9**, 238–241.

Evans, M. B. (1972). The relative effects of treatment specific and demand characteristic variables in the pre post behaviour therapy outcome research paradigm. Unpublished doctoral dissertation, University of Illinois.

Evans, P. D. and Kellam, A. M. P. (1973). Semi-automated desensitization: A controlled clinical trial, *Behaviour Research and Therapy,* **11**, 641–646.

Everaerd, W. T., Rijken, H. M., and Emmelkamp, P. M. (1973). A comparison of flooding and successive approximation in the treatment of agoraphobia, *Behaviour Research and Therapy,* **11**, 105–117.

Eysenck, H. J. (1964). *Manual of the Eysenck Personality Inventory*, University of London Press, London.

Eysenck, H. J. (1968). A theory of the incubation of anxiety-fear responses, *Behaviour Research and Therapy,* **6**, 309–321.

Eysenck, H. J. (1976). The learning theory model of neurosis—A new approach, *Behaviour Research and Therapy,* **14**, 251–267.

Eysenck, H. J. and Beech, H. R. (1971). Counterconditioning and related methods, in *Handbook of Psychotherapy and Behavior Change* (Eds A. E. Bergin and S. L. Garfield), Wiley, New York.

Eysenck, H. J., and Rachman, S. (1965). *The Causes and Cures of Neurosis*, Routledge & Kegan Paul, London.

Eysenck, H. J., Warzburt, W. A. and Berne, R. M. (1972). *Encyclopaedia of Psychology*, Search Press, London.

Feist, J. R. and Rosenthal, T. L. (1973). Serpent versus surrogate and other determinants of runway fear differences, *Behaviour Research and Therapy*, **11**, 483–489.

Feldman, M. P. and MacCulloch, M. J. (1971). *Homosexual Behaviour: Therapy and Assessment*, Pergamon Press, Oxford.

Field, G. E. and Boren, J. J. (1963). An adjusting avoidance procedure with multiple auditory and visual warning stimuli, *Journal of the Experimental Analysis of Behavior,* **6**, 537–543.

Findley, J. D., Schuster, C. R., and Zimmerman, J. (1966). Second-order avoidance behavior in monkeys, *Journal of the Experimental Analysis of Behavior*, **9**, 703–708.

Fishman, S. (1980). *Agoraphobia: Multiform Behavioral Treatment*, BMA Audio-Cassette Publications, New York.

Fix, A. J. and Haffke, E. A. (1976). *Basic Psychological Therapies: Comparative Effectiveness*, Human Sciences Press, New York.

Foa, E. B., Jameson, J. S., Turner, R. M., and Payne, L. L. (1980). Massed vs. spaced exposure sessions in the treatment of agoraphobia, *Behaviour Research and Therapy,* **18**, 333–338.

Fodor, I. G. (1974). The phobic syndrome in women, in *Women in therapy* (Eds. V. Franks and V. Burtle), Brunner/Mazel, New York.

Fodor, I. G. (1978). *Phobias in Women: Therapeutic Approaches*, BMA Audio-Cassette Publications, New York.

Foulds, G. A. and Hope, K. (1968). *Manual of the Symptom-Sign Inventory*, University of London Press, London.

Frank, J. D. (1973). *Persuasion and Healing*, Johns Hopkins University Press, Baltimore.

Frank, J. D. (1975). Evaluation of psychiatric treatment, in *Comprehensive Textbook of Psychiatry—II* (Eds. A. M. Freedman, H. I. Kaplan, and B. J. Sadock), Williams and Wilkins, Baltimore.

Franks, C. M. and Wilson, G. T. (Eds) (1975). *Annual Review of Behavior Therapy: Theory and Practice*, Vol. 3, Brunner/Mazel, New York.

Franks, C. M. and Wilson, G. T. (Eds) (1978). *Annual Review of Behavior Therapy: Theory and Practice*, Vol. 6, Brunner/Mazel, New York.

Franks, C. M. and Wilson, G. T. (Eds) (1979). *Annual Review of Behavior Therapy: Theory and Practice,* Vol. 7, Brunner/Mazel, New York.

Frazier, S. H. and Carr, A. C. (1967). Phobic reactions, in *Comprehensive Textbook of Psychiatry* (Eds. A. M. Freedman and H. I. Kaplan), Williams and Wilkins, Baltimore.

Freud, S. (1894). The justification for detaching from neurasthenia a particular syndrome: The anxiety neurosis, in *Collected Works*, Vol. I, Hogarth Press and Institute of Psychoanalysis, London, 78–106.

Freud, S. (1919). Turnings in the world of psychoanalytic therapy, in *Collected Papers*, Vol. 2, Hogarth Press and Institute of Psychoanalysis, London. pp. 399–400.

Friedman, D. E. (1966). A new technique for the systematic desensitization of phobic symptoms, *Behaviour Research and Therapy,* **4**, 139–140.

Fry, W. (1962). The marital content of an anxiety syndrome, *Family Process*, **1**, 245–252.

Galassi, J. P., DeLo, J. S., Galassi, M. D., and Bastien, S. (1974). A college self-expression scale: A measure of assertiveness, *Behavior Therapy,* **5**, 165–171.

Garcia, J., Ervin, F., and Koelling, R. (1966). Learning with prolonged delay of reinforcement, *Psychonomic Science,* **5**, 121–122.

Garcia, J. and Koelling, R. A. (1966). Relation of cue to consequence in avoidance learning, *Psychonomic Science,* **4**, 123–124.

Gathercole, C. E. (1968). *Assessment in Clinical Psychology*, Penguin Books, Harmondsworth.

Gelder, M. G., Bancroft, J. H. J., Gath, D. H., Johnston, D. W., Mathews, A. M., and Shaw, P. M. (1973). Specific and non-specific factors in behaviour therapy, *British Journal of Psychiatry,* **123**, 445–462.

Gelder, M. G. and Marks, I. M. (1966). Severe agoraphobia: A controlled prospective trial of behaviour therapy, *British Journal of Psychiatry,* **112**, 309–319.

Gelder, M., Marks, I. M., and Wolff, H. (1967). Desensitization and psychotherapy in the treatment of phobic states, *British Journal of Psychiatry,* **113**, 53–73.

George, A. J. (1982). School of Pharmacy, Liverpool Polytechnic. Personal Communication.

Gillan, P. and Rachman, S. (1974). An experimental investigation of desensitization in phobic patients, *British Journal of Psychiatry,* **124**, 392–401.

Goldfried, M. R. and D'Zurilla, T. (1969). A behaviour analytic model for assessing competence, in *Current Topics in Clinical and Community Psychology*, Vol. 1 (Ed. C. D. Spielberger), Academic Press, New York.

Goldstein, A. J. (1970). Case conference: Some aspects of agoraphobia, *Journal of Behavior Therapy and Experimental Psychiatry,* **1**, 305–313.

Goldstein, A. J. (1978). Case conference: The treatment of a case of agoraphobia by a multifaceted treatment program, *Journal of Behavior Therapy and Experimental Psychiatry,* **9**, 45–51.

Goldstein, A. J. and Chambless, D. L. (1978). A reanalysis of agoraphobia, *Behavior Therapy*, **9**, 47–59.

Gosling, J. (1980). Behaviour therapy: when a foe becomes a friend, *Nursing Mirror,* **151**, 21, 28–31.

Gottman, J. M. and Leiblum, S. R. (1974). *How to do Psychotherapy and How to Evaluate it*, Holt, Rinehart and Winston, New York.

Greer, J. H. (1965). The development of a scale to measure fear, *Behaviour Research and Therapy,* **3**, 45–53.

Greist, J. H., Marks, I. M., Berlin, F., Gournay, K., and Noshirvani, H. (1980). Avoidance versus confrontation of fear, *Behavior Therapy,* **11**, 1–14.

Grossberg, J. M. and Wilson, H. K. (1965). A correlational comparison of the Wolpe-Lang fear survey schedule and Taylor manifest anxiety scale, *Behaviour Research & Therapy,* **3**, 125–128.

Hafner, R. J. (1976). Fresh symptom emergence after intensive behavior therapy, *British Journal of Psychiatry,* **129**, 378–383.

Hafner, R. J. (1977a). The husbands of agoraphobic women: Assortative mating or pathogenic interaction? *British Journal of Psychiatry,* **130**, 233–239.

Hafner, R. J. (1977b). The husbands of agoraphobic women and their influence on treatment outcome, *British Journal of Psychiatry,* **131**, 289–294.

Hafner, R. J. (1979). Agoraphobic women married to abnormally jealous men, *British Journal of Medical Psychology,* **52**, 99–104.

Hafner, R. J. and Marks, I. (1976). Exposure *in vivo* of agoraphobics: Contributions of diazepam, group exposure, and anxiety evocation, *Psychological Medicine*, **6**, 71–88.

Hafner, J. and Milton, F. (1977). The influence of propranolol on the exposure *in vivo* of agoraphobics, *Psychological Medicine,* **7**, 419–425.

Hallam, R. S. (1978). Agoraphobia: A critical review of the concept, *British Journal of Psychiatry,* **133**, 314–319.

Hallam, R. S. and Hafner, R. J. (1978). Fears of phobic patients: Factor analyses of self-report data, *Behaviour Research and Therapy,* **16**, 1–6.

Hand, I. and Lamontagne, Y. (1976). The exacerbation of interpersonal problems after rapid phobia-removal, *Psychotherapy: Theory, Research, and Practice,* **13**, 405–411.

Hand, I., Lamontagne, Y., and Marks, I. M. (1974). Group exposure (flooding) *in vivo* for agoraphobics, *British Journal of Psychiatry*, **124**, 588–602.

Hare, E. H. (1965). *Triennial Statistical Report, 1961–63*, Bethlem Royal and Maudsley Hospital, London.

Harper, M. and Roth, M. (1962). Temporal lobe epilepsy and the phobic-anxiety-depersonalisation syndrome, *Comprehensive Psychiatry,* **3**, 129–151.

Harris, B. (1979). Whatever happened to little Albert? *American Psychologist,* **34**, 151–160.

Harzem, P. and Miles, T. R. (1978). *Conceptual Issues in Operant Psychology*, Wiley, Chichester.

Hawkrigg, J. J. (1975). Agoraphobia, *Nursing Times*, **71**, 33, 1280–1282.

Heimberg, R. G. and Harrison, D. F. (1980). Use of the Rathus Assertiveness Schedule with offenders: A question of questions, *Behavior Therapy,* **11**, 278–281.

Hendry, D. P. (Ed.) (1969). *Conditioned Reinforcement,* Dorsey, Homewood, Illinois.

Herrnstein, R. J. (1969). Method and theory in the study of avoidance, *Psychological Review,* **76**, 49–69.

Herrnstein, R. J. and Hineline, P. N. (1966). Negative reinforcement as shock-frequency reduction, *Journal of the Experimental Analysis of Behavior,* **9**, 421–430.

Hersen, M. (1973). Self assessment of fear, *Behaviour Therapy,* **4**, 241–257.

Hersen, M., Eisler, R., Miller, P. M., Johnson, M. B., and Pinkston, S. G. (1973). Effects of practice, instructions and modeling on components of assertive behaviour, *Behaviour Research and Therapy,* **11**, 443–451.

Hineline, P. (1977). Negative reinforcement and avoidance, in *Handbook of Operant Behavior* (Eds. W. K. Honig and J. E. R. Staddon), Prentice-Hall, Englewood Cliffs, New Jersey.

Hollingshead, A. B. and Redlich, F. C. (1958). *Social Class and Mental Illness*, Wiley, New York.

Holmes, T. H. and Rahe, R. H. (1967). The Social Readjustment Rating Scale, *Journal of Psychosomatic Research,* **11**, 213–218.

Hudson, B. (1974). The families of agoraphobics treated by behaviour therapy, *British Journal of Social Work,* **4**, 51–59.

Hull, C. L. (1952). *A Behavior System*, Yale University Press, New Haven, Connecticutt.

Hussain, M. Z. (1971). Desensitization and flooding (implosion) in the treatment of phobias, *American Journal of Psychiatry,* **127**, 1509–1514.

Jacobson, E. (1938). *Progressive Relaxation,* University of Chicago Press, Chicago.

Jannoun, L., Munby, M., Catalan, J., and Gelder, M. (1979). A home-based treatment programme for agoraphobia: Replication and controlled evaluation, *Bulletin of the British Psychological Society,* **32**, 201 (Abstract).

Jannoun, L., Munby, M., Catalan, J., and Gelder, M. (1980). A home-based treatment program for agoraphobia: Replication and controlled evaluation, *Behavior Therapy,* **11**, 294–305.

Johnston, D. and Gath, D. (1973). Arousal levels and attribution effects in diazepam-assisted flooding, *British Journal of Psychiatry,* **123**, 463–466.

Johnston, D. W., Lancashire, M., Mathews, A. M., Munby, M., Shaw, P. M., and Gelder, M. G. (1976). Imaginal flooding and exposure to real phobic situations: Changes during treatment, *British Journal of Psychiatry,* **129**, 372–377.

Johnston, D. W. and Munby, M. (1980). Agoraphobia: The long-term outcome of behavioural treatment, *Bulletin of the British Psychological Society,* **33**, 189–190 (Abstract).

Johnston, M., Johnston, D. W., Wilkes, H., Burns, L. E., and Thorpe, G. L. (1982). *Cumulative Scales for the Measurement of Agoraphobia*, manuscript submitted for publication.

Jones, R. B., Sinnott, A. and Fordham, A. S. (1980). Group *in vivo* exposure augmented by the counselling of significant others in the treatment of agoraphobia, *Behavioural Psychotherapy,* **8**, 31–35.

Kanfer, F. H. and Saslow, G. (1969). Behavioral diagnosis, in *Behavior Therapy: Appraisal and Status* (Ed. C. M. Franks), McGraw-Hill, New York.

Kantor, J. S., Zitrin, C. M., and Zeldis, S. M. (1980). Mitral valve prolapse syndrome in agoraphobic patients, *American Journal of Psychiatry,* **137**, 467–469.

Kazdin, A. E. (1979a). Situational specificity: The two-edged sword of behavioral assessment, *Behavioral Assessment,* **1**, 57–75.

Kazdin, A. E. (1979b). Therapy outcome questions requiring control of credibility and treatment-generated expectancies, *Behavior Therapy,* **10**, 81–93.

Kazdin, A. E. and Wilcoxon, L. A. (1976). Systematic desensitization and nonspecific treatment effects: a methodological evaluation, *Psychological Bulletin,* **83**, 5, 729–758.

Kedwood, H. B. and Cooper, B. (1966). Neurotic disorders in urban practice; a three year follow-up, *Journal of College of General Practitioners,* **12**, 148–163.

Keehn, J. D. (1966). Avoidance responses as discriminated operants, *British Journal of Psychology,* **57**, 375–380.

Kendall, P. C. and Korgeski, G. P. (1979). Assessment and cognitive-behavioral interventions, *Cognitive Therapy and Research,* **3**, 1–21.

Kimble, G. A. (1961). *Hilgard and Marquis' Conditioning and Learning* (2nd edn), Methuen, London.

Klein, D. F. (1964). Delineation of two drug-responsive anxiety syndromes, *Psychopharmacologia,* **5**, 397–408.

Klein, D. F. and Fink, M. (1962). Psychiatric reaction patterns to imipramine, *American Journal of Psychiatry,* **119**, 432–438.

Klein, D. F., Zitrin, C. M., and Woerner, M. G. (1977). Imipramine and phobia, *Psychopharmacological Bulletin,* **13**, 24–27.

Kolb, L. C. (1973). *Modern Clinical Psychiatry,* Saunders, Philadelphia.

Kraepelin, E. (1906). *Lectures on Clinical Psychiatry*, Bailliere Tindall, London.

Krumboltz, J. D. and Thoresen, C. E. (1976). *Counselling methods*, Holt, Rinehart and Winston, New York.

Lader, M. and Marks, I. M. (1971). *Clinical anxiety*, Heinemann, London.

Lang, P. J. (1968). Fear reduction and fear behavior: Problems in treating a construct, in *Research in Psychotherapy,* Vol. 3, (Ed. J. M. Shlien), American Psychological Association, Washington, DC.

Lang, P. J. (1969). The mechanics of desensitization and the laboratory study of human fear, in *Behaviour Therapy: Appraisal and Status* (Ed. C. M. Franks), McGraw Hill, New York.

Lang, P. J. (1971). The application of psychophysiological methods to the study of psychotherapy and behavior modification, in *Handbook of psychotherapy and behavior change*. (Eds. A. E. Bergin and S. L. Garfield) Wiley, New York.

Lang, P. J., and Lazovik, A. D. (1963). The experimental desensitization of a phobia. *Journal of Abnormal and Social Psychology,* **66**, 519–525.

Langner, T. S. and Michael, S. T. (1963). *Life Stress and Mental Illness*, Wiley, New York.

Lapouse, R. and Monk, M. A. (1959). Fears and worries in a representative sample of children, *American Journal of Orthopsychiatry*, **29**, 803–818.

Last, C. G., Barlow, D. H., and O'Brien, G. T. (1981). *Cognitive Changes During In Vivo Exposure in an Agoraphobic*, Paper presented at the 15th Annual AABT Convention, Toronto.

Law, S. (1975). *Inspired Freedom. Agoraphobia: A Battle Won*, Regency Press, London.

Lazarus, A. A. (1966). Broad-spectrum behaviour therapy and the treatment of agoraphobia, *Behaviour Research and Therapy,* **4**, 95–97.

Lazarus, A. A. (1971). *Behaviour Therapy and Beyond*, McGraw Hill, New York.

Lazarus, A. A. (1975). Group therapy and the BASIC ID, in *Annual Review of Behavior Therapy: Theory and Practice*, Vol. 3 (Eds. C. M. Franks and G. T. Wilson), Brunner/Mazel, New York.

Lazarus, A. A. (1976). *Multimodal Behavior Therapy*, Springer, New York.

Lazell, D. (1973). *I Couldn't Catch the Bus Today*. Lutterworth Press, Guildford and London.

Ledwidge, B. (1978). Cognitive behavior modification: A step in the wrong direction? *Psychological Bulletin,* **85**, 353–375.

Legrand du Saule, H. (1885). De l'agoraphobie, *Practicien*, **8**, 208–210.

Leitenberg, H., Agras, W. S., Allen, R., and Butz, R. A. (1975). Feedback and therapist praise during treatment of phobia, *Journal of Consulting and Clinical Psychology,* **43**, 396–404.

Leitenberg, H., Agras, W. S., Edwardes, J. A., Thompson, L. E., and Wincze, J. P. (1970). Practice as a psychotherapeutic variable: An experimental analysis within single cases, *Journal of Psychiatric Research,* **7**, 215–225.

Leitenberg, H., Agras, W. S., Thompson, L. E., and Wright, D. E. (1968). Feedback in behavior modification: An experimental analysis in two phobic cases, *Journal of Applied Behavior Analysis,* **1**, 131–137.

Lemkau, P., Tietze, C., and Cooper, M. (1942). Mental-hygiene problems in an urban district, *Mental Hygiene*, **26**, 100–119.

Leonard, W. E. (1928). *The Locomotive God*. Chapman & Hall, London.

Lick, J. R. (1973). Statistical vs clinical significance in research on the outcome of psychotherapy, *International Journal of Mental Health*, **2**, 26–37.

Lick, J. R. and Katkin, E. S. (1976). Assessment of anxiety and fear, in *Behavioral* Assessment: A Practical Handbook (Eds. M. Hersen and S. Bellack) Pergamon Press, New York.

Liddell, H. (1944). Conditioned reflex method and experimental neurosis, in *Personality and the Behavior Disorders* (Ed. J. McV. Hunt), Ronald Press, New York.

Linder, L. H. (1981). Group behavioral treatment of agoraphobia: A preliminary report, *Comprehensive Psychiatry,* **22**, 226–233.

Liotti, G. and Guidano, V. (1976). Behavioral analysis of marital interaction in agoraphobic male patients, *Behaviour Research and Therapy,* **14**, 161–162.

Lipsedge, M. S., Hajioff, J., Huggins, P., Napier, L., Pearce, J., Pike, D. J., and Rich, M. (1973). The management of severe agoraphobia: A comparison of Iproniazid and systematic desensitization, *Psychopharmacologia*, **32**, 67–80.

Lowen, A. (1967). *The Betrayal of the Body*, Macmillan, New York.

Mahoney, M. J. (1980). *Abnormal Psychology: Perspectives on Human Variance*, Harper & Row, San Francisco.

Mancini, F., Sassaroli, S., and Semerari, A. (1977). Cognitive restructuring and prescription of behavior in the psychotherapy of an agoraphobic, *Archivio di Psicologia neurologia e Psichiatria*, **38**, 473–485.

Manosevitz, M. and Lanyon, R. I. (1965). Fear survey schedule: a normative study. *Psychological Reports*, **17**, 699–703.

Marks, I. M. (1967). Components and correlates of psychiatric questionnaires, *British Journal of Medical Psychology,* **40**, 261–272.

Marks, I. M. (1969). *Fears and Phobias*, Academic Press, New York.

Marks, I. M. (1970). Agoraphobic syndrome (phobic anxiety state), *Archives of General Psychiatry,* **23**, 538–553.

Marks, I. M. (1972a). Flooding (implosion) and related treatments, *Behavior Modification: Principles and Clinical Applications* (Ed. W. S. Agras), Little, Brown, Boston.

Marks, I. M. (1972b). Perspective on flooding, *Seminars in Psychiatry,* **4**, 129–138.

Marks, I. M. (1975). Behavioral treatments of phobic and obsessive-compulsive disorders: A critical appraisal, in *Progress in behavior modification*, (Eds. M. Hersen, R. M. Eisler, and P. M. Miller), Vol. 1 Academic Press, New York.

Marks, I. M. (1980). *Toward an Empirical Clinical Science*, invited address presented at the meeting of the Association for Advancement of Behavior Therapy, New York.

Marks, I. M. (1981a). Behavioural concepts and treatments of neuroses, *Behavioural Psychotherapy,* **9**, 137–154.

Marks, I. M. (1981b). *Cure and Care of Neuroses: Theory and Practice of Behavioural Psychotherapy*, Wiley, New York.

Marks, I. M. (1981c). Personal Communication.

Marks, I. M. (1981d). New developments in psychological treatments of phobias. In *Phobia: Psychological and Pharmacological Treatments* (Eds. M. Mavissakalian and D. H. Barlow) Guilford Press, New York.

Marks, I. M. and Bebbington, P. (1976). Space phobia: Syndrome or agoraphobic variant? *British Medical Journal,* 6031, 345–347.

Marks, I. M., Birley, J. L. T. and Gelder, M. G. (1966). Modified leucotomy in severe agoraphobia: A controlled serial inquiry, *British Journal of Psychiatry,* **112**, 757–769.

Marks, I. M., Boulougouris, J., and Marset, P. (1971). Flooding versus desensitisation in the treatment of phobic patients: A crossover study, *British Journal of Psychiatry*, **119**, 353–375.

Marks, I. M. and Gelder, M. G. (1965). A controlled retrospective study of behaviour therapy in phobic patients, *British Journal of Psychiatry*, **111**, 571–573.

Marks, I. M. and Gelder, M. G. (1966). Different onset ages in varieties of phobia, *American Journal of Psychiatry*, **111**, 571–573.

Marks, I. M. and Herst, E. R. (1970). A survey of 1200 agoraphobics in Britain: Features associated with treatment and ability to work, *Social Psychiatry*, **5**, 16–24.

Marks, I. M. and Mathews, A. M. (1979). Brief standard self-rating for phobic patients, *Behaviour Research and Therapy*, **17**, 263–267.

Marks, I. M., Viswanathan, R., Lipsedge, M. S., and Gardner, R. (1972). Enhanced relief of phobias by flooding during waning Diazepam effect, *British Journal of Psychiatry*, **121**, 493–505.

Masserman, J. H. (1943). *Behavior and Neurosis*, University of Chicago Press, Chicago.

Masserman, J. H. (1971). The principle of uncertainty in neurotigenesis, in *Experimental Psychopathology: Recent Research and Theory* (Ed. H. D. Kimmel) Academic Press, New York.

Mathews, A. (1971). *Specific and Non-specific Factors in Behaviour Therapy*. Paper presented at the Third Annual Conference of the Behavioural Engineering Association, Wexford, Ireland.

Mathews, A. (1977a). Behavioural treatment of agoraphobia: New findings, new problems, in *The Treatment of Phobic and Obsessive Compulsive Disorders* (Eds J. C. Boulougouris and A. Rabavilas) Pergamon Press, Oxford.

Mathews, A. (1977b). Recent developments in the treatment of agoraphobia, *Behavioural Analysis and Modification*, **2**, 64–75.

Mathews, A. (1978). Fear-reduction research and clinical phobias, *Psychological Bulletin*, **85**, 390–404.

Mathews, A. M., Gelder, M. G., and Johnston, D. W. (1981). *Agoraphobia: Nature and Treatment*, The Guilford Press, New York.

Mathews, A. M., Johnston, D. W., Lancashire, M., Munby, M., Shaw, P. M., and Gelder, M. G. (1976). Imaginal flooding and exposure to real phobic situations: Treatment outcome with agoraphobic patients, *British Journal of Psychiatry*, **129**, 362–371.

Mathews, A. M., Johnston, D. W., Shaw, P. M., and Gelder, M. G. (1974). Process variables and the prediction of outcome in behaviour therapy, *British Journal of Psychiatry*, **125**, 256–264.

Mathews, A. M. and Rezin, V. (1977). Treatment of dental fears by imaginal flooding and rehearsal of coping behaviour, *Behaviour Research and Therapy*, **15**, 321–328.

Mathews, A. M. and Shaw, P. (1973). Emotional arousal and persuasion effects in flooding. *Behaviour Research and Therapy*, **11**, 587–598.

Mathews, A., Teasdale, J., Munby, M., Johnston, D., and Shaw, P. (1977). A home-based treatment program for agoraphobia, *Behavior Therapy*, **8**, 915–924.

Mavissakalian, M. and Barlow, D. H. (1981). Phobia: an overview, in *Phobia—Psychological and Pharmacological Treatment* (Eds. M. Mavissakalian and D. H. Barlow) Guilford Press, New York.

McDonald, R., Sartory, G., Grey, S. J., Cobb, J., Stern, R., and Marks, I. (1979). The effects of self-exposure instructions on agoraphobic outpatients, *Behaviour Research and Therapy*, **17**, 83–85.

McFall, R. M. and Twentyman, C. T. (1973). Four experiments on the relative contributions of rehearsal, modeling, and coaching to assertion training, *Journal of Abnormal Psychology*, **81**, 199–218.

McGennis, A., Hartman, M., and Nolan, G. (1977). The role of a self-help association in agoraphobia: One year's experience with 'out and about', *Journal of the Irish Medical Association,* **70**, 10–13.

McPherson, F. M., Brougham, L., and McLaren, S. (1980). Maintenance of improvement in agoraphobic patients treated by behavioural methods—a four-year follow-up, *Behaviour Research and Therapy,* **18**, 150–152.

Meichenbaum, D. (1972). Cognitive modification of test anxious college students, *Journal of Consulting and Clinical Psychology,* **39**, 370–380.

Meichenbaum, D. (1973). *A Self-instructional Approach to Stress Management: A Proposal for Stress Inoculation Training*, Paper presented at NATO Conference, Murnau, Germany.

Meichenbaum, D. (1975a). *Cognitive Factors as Determinants of Learning Disabilities: A Cognitive-functional Approach*, Paper presented at NATO Conference on 'The Neuropsychology of Learning Disorders: Theoretical Approaches'. Korsor, Denmark.

Meichenbaum, D. (1975b). *Toward a Cognitive Theory of Self-control*, Research Report No. 48, Department of Psychology, University of Waterloo.

Meichenbaum, D. (1975c). *Towards a Cognitive Theory of Self Control*. Research Report No. 48, Psychology Dept., University of Waterloo, Ontario.

Meichenbaum, D. (1976). Cognitive behaviour modification, in *Behavioural Approaches to Therapy* (Eds. J. T. Spence, R. C. Carson, and J. W. Thibaut) General Learning Press, Morristown, New Jersey.

Meichenbaum, D. (1977). *Cognitive-behavior Modification: An Integrative Approach*. Plenum, New York.

Meichenbaum, D. and Cameron, R. (1974). *An Examination of Cognitive and Contingency Variables in Anxiety Relief Procedures*. Unpublished manuscript, University of Waterloo.

Meichenbaum, D., Gilmore, J. B., and Fedoravicius, A. (1971). Group insight versus group desensitization in treating speech anxiety, *Journal of Consulting and Clinical Psychology,* **36**, 410–421.

Meichenbaum, D. and Turk, D. (1975). *The Cognitive-behavioural Management of Anxiety, Anger and Pain*. Proceedings of 7th Banff International Conference. Research Press.

Meyer, V. and Gelder, M. G. (1963). Behaviour therapy and phobic disorders, *British Journal of Psychiatry*, **109**, 19–28.

Miller, M. L. (1953). On street fear, *International Journal Psychoan,* **34**, 232–252.

Miller, N. E. (1944). Experimental studies of conflict, in *Personality and the Behavior Disorders* (Ed. J. McV. Hunt), Ronald Press, New York.

Milton, F. and Hafner, J. (1979). The outcome of behavior therapy for agoraphobia in relation to marital adjustment, *Archives of General Psychiatry,* **36**, 807–811.

Mineka, S. and Kihlstrom, J. F. (1978). Unpredictable and uncontrollable events: A new perspective on experimental neurosis, *Journal of Abnormal Psychology,* **87**, 256–271.

Mischel, W. (1968). *Personality and Assessment*, Wiley, New York.

Mittelman, B. (1956). Analysis of reciprocal neurotic patterns in family relationships, in *Neurotic Interactions in Marriage* (Ed. V. Eisenstein), Tavistock, London.

Mowrer, O. H. (1947). On the dual nature of learning as a reinterpretation of 'conditioning' and 'problem-solving', *Harvard Educational Review,* 102–148.

Mowrer, O. H. (1960). *Learning Theory and Behavior*, Wiley, New York.

Mullaney, J. A. and Trippett, C. J. (1979). Alcohol dependence and phobias: Clinical description and relevance, *British Journal of Psychiatry,* **135**, 565–573.

Munby, M. and Johnston, D. W. (1980). Agoraphobia: The long-term follow-up of behavioural treatment, *British Journal of Psychiatry,* **137**, 418–427.

Napalkov, S. V. (1963). Information process and the brain, in *Progress in brain research*, Vol. 2 (Eds. N. Wiener and J. Schadel) Elsevier, Amsterdam.
Nelson, R. O. and Hayes, S. C. (1979). Some current dimensions of behavioral assessment, *Behavioral Assessment,* **1**, 1–16.
Nemiah, J. C. (1975). Depersonalisation neurosis, in *Comprehensive Textbook of Psychiatry*, Vol. 1, 2nd edn (Eds. A. M. Freedman, H. I. Kaplan, and B. J. Sadock) Williams & Wilkins, Baltimore.
Nietzel, M. T. (1973). *The Effects of Assessment and Treatment Mediated Demand Characteristics in a Psychotherapy Outcome Study*, Unpublished doctoral dissertion, University of Illinois.
Nietzel, M. T. and Berstein, D. A. (1975). *No-treatment Control Groups: The Effect of Rationale on Subsequent Avoidance Behaviour*, paper read at the Midwestern Psychological Association.
O'Brien, J. S. (1979). A modified thought stopping procedure for the treatment of agoraphobia, *Journal of Behavior Therapy and Experimental Psychiatry,* **10**, 121–124.
Öhman, A., Fredrikson, M., and Hugdahl, K. (1978). Towards an experimental model for simple phobic reactions, *Behavioural Analysis and Modification,* **2**, 97–114.
Orwin, A. (1973). 'The running treatment': A preliminary communication on a new use for an old therapy (physical activity) in the agoraphobic syndrome, *British Journal of Psychiatry,* **122**, 175–179.
Ost, L. G., Jerremalm, A., and Johansson, J. (1981). Individual response patterns and the effects of different behavioral methods in the treatment of social phobia, *Behaviour Research and Therapy,* **19**, 1–16.
Overmier, J. B. and Seligman, M. E. P. (1967). Effects of inescapable shock upon subsequent escape and avoidance learning, *Journal of Comparative and Physiological Psychology,* **63**, 23–33.
Parker, G. (1979). Reported parental characteristics of agoraphobics and social phobics, *British Journal of Psychiatry,* **135**, 555–560.
Patterson, C. H. (1980). *Theories of Counseling and Psychotherapy* (3rd edn), Harper & Row, New York.
Pavlov, I. P. (1927). *Conditioned Reflexes: An Investigation of the Physiological Activity of the Cerebral Cortex* (Translated by G. V. Anrep), Oxford University Press, London.
Phares, E. J. (1967). The deviant personality. in *Contemporary Approaches to Psychology* (Eds. H. Helson and W. Bevan), Van Nostrand, New York.
Popler, K. (1977). Agoraphobia: Indications for the application of the multimodal behavioral conceptualization, *Journal of Nervous and Mental Disease*, **164**, 97–101.
Prince, M. and Putnam, J. J. (1912). Clinical study of a case of phobia: a symposium. *Journal of Abnormal Social Psychology,* **7**, 259–303.
Rabavilas, A. D., Boulougouris, J. C., and Perissaki, C. (1979). Therapist qualities related to outcome with exposure *in vivo* in neurotic patients, *Journal of Behavior Therapy and Experimental Psychiatry,* **10**, 293–294.
Rachman, S. (1977). The conditioning theory of fear acquisition: A critical examination, *Behaviour Research and Therapy,* **15**, 375–387.
Ramsay, R. (1975). Research on anxiety and phobic reactions, in *Stress and Anxiety*, Vol. 1, (Eds. C. D. Spielberger and I. Sarason) Wiley, New York.
Rathus, S. A. (1973). A 30-item schedule for assessing assertive behavior, *Behavior Therapy,* **4**, 398–406.
Rathus, S. A. and Nevid, J. S. (1977). Concurrent validity of the 30-item assertiveness schedule with a psychiatric population, *Behavior Therapy,* **8**, 393–397.
Raven, J. C. (1960). *Guide to the Standard Progressive Matrices*, Lewis, London.
Raven, J. C. (1965). *Guide to Using the Mill Hill Vocabulary Scale*, Lewis, London.

Raymond, E. (1946). *The Autobiography of David*, Gollancz, London.

Reiss, S. (1980). Pavlovian conditioning and human fear: An expectancy model, *Behavior Therapy,* **11**, 380–396.

Rescorla, R. A. and Solomon, R. L. (1967). Two-process learning theory: Relationships between Pavlovian conditioning and instrumental learning, *Psychological Review,* **74**, 151–182.

Rimm, D. C., Janda, L. H., Lancaster, D. W., Nahl, M., and Dittmar, K. (1977). An exploratory investigation of the origin and maintenance of phobias. *Behaviour Research and Therapy*, **15**, 231–238.

Roberts, A. H. (1964). Housebound housewives—a follow-up study of a phobic anxiety state, *British Journal of Psychiatry,* **110**, 191–197.

Rosenthal, D. (1970). *Genetic Theory and Abnormal Behavior,* McGraw-Hill, New York.

Ross, J. (1979). *The Use of Former Phobics in the Treatment of Phobias*, Presented at the 132nd Annual Meeting of the American Psychiatric Association, Chicago, Illinois.

Roth, M. (1959). The phobic-anxiety-depersonalisation syndrome, *Proceedings of the Royal Society of Medicine,* **52**, 587–595.

Roth, M., Garside, R., and Gurney, C. (1965). Clinical statistical enquiries into the classification of anxiety states and depressive disorders, in: *Proceedings of Leeds Symposium on Behavioural Disorders*, May and Baker, London.

Roth, M., Garside, R. F., and Kerr, T. A. (1972). Studies in classification of affective disorders, *British Journal of Psychiatry,* **121**, 147–161.

Rotter, J. B. (1966). Generalized expectancies for internal vs. external control of reinforcement, *Psychological Monographs,* **80**, 1–28.

Rudestam, K. E. and Bedrosian, R. (1977). An investigation of the effectiveness of desensitization and flooding with two types of phobia, *Behaviour Research and Therapy*, **15**, 23–30.

Rutner, I. V. (1973). The effects of feedback and instructions on phobic behaviour, *Behaviour Therapy,* **4**, 338–348.

Rutter, M., Tizard, J., and Whitmore. K. (1968). *Education, Health and Behaviour*, Longmans, London.

Rycroft, C. (1968). *A critical Dictionary of Psychoanalysis*, Nelson, London.

Sauvages, F. B. de, (1770). *Nosologie Methodique*, Vol. II (Translated by J. Nicolas) Herissant, Paris. pp. 606–617.

Schachter, S. (1966). The interaction of cognitive and physiological determinants of emotional state, in *Anxiety and Behaviour* (Ed. C. Speilberger) Academic Press, New York.

Shapira, K., Kerr, T. A., and Roth, M. (1970). Phobias and affective illness, *British Journal of Psychiatry,* **117**, 25–32.

Scherer, M. W. and Nakamura, C. Y. (1968). A fear survey schedule for children (FSS-FC); a factor analytic comparison with manifest anxiety, *Behaviour Research & Therapy*, **6**, 173–182.

Seligman, M. E. P. (1971). Phobias and preparedness, *Behavior Therapy*, **2**, 307–320.

Seligman, M. E. P. (1975). *Helplessness: On Depression, Development and Death*. W. H. Freeman, San Francisco.

Seligman, M. E. P. and Hager, J. L. (Eds.) (1972). *Biological Boundaries of Learning*, Appleton, New York.

Shafar, S. (1976). Aspects of phobic illness—a study of 90 personal cases, *British Journal of Medical Psychology*, **49**, 221–236.

Shapiro, A. K., and Morris, L. A. (1978). Placebo effects in medical and psychological therapies, in *Handbook of Psychotherapy and Behaviour Change* (Eds. S. L. Garfield and A. E. Bergin) 2nd edn., Wiley, New York.

Sidman, M. Two temporal parameters of the maintenance of avoidance behavior by the white rat. *Journal of Comparative and Physiological Psychology,* 1953, **46**, 253–261.

Sidman, M. (1966). Avoidance behavior, in *Operant Behavior: Areas of Research and Application* (Ed. W. K. Honig) Appleton-Century-Crofts, New York.

Sinnott, A., Jones, R. B., Scott-Fordham, A., and Woodward, R. (1981). Augmentation of *in vivo* exposure treatment for agoraphobia by the formation of neighbourhood self-help groups. *Behaviour Research and Therapy*, **19**, 339–347.

Skinner, B. F. (1966). Operant behavior, in *Operant Behavior: Areas of Research and Application* (Ed. W. K. Honig) Appleton-Century-Crofts, New York.

Slater, E. and Roth, M. (1969). *Clinical Psychiatry* (3rd Edn), Bailliere, Tindall & Cassell, London.

Smith, R. E., Diener, E., and Beman, A. L. (1974). Demand characteristics and the behavioural avoidance measure of fear in behaviour therapy analogue research, *Behaviour Therapy*, **5**, 172–182.

Snaith, R. P. (1968). A clinical investigation of phobias, *British Journal of Psychiatry,* **114**, 673–698.

Solyom, L., Beck, P., Solyom, C. and Hugel, R. (1974). Some aetiological factors in phobic neurosis. *Canadian Psychiatric Association Journal*, **19**, 69–78.

Solyom, L., Heseltine, G. F. D., McClure, D. J., Solyom, C., Ledwidge, B., and Steinberg, G. (1973). Behaviour therapy versus drug therapy, *Canadian Psychiatric Association Journal*, **18**, 25–31.

Solyom, C., Solyom, L., LaPierre, Y., Pecknold, J., and Morton, L. (1981). Phenelzine and exposure in the treatment of phobias, *Biological Psychiatry,* **16**, 239–247.

Stampfl, T. G. and Levis, D. J. (1967). Essentials of implosive therapy: A learning-theory-based psychodynamic behavioral therapy, *Journal of Abnormal Psychology,* **72**, 496–503.

Stern, R. S. and Marks, I. M. (1971). *Long and Short Flooding in Phobic Disorders*, paper presented at the Third Annual Conference of the Behavioural Engineering Association, Wexford, Ireland.

Stern, R. S. and Marks, I. M. (1973a). Brief and prolonged flooding: A comparison in agoraphobic patients, *Archives of General Psychiatry,* **28**, 270–276.

Stern, R. A. and Marks, I. M. (1973b). Contract therapy in obsessive-compulsive neurosis with marital discord. *British Journal of Psychiatry,* **123**, 681–684.

Stuart, R. B. (1980). *Helping Couples Change: A Social Learning Approach to Marital Therapy*, The Guilford Press, New York.

Teasdale, J. D., Walsh, P. A., Lancashire, M., and Mathews, A. M. (1977). Group exposure for agoraphobics: A replication study, *British Journal of Psychiatry,* **130**, 186–193.

Terhune, W. (1949). The phobic syndrome: A study of 86 patients with phobic reactions, *Archives of Neurological Psychiatry*, **62**, 162–172.

Thompson, R. F. and Spencer, W. A. (1966). Habituation: A model phenomenon for the study of neuronal substrates of behavior, *Psychological Review,* **73**, 16–43.

Thorpe, G. L. (1972). Learning paradigms in the anticipatory avoidance technique: A comment on the controversy between MacDonough and Feldman, *Behavior Therapy,* **3**, 614–618.

Thorpe, G. L. (1975). Desensitization, behavior rehearsal, self-instructional training and placebo effects on assertive-refusal behavior, *European Journal of Behavioural Analysis and Modification*, **1**, 30–44.

Thorpe, G. L. (1979). A big hand for Neil Cheshire; but . . . (Correspondence), *Bulletin of the British Psychological Society*, **32**, 429–430.

Thorpe, G. L., Amatu, H. I., Blakey, R. S., and Burns, L. E. (1976). Contributions of overt instructional rehearsal and 'specific insight' to the effectiveness of self-instructional training: A preliminary study, *Behavior Therapy*, **7**, 504–511.

Thorpe, G. L. and Barnes, G. S. (1981). Agoraphobia: Multiform Behavioural Treatment. Audio-Cassette Review, *Journal of Mind and Behavior*, **2**, 357–361.

Thorpe, G. L., Burns, L. E., Smith, P. J., and Blier, M. J. (1982). Agoraphobia: Research developments and clinical implications, *Child & Family Behavior Therapy*. Fall Supplement (In Press).

Thorpe, G. L., Cavallaro, L., Zwerdling, A. B., Barnes, G. S., Freedman, E. G., and Kulberg, G. (1982). *Group Exposure Treatment for Agoraphobics: Efficacy Expectations and Adequacy of Interpersonal Functioning as Correlates of Phobia-removal.* Research in progress.

Thorpe, G. L. and Wilkins, W. W. (1977). Review of A. A. Lazarus: Multi-modal Behavior Therapy, *European Journal of Behavioural Analysis and Modification,* **1**, 292–293.

Torpy, D. and Measey, G. (1974). Marital interaction in agoraphobia, *Journal of Clinical Psychology,* **30**, 351–354.

Tucker, W. I. (1956). Diagnosis and treatment of the phobic reaction, *American Journal of Psychiatry,* **112**, 825.

Twentyman, C. T. and McFall, R. M. (1975). Behavioural training of social skills in shy males, *Journal of Consulting and Clinical Psychology,* **43**, 384–395.

Tyrer, P., Candy, J., and Kelly, D. (1973). A study of the clinical effects of phenelzine and placebo in the treatment of phobic anxiety, *Psychopharmacologia*, **32**, 237–254.

Tyrer, P., Horn, S., and Lee, I. (1978). Treatment of agoraphobia by subliminal and supraliminal exposure to phobic cine film, *Lancet*, **1**, 358–360.

Tyrer, P. and Steinberg, D. (1975). Symptomatic treatment of agoraphobia and social phobias: A follow-up study, *British Journal of Psychiatry,* **127**, 163–168.

Ullrich, R., Ullrich, R., Crombach, G., and Peikert, V. (1972). *Three Flooding Procedures in the Treatment of Agoraphobia*, paper presented at the Second European Conference on Behaviour Modification, Wexford, Ireland.

'Vincent' (1919). Confessions of an agoraphobic victim, *American Journal of Psychology,* **30**, 295–299.

Vose, R. H. (1981). *Agoraphobia*, Faber & Faber, London.

Wagner, A. R. and Rescorla, R. A. (1972). Inhibition in Pavlovian conditioning: Applications of a theory, in *Inhibition and Learning*, (Eds R. A. Boakes and M. S. Halliday), Academic Press, New York.

Warburton, J. W. (1963). *Some Observations on the Aetiology of Phobic Anxiety*, Unpublished.

Watson, D. and Friend, R. (1969). Measurement of social-evaluative anxiety, *Journal of Consulting and Clinical Psychology,* **33**, 448–457.

Watson, J. B. and Rayner, R. (1920). Conditioned emotional reactions, *Journal of Experimental Psychology,* **3**, 1–14.

Watson, J. P., Gaind, R., and Marks, I. M. (1971). Prolonged exposure: A rapid treatment for phobias, *British Medical Journal,* **1**, 13–15.

Watson, J. P., Gaind, R., and Marks, I. M. (1972). Physiological habituation to continuous phobic stimulation, *Behaviour Research and Therapy,* **10**, 269–278.

Watson, J. P. and Marks, I. M. (1971). Relevant and irrelevant fear in flooding—A crossover study of phobic patients, *Behavior Therapy,* **2**, 275–293.

Watson, J. P., Mullett, G. E., and Pillay, H. (1973). The effects of prolonged exposure to phobic situations upon agoraphobic patients treated in groups, *Behaviour Research and Therapy,* **11**, 531–545.

Webster, A. S. (1953). The development of phobias in married women, *Psychological Monographs,* **67** (Whole No. 367).

Weekes, C. (1978). Simple, effective treatment of agoraphobia, *American Journal of Psychotherapy,* **32**, 357–369.
Weinman, B., Gelbart, P., Wallace, M., and Post, M. (1972). Inducing assertive behavior in chronic schizophrenics: A comparison of socioenvironmental, desensitization and relaxation therapies, *Journal of Consulting and Clinical Psychology,* **39**, 246–252.
Westphal, C. (1871–72). Die agoraphobie: eine neuropathische erscheinung, *Archiv für Psychiatrie und Nervenkrankheiten,* **3**, 138–171, 219–221.
Wheeler, E. O., White, P. D., Reed, E. W., and Cohen, M. E. (1950). Nemocirculatory asthenia (Anxiety neurosis, effort syndrome, neurasthenia), *Journal of American Medical Association*, **142**, 878–888.
Wilder, J. (1957). The law of initial value in neurology and psychiatry, *Journal of Nervous and Mental Disease,* **125**, 73.
Wilkins, W. (1973). Systematic desensitization and implosion: A theoretical rapprochement, *Psychotherapy: Theory, Research, and Practice*, **10**, 312–314.
Wilkins, W. (1979). Getting specific about nonspecifics, *Cognitive Therapy and Research,* **3**, 319–329.
Wilkins, W. and Thorpe, G. L. (1978). Critique and reformulation of multimodal behavior therapy, *Behavior Therapy,* **9**, 635–639.
Wilson, C. D. (1967). Social desirability and sex differences in expressed fear, *Behaviour Research & Therapy*, **5**, 136–137.
Wilson, G. T. (1973). Counterconditioning versus forced exposure in extinction of avoidance responding and conditioned fear in rats, *Journal of Comparative and Physiological Psychology,* **82**, 105–114.
Wilson, G. T. (1981a). Behavioural concepts and treatments of neuroses: Comments on Marks, *Behavioural Psychotherapy,* **9**, 155–166.
Wilson, G. T. (1981b). *Psychotherapy Process and Procedure: The Behavioral Mandate*. Presidential address to the 15th Annual AABT Convention, Toronto.
Wilson, G. T. and Davison, G. C. (1971). Processes of fear reduction in systematic desensitization: Animal studies, *Psychological Bulletin,* **76**, 1–14.
Wolfe, J. L. and Fodor, I. G. (1977). Modifying assertive behavior in women: A comparison of three approaches, *Behavior Therapy,* **8**, 567–574.
Wolman, B. B. (1973). *Dictionary of Behavioural Sciences*, MacMillan, London.
Wolpe, J. (1958). *Psychotherapy by Reciprocal Inhibition*, Stanford University Press, California.
Wolpe, J. (1969). *The Practice of Behavior Therapy*, Pergamon Press, New York.
Wolpe, J. (1970). Identifying the antecedents of an agoraphobic reaction: A transcript, *Journal of Behavior Therapy and Experimental Psychiatry*, **1**, 299–304.
Wolpe, J. (1973). *The Practice of Behavior Therapy* (2nd ed), Pergamon Press, New York.
Wolpe, J. (1976). Behavior therapy and its malcontents: II. Multimodal eclecticism, cognitive exclusivism and 'exposure' empiricism, *Journal of Behavior Therapy and Experimental Psychiatry,* **7**, 109–116.
Wolpe, J. and Lang, P. S. (1964). A fear survey schedule for use in behaviour therapy, *Behaviour Research and Therapy,* **2**, 27–30.
Wolpe, J. and Lazarus, A. A. (1966). *Behaviour Therapy Techniques,* Pergamon Press, Oxford.
Wood, P. (1941). De Costa's syndrome (or effort syndrome), *British Medical Journal*, **767**, 895.
Yates, A. J. (1962). *Frustration and Conflict*, Methuen, London.
Zaccheo, D. and Palmer, M. B. (1980). Agoraphobic-like behavior treated by recognition of and systematic desensitization to the theme, loss of control: A case report, *The Behavior Therapist,* **3**, 7–8.

Zitrin, C. M., Klein, D. F., Lindemann, C., Tobak, P., Rock, M., Kaplan, J. H., and Ganz, V. H. (1976). Comparison of short-term treatment regimens in phobic patients: A preliminary report, in *Evaluation of psychological therapies* (Eds R. Spitzer and D. Klein), Johns Hopkins University Press, Baltimore.

Zitrin, C., Klein, D. F., and Woerner, M. G. (1980). Treatment of agoraphobia with group exposure *in vivo* and imipramine, *Archives of General Psychiatry*, **37**, 63–72.

Author Index

(underlined page numbers refer to entries in the *References* Section)

Abraham, K., 3, *207*
Adams, N. E., 67, 183, *207*
Agras, W. S., 7, 81, 82, 138, 182, *207, 210, 215*
Agulnik, P., 42, *207*
Allen, R., *215*
Amatu, H. I., *222*
American Psychiatric Association, 72, *207*
Anger, D., 171, *207*
Arrindell, W. A., 6, *207*
Ascher, L. M., 78, 91, 104, *207*
Asso, D., 9, 23, 37, 50, *207*
Ayllon, T., 34, *207*

Bancroft, J. H. J., *212*
Bandura, A., 51, 67, 71, 73, 74, 77, 82, 95, 97, 98, 101, 104, 142, 176, 183, 186, 188, 189, 191, *207*
Barlow, D. H., 1, 45, 71, 77, 98, *207*, 208, 215
Barnes, G. S., 37, *222*
Bastien, S., *212*
Bebbington, P., 64, *216*
Beck, A. T., 68, *208*
Bedrosian, R., 94, *220*
Beech, H. R., 9, 23, 37, 50, 103, 114, *207, 211*
Beman, A. L., *221*
Benedikt, V., xvii, 3, *208*
Benjamin, S., 80, *208*
Berg, I., 8, 10, *208*
Berlin, F., *213*
Berne, R. M., *211*
Bernstein, D. A., 73, 75, 145, *207*, *208*
Biran, M., 97, 98, *208*
Blake, B. G., 108, *208*
Blakey, R. S., *222*
Bland, K., 8, 46, *208*
Blier, M. J., *222*
Boren, J. J., 171, 183, *211*
Boulougouris, J. C., 37, 82, 93, *208*, *217*, *219*
Bowen, R. C., 5, 8, 16, *208*
Bowlby, J., 51, 54, *208*
Brougham, L., *218*
Brown, R., 172, *208*
Buglass, D., 8–10, 15–17, 24, 29, 39, 40, 42, 50, 196, *208*
Burgess, I. S., 188, *208*
Burlington, M. A., *207*
Burns, L. E., 1, 6, 7, 19, 29, 31, 37, 39, 40, 50, 68, 79, 111, 112, 114, 145, *208, 209, 214, 222*
Burton, R., 2, *209*
Butz, R. A., *215*

Caine, T. M., 67, *209*
Cameron, R., 117, *218*
Candy, J., *222*
Carr, A. C., 7, 9, *212*
Catalan, J., *214*
Cattell, R. B., 61, 67, 86, 111, *209*
Cavallaro, L., *222*
Chambless, D. L., 9, 17, 18, 38, 40, 41, 51, 53, 54, 56, 58–61, 63–66, 68, 80, 100, 101, 103, 177–185, 189–191, 198, 203, 205, *209, 212*
Cheshire, N. M., 34, 63, 76, *209*
Chiari, G., 78, *209*

Clapman, H. I., 7, *209*
Clarke, J., *208*
Clevenger, S. W., 4, *209*
Cobb, J. P., 47, *209, 217*
Cohen, M. E., *223*
Cohen-Kettenis, P., 40, *210*
Coleman, J. V., 7, *211*
Coleman, R. E., 70, 78, *209*
Cone, J. D., 70, 71, 72, *209*
Cooper, B., 9, *214*
Cooper, M., 6, 9, *216*
Cordes, E., 4, *210*
Costello, C. G., 171, 181, *210*
Crisp, A. H., 67, *210*
Crombach, G., *222*
Crowe, M. J., 66, 67, 92, 138, 193, *210*
Crown, S., 67, *210*

D'Amato, M. R., 169, *210*
Davison, G. C., 15, 38, 64, 80, 171, 177, 180, *210, 223*
DeLo, J. S., *212*
Delprato, D. J., 35, 170, 174, 175, *210*
De Monchaux, C., *210*
De Silva, P., 173, *210*
Diener, E., *221*
DiLoreto, A. O., 69, *210*
Dinsmoor, J. A., 171, *210*
Dittmar, K., *220*
Dixon, J. J., 5, 136, *210*
Dugas, L., 15, *210*
D'Zurilla, T., 145, *212*

Edwardes, J. A., *215*
Eggeratt, J. B., *211*
Eisler, R., *214*
Ellis, A., 96, 104, 107, 201, *210*
Emmelkamp, P. M. G., 37, 40, 41, 45–48, 55, 56, 72, 73, 75, 76, 81, 83, 85, 86, 96, 97, 105, 136, 138, 145, 170, 174, 176, 178, 181, 186, 187, 189, 190, *210, 211*
Emmelkamp-Benner, A., 47, *210*
Errera, P., 7, *211*
Ervin, F., *212*
Evans, I. M., 52, *211*
Evans, M. B., 144, *211*
Evans, P. D., 80, 136, 141, *211*
Everaerd, W. T., 90, 91, 138, 193, *211*
Eysenck, H. J., 2, 69, 103, 112, 167, 170, 171, 175–177, 179, 191, *211*

Fedoravicius, A., *218*
Feist, J. R., 143, *211*
Feldman, M. P., 168, *211*
Field, G. E., 171, 183, *211*
Findley, J. D., 171, *211*
Fink, M., 99, *215*
Fishman, S., 37, 52, 53, *211*
Fix, A. J., 146, *211*
Flint, G. A., *210*
Foa, E. B., 85, 186, *209, 211*
Fodor, I., 9, 36, 38, 66, 95, 183, 184, *211, 223*
Foulds, G. A., 114, *209, 212*
Frank, J. D., 141, 144, *212*
Franks, C. M., 77, 95, 96, 101, 102, 170, 171, 174, 176, 187, *212*
Frazier, S. H., 7, 9, *212*
Fredrikson, M., *219*
Freedman, E. G., *222*
Freeman, N. T., 7, *209*
Freud, S., 3, 4, 81, *212*
Friedman, D. E., 23, 50, *212*
Friend, R., 69, 112, 136, *222*
Fry, W., 42, 44, *212*

Gaind, R., *222*
Galassi, J. P., 67, *212*
Galassi, M. D., *212*
Ganz, V. H., *224*
Garcia, J., 174, 175, *212*
Gardner, R., *217*
Garside, R. T., 5, *220*
Gath, D. H., 101, *212, 214*
Gathercole, C. E., 67, *212*
Gelbart, P., *223*
Gelder, M. G., 8, 9, 10, 11, 17, 20, 21, 39, 40, 48, 64, 69, 72, 73, 79, 80, 82, 89, 93, 94, 99, 103, 131, 134, 136, 144, 189, 190, 193, *212, 214, 217, 218*
George, A. J., 9, *212*
Gillan, P., 11, 80, 131, 134, 136, 138, 169, 183, *212*
Gilmore, J. B., *218*
Goldfried, M. R., 145, *212*
Goldstein, A. J., 9, 17, 18, 22, 38, 40–42, 52–54, 56, 58–61, 63–65, 80, 101, 177, 179–184, 190, 191, 198, 203–205, *209, 212*
Golombok, S., 66
Gosling, J., 145, *213*
Gottman, J. M., 141, *213*
Gournay, K., *213*
Greer, J. H., 6, *213*
Greist, J. H., 83, *213*
Grey, S. J., *217*
Grossberg, J. M., 62, *13*

Groves, G. A., *209*
Guidano, V., 45, *216*
Gurnay, C., *220*

Haffke, E. A., 146, *211*
Hafner, R. J., 5, 38, 41, 42, 44–47, 61, 66–68, 72, 89, 90, 101, 105, 188, 189, *213, 218*
Hager, J. L., 170, 173, *220*
Hajioff, J., *216*
Hallam, R. S., 5, 6, 8, 37, 38, 41, 46, 49, 58, 60, 65, 68, 72, 75, *208, 213*
Hand, I., 38, 41, 43, 44, 47, 48, 61, 75, 85, 88–91, 95, 96, 187, 188, *213*
Hardy, A. B., *207*
Hare, E. H., 7, *213*
Harper, M., 4, 10, 15, 22, 39, *213*
Harper, R. A., 107, *210*
Harris, B., 170, *213*
Harrison, D. F., 67, *213*
Hartman, M., *218*
Harzem, P., 62, *213*
Haughton, E., *207*
Hawkrigg, J. J., 13, 15, 16, *213*
Hay, L. R., *208*
Hayes, S. C., 70, *219*
Heimberg, R. G., 67, *213*
Henderson, A. S., *208*
Hendry, D. P., 171, 183, *213*
Hernstein, R. J., 172, 177, 183, *213*
Hersen, M., 5, 142, *214*
Herst, E. R., 5, 8, 11, 12, 19, 68, 72, *217*
Heseltine, G. F. D., *221*
Hineline, P., 77, 168, 172, 183, *213, 214*
Hollingshead, A. B., 6, 7, *214*
Holmes, T. H., 62, *214*
Hope, K., 114, *209, 212*
Horn, S., *222*
Howells, G. N., *207*
Hudson, B., 46, *214*
Hugdahl, K., *219*
Huggins, P., *216*
Hughes, H. B., *207*
Hull, C. L., 169, *214*
Huson, J., *208*
Hussain, M. Z., 93, 100, *214*

Jacobsen, E., 114, *214*
Jameson, J. S., *211*
Janda, L. H., *220*
Jannoun, L., 70, 83, 91, *214*
Jerremalm, A., *219*
Johansson, J., *219*
Johnston, D. W., 6, 48, 87, 101, 188, 190, 194, *212, 214, 217, 218*
Johnston, M., 68, *214*
Jones, R. B., 90, *214, 221*

Kanfer, F. H., 57, 65, *214*
Kantor, J. S., 36, *214*
Kaplan, J. H., *224*
Katkin, E. S., 65, 69, 71, 73, 75–77, *216*
Kazdin, A. E., 72, 74–76, 87, 146, *214*
Kedwood, H. B., 9, *214*
Keehn, J. D., 172, *214*
Kellam, A. M. P., 80, 136, 141, *211*
Kelly, D., *222*
Kendall, P. C., 70, *214*
Kerr, T. A., 5, *220*
Kihlstrom, J. F., 179, 181, 182, *218*
Kimble, G. A., 179, *215*
Klein, D. F., 3, 9, 99, 102, *215, 224*
Koelling, R. A., 174, *212*
Kohout, J., 5, 16, *208*
Kolb, L. C., 9, *215*
Korgeski, G. P., 70, *214*
Kraepelin, E., 4, *215*
Kreitman, N., *208*
Krumboltz, J. D., 114, *215*
Kuipers, A. C. M., 47, 138, *210, 211*
Kulberg, G., *222*

Lader, M., 8, *215*
Lamontagne, Y., 41, 43, 44, 47, 61, 188, *213*
Lancashire, M., *214, 217, 221*
Lancaster, D. W., *220*
Lang, P. J., 70, 71, 75, 142, *215*
Lang, P. S., 68, *223*
Langner, T. S., 6, *215*
Lanyon, R. I., 6, *216*
LaPierre, Y., *221*
Lapouse, R., 22, *215*
Last, C. G., 98, *215*
Law, S., 5, *215*
Lazarus, A. A., 38, 41, 53, 57–59, 63, 70, 95, 107, 108, 116, 184, 189, *215*
Lazell, D., 5, *215*
Lazovik, A. D., 75, *215*
Ledwidge, B., 95, *215, 221*
Lee, I., *222*
Legrand du Saule, H., 4, 14, *215*
Leiblum, S. R., *213*
Leitenberg, H., 70, 81, 138, 145, 193, *207, 210, 215*
Lemkau, P., 6, *216*
Leonard, W. E., 4, 5, 13, 14, *216*

Levis, D. J., 79, *221*
Lick, J. R., 65, 69, 71, 73, 75–77, 146, *216*
Liddell, H., 179, *216*
Lindemann, C., *224*
Linder, L. H., 78, *216*
Liotti, G., 45, *216*
Lipsedge, M. S., 10, 99, 100, *208, 216, 217*
Lowen, A., 107, *216*

MacCulloch, M. J., 168, *211*
Mahoney, M. J., 52, *216*
Mancini, F., 78, *216*
Manosevitz, M., 6, *216*
Marks, I. M., 5, 7, 8, 9, 10, 11, 12, 14, 15, 16, 19, 20, 21, 22, 23, 25, 34, 35, 39, 40, 42, 47, 52, 53, 56, 60, 64, 67, 68, 72, 73, 78, 79, 81–85, 88–93, 95, 99, 101–103, 105, 111, 134, 135, 141, 145, 166, 170, 174, 177, 178, 185–187, 190, 191, *208–210, 212, 213, 216, 217, 221, 222*
Marset, P., *208, 217*
Masserman, J. H., 179, 182, *217*
Mathews, A. M., 36, 38, 48, 49, 56, 63–65, 70, 72, 73, 75, 79, 82–87, 91, 92, 94, 95, 131, 134, 136, 138, 144, 170, 178, 183–185, 187–190, 193, 195, 196, *212, 214, 217, 221*
Mavissakalian, M., 1, *208*
McClure, D. J., *221*
McDonald, R., 8, 90, 91, *209, 217*
McFall, R. M., 66, 108, 142, *217*
McGennis, A., 39, 218
McGuire, R., 10, *208*
McLaren, S., *218*
McPherson, F. M., 9, 49, *218*
Measey, G., 42, *222*
Meichenbaum, D., 69, 95, 96, 108, 117, 163, *218*
Meyer, V., 79, *218*
Michael, S. T., 6, *215*
Miles, T. R., 62, *213*
Miller, M. L., 3, *218*
Miller, N. E., 179, *218*
Miller, P. M., *214*
Milton, F., 41, 44, 45, 47, 66, 67, 101, 188, *213, 218*
Mineka, S., 179, 181, 182, *218*
Mischel, W., 142, *218*
Mittelman, B., 42, *218*
Monk, M. A., 22, *215*
Morris, L. A., *220*
Morton, L., *221*
Mosticone, R., 78, *209*
Moutier, F., 15, *210*
Mowrer, O. H., 167, 169, *218*
Mullaney, J. A., 41, *218*
Mullett, G. E., *222*
Munby, M., 6, 48, *214, 217, 218*

Nahl, M., *220*
Nakamura, C. Y., 7, *220*
Napalkov, S. V., 175, *219*
Napier, L., *216*
Neale, J. M., 38, 64, 180, *210*
Nelson, R. O., 70, *219*
Nemiah, J. C., 15, *219*
Nevid, J. S., 67, *219*
Nietzel, M. T., 73, 75, 144, 145, *207, 208, 219*
Nolan, G., *218*
Noshirvani, H., *213*

O'Brien, G. T., 98, *215*
O'Brien, J. S., 78, *219*
Ohman, A., 170, 173, 174, *219*
Oliveau, D., *207*
Orwin, A., 78, *219*
Ost, L. G., 36, *219*
Overmier, J. B., 182, *219*

Palmer, M. B., 52, 60, 80, *223*
Parker, G., 40, 41, *219*
Patterson, C. H., 179, *219*
Pavlov, I. P., 179, *219*
Payne, L. L., *211*
Pearce, J., *216*
Pecknold, J., *221*
Peikert, V., *222*
Perissaki, C., *219*
Phares, E. J., 64, *219*
Pike, D. J., *216*
Pillay, H., *222*
Pinkston, S. G., *214*
Popler, K., 78, *219*
Post, M., *223*
Presley, A. S., *208*
Prince, M., 4, *219*
Putman, J. J., 4, *219*

Rabavilas, A. D., 194, *219*
Rachman, S., 11, 51, 80, 131, 134, 136, 138, 167, 169, 170, 174, 176, 179, 183, 191, *210–212, 219*
Rahe, R. H., 62, *214*
Ramsay, R., 12, *219*

Rathus, S. A., 67, *219*
Raven, J. C., 11, 111, *219*
Raymond, E., 5, *220*
Rayner, R., 34, 170, *222*
Redlich, F. C., 6, 7, *214*
Reed, E. W., *223*
Reiss, S., 167, 176, 186, 188, *220*
Rescorla, R. A., 167, 176, *220, 222*
Rezin, V., 95, *217*
Rich, M., *216*
Rijken, H. M., *211*
Rimm, D. C., 51, *220*
Roberts, A. H., 22, 39, *220*
Rock, M., *224*
Rosenthal, D., 35, *220*
Rosenthal, T. L., 143, *211*
Ross, J., 146, *220*
Roth, M., 2, 3, 4, 5, 9, 10, 15, 22, 23, 39, 40, 50, *213, 220, 221*
Rotter, J. B., 40, 47, *220*
Rudestam, K. E., 94, *220*
Rutner, I. V., 142, *220*
Rutter, M., 8, 23, *220*
Rycroft, C., 2, *220*

Sandler, J., *210*
Sartory, G., *217*
Saslow, G., 57, 65, *214*
Sassaroli, S., *216*
Sauvages, F. B. de, 2, *220*
Schachter, S., 117, 162, *220*
Schapira, K., 5, *220*
Scherer, M. W., 7, *220*
Schofield, L. D., *208*
Schuster, C. R., *211*
Sclare, E. B., 7, *209*
Scott-Fordham, A., *214, 221*
Seligman, M. E. P., 34, 55, 168, 170, 173, 182, *210, 219, 220*
Semerari, A., *216*
Shafar, S., 8, 9, 10, 12, 17, 39, 40, 51, *220*
Shapiro, A. K., 144, *220*
Shaw, P. M., 84, 95, 185, *212, 214, 217*
Shenger-Krestovnikova, N. R., 179
Sidman, M., 168, 171, *221*
Sinnott, A., 38, 91, 193, *214, 221*
Skinner, B. F., 188, *221*
Slater, E., 2, *221*
Smith, P. J., 205, *222*
Smith, R. E., 143, *221*
Smith, R. F., *210*
Snaith, R. P., 3, 5, 9, 39, *221*
Solomon, R. L., 167, *220*
Solyom, C., 102, *221*
Solyom, L., 8, 9, 99, *221*
Spencer, W. A., 186, *221*
Stampfl, T. G., 79, *221*
Steinberg, D., 99, *222*
Steinberg, G., *221*
Stern, R. S., 47, 84, 85, 186, *209, 217, 221*
Stuart, R. B., 67, *221*
Sylvester, D., *207*

Teasdale, J. D., 73, 75, 89, 90, 91, 141, *217, 221*
Terhune, W., 7, 39, 40, *221*
Thompson, L. E., *215*
Thompson, R. F., 186, *221*
Thorpe, G. L., 6, 7, 19, 37, 39, 40, 50, 59–61, 63, 66, 68, 70, 74, 76–78, 95, 168, 188, *209, 214, 221—223*
Thoreson, C. E., 114, *215*
Tietza, C., 6, *216*
Tizzard, J., *220*
Tobak, P., *224*
Torpy, D., 42, *222*
Trippett, C. J., 41, *218*
Tucker, W. I., 9, *222*
Turk, D., 117, *218*
Turner, R. M., *211*
Twentyman, C. I., 66, 142, *217*
Tyrer, P., 78, 99, *222*

Ullrich, R., 100, *222*
Ultee, K. A., 47, 81, *211*

Viemeister, N. F., *210*
'Vincent', 4, *222*
Viswanathan, R., *217*
Vose, R. H., 14, *222*

Wagner, A. R., 176, *222*
Wallace, M., *223*
Walsh, P. A., *221*
Warburton, J. W., 9, *222*
Warzburt, W. A., *211*
Watson, D., 69, 112, 136, *222*
Watson, J. B., 34, 170, *222*
Watson, J. P., 47, 72, 73, 75, 77, 82, 83, 87–89, 138, 144, 177, 178, 185, *222*
Webster, A. S., 9, 41, *222*
Weekes, C., 201, *223*
Weinman, B., 69, *223*
Wessels, H., 47, 85, 86, 138, *211*
Westphal, C., xxvii, 2, 3, 12, 14, 25, 60, *223*

Wheeler, E. D., 9, *223*
White, P. D., 9, *223*
Whitmore, K., *220*
Wilcoxon, L. A., 146, *214*
Wilder, J., 141, *223*
Wilkes, H., *214*
Wilkins, W., 59–61, 70, 79, 188, 189, *222, 223*
Wilson, C. D., 9, *223*
Wilson, G. T., 77, 95–98, 101, 102, 168–171, 174, 176, 177, 180, 186, 187, 198, *208, 212, 223*
Wilson, H. K., 6, *213*
Wincze, J. P., *215*
Woerner, M. G., *215, 224*
Wolfe, J. L., 66, 95, *223*
Wolff, H., *212*
Wolman, B. B., 2, *223*
Wolpe, J., 22, 42, 52, 54, 60, 67, 68, 70, 78, 80, 98, 99, 116, 166, 169, 179, 180, 184, 185, *223*
Wood, P., 9, *223*
Woodward, R., *221*
Wright, D. E., *215*

Yates, A. J., 179, 191, *223*

Zaccheo, D., 52, 60, 80, *223*
Zeldis, S. M., *214*
Zimmerman, J., *211*
Zitrin, C. M., 102, 177, *214, 215, 224*
Zwerdling, A. B., *222*

Subject Index

ABAB design, 81
'acceptance', 201
additive research strategy, 106
adjusting avoidance, 171
aetiological factors, 34–55
  correlational nature of data, 34
age of onset, 8, 23, 135
agoraphobia as a distinct clinical entity, 5, 6
agoraphobia questionnaire (Burns, 1977), 111, 115, 122, 126
  section 36, 29–31, 111–113, 115, 123, 124, 126–128, 130, 132–134, 136, 141, 150, 151
  section 39, 31–33, 111–113, 115, 123, 124, 126–128, 130, 132–134, 136, 138, 139, 141, 142, 152, 153, 165
agoraphobia questionnaires, 68
'Alan' (case illustration), 202–203
'Albert B.', 170
alcohol, 3
alcoholism, 37, 41, 44
Alprenelol, 100
Anatomy of Melancholy, 2
anti-depressant medication, 44, 88, 99, 194
anxiety hierarchy, 74, 79, 93, 120
anxiety hysteria, 3
anxiety neurosis, *see* generalized anxiety disorder
anxiety syndrome, 3
'anxious-patient' families, 46
apprehension, 3
assertiveness, 53, 54, 58, 61–63, 95, 183, 189, 200
assessment, 56–77
associated symptomatology, 15–17
assortative mating, 42–44, 47
asynchrony of response measures, 71
attention-placebo groups, 87
attribution effects, 99, 101, 202
autobiographical accounts, 4, 5
autonomic measures, *see* psychophysiological assessment
aversion relief, 99
aversion therapy, 168
avoidance, 168, 170–172

'BASIC ID', 59, 60, 108
Beck Depression Inventory, 68
'Becky' (case illustration), 204–205
behaviour analytic model, 145
behavioural assessment, 69, 74–76, 83–86, 182
behavioural avoidance tests, 70, 75
behavioural counselling (modified), 114, 120, 160, 161
'behavioural forgery', 34
behavioural system, 1
behavioural tests
  Arndale Centre, 113–115, 121, 122, 125, 133, 138, 139, 143
  top three hierachy items, 113–115, 121, 125, 128, 133, 136, 138, 139, 143
  unaccompanied walk, 112, 113, 115, 122, 123, 125–128, 131–134, 137–141, 143, 144, 165
benefit ratings, 112, 115, 122, 123, 126, 130–133
bereavement, 10, 23, 24, 50, 205
Bernreuter Personality Inventory, 67
bioenergetics, 107

biofeedback, 78
birth, 24
bizarre behaviour, 34
blocking (response-prevention), 180
blood-injury phobia, 72
blushing, 3, 52
brief standard self-rating form, 72
broad spectrum behaviour therapy, 53

case manager, 57
characteristics of phobias, 1, 2
childhood problems, 10, 11, 21, 22
Chlordiazepoxide, 99
Chlorpromazine, 98
cinematic films of phobic material, 78
classical conditioning, 51, 53, 167–170, 173–177
climacteric, 9
clinical descriptions of agoraphobia, 60
clinical paradigm for exposure treatment, 166, 186
clinical series, 78, 83
clinicians' assessments, 113, 115, 122, 125, 131, 132, 143, 154
Codeine, 98
cognitive assessment, 70
cognitive-behaviour therapy, *see* cognitive restructuring
'cognitive modality', the, 4, 14, 29, 58, 104
cognitive restructuring, 45, 60, 69, 78, 95–98, 194, 198, 201–202
  compared with *in vivo* exposure, 96–97
cognitive set, 89, 91, 104, 187
cognitive system, 1
College Self–Expression Scale, 67
complex agoraphobia, 17, 18, 41, 54, 58, 64, 65, 180, 183, 203, 205
'compulsory marriage', 44
conditioned aversive temporal stimuli, 172
conditioned inhibition, 169, 179
conditioned response, 167–172
conditioned stimulus, 167–172
  and anxiety expectations, 188
conditioning events, 51
conflict, 179–182
contract, 110, 122, 146, 147
controlled trial
  discussion, 136–146
  Experiment I
    definition of
    assessment, 111–114, 115
    agoraphobia, 109, 110
    discussion, 129–134
    procedure, 117–121
    researchers, 111
    results, 122–126
    subjects, 110, 111
    therapists, 111
    treatment, 114, 116, 117
  Experiment II
    procedure, 121, 122
    rationale, 121
    results, 126–129
  hypotheses, 109
  rationale, 107, 108
converging operational definitions, 141
conversion reactions (somatoform disorder), 38, 41, 179–180
coping strategies, 29, 58, 65, 83, 85, 89, 95, 108, 178
covert conditioning, 176
cross-over studies, 47, 80–82, 91–92, 96, 100
crowds, 4
cumulative scales, 68–69

daily record of counter-phobic activities, 70, 201
Daily Record of Dysfunctional thoughts, 70
definition of agoraphobia, 146, 147
delusions, 3, 16
demand characteristics, 73, 75–76, 143–146
dental phobia, 95
dependency, 38, 40–41, 53–54, 61
depersonalization, 5, 8, 15, 72, 196
depression, 5, 6, 8, 11, 16, 43–44, 47–49, 59, 61, 66, 72, 188, 193, 194
  and prognosis for agoraphobia treatment, 88, 194
derealization, 8, 15
diagnostic classifications, 64
Diazepam, 89, 99–101, 105
  and group *in vivo* exposure, 101
  and *in vivo* exposure, 100–101
Die Agoraphobie, 2
direct associative experience, 51
discrimination theory, of extinction of avoidance behaviour, 169
discriminative stimulus, 171
drive-reduction, 169
drug dependency, 60
duration of illness, 30, 33
dynamic unconscious, 191

dysphoric mood, 98

early accounts, 2–4
educating the patient, 195–196
educational status, 11
electrodermal response, 35, 77, 82–84, 92, 182
emotional arousal and conditioning, 37
  child-birth, 37
  menstrual cycle, 37
  pregnancy, 37
emotional stability, 38, 86
enuresis, 10, 21
epidemiology, 6, 7
epilepsy, 3, 15
equipotentiality, 170, 173
escape, 168, 170–172
ethical issues, 203–206
evoked response, 186
evoking stimulus, 186
expectancy
  in classical conditioning, 176
  of benefit, 69, 93–94, 99, 189–190
  of harm, 183
expectancy ratings, 112, 115, 122, 123, 129–130, 136, 139, 140
experimental neurosis, 179, 181
experimental subjects, characteristics, 148, 149
extincton, 78, 84, 91, 167–184, 185
extraversion scale (E), 123, 127, 130, 131, 133, 134, 136, 138–140
eyeblink responses, 35
Eysenck Personality Inventory, 69, 94, 112, 113, 115, 123, 126, 127, 130–134, 138, 139

factor-analytic studies, 5, 6, 68, 72
failure of extinction, 174
family background, 39, 46
family nervous disorder, 22, 30, 33
fear of fear, 14, 18
Fear of Negative Evaluation Scale, 69, 112, 113, 115, 122, 123, 126, 127, 130, 133–135, 138, 139
Fear Survey Schedule, 6, 68
fears
  childhood, 21
  confinement, 13
  fainting, 24
  situational, 12
features associated with treatment, 12
flooding, 82–106
  see also imaginal *and in vivo* exposure
fluctuations, 14, 25, 26
follow-up studies, 47–49, 79–87, 89–92, 99–103
fore-arm blood flow, 35
former agoraphobics as therapists, 97, 146
free association, 92, 189
'free-floating' anxiety, 88

'Garcia effect', 174
general benefit ratings, 113–115, 122, 124, 131
generalization, of treatment effects, 75, 82, 97
generalized anxiety disorder, 5, 6, 16, 35, 41, 58, 60
genetic contributions, 35
Gestalt therapy, 107
graded practice, 79, 81–82, 90, 92–93, 169, 193–194
  compared with imaginal exposure and systematic desensitization, 92–93
  see also reinforced graded practice
'group panic', 89
group treatment, 38, 48, 78, 87–92, 101–102, 194
  and Diazepam, 101
  and Imipramine, 102
  and Propranolol, 101–102
guilt feelings, 26–28
Guttman scaling, 68

habituation, 35, 78, 84, 91, 94, 178, 185–186
  of electrodermal response, 35
Hawthorne effect, 76
heart rate, 36, 71, 77, 82–92, 92, 94, 98, 182
Hippocrates, 2
home-based treatment, 49, 65, 83, 87, 91, 187, 193
  follow-up study, 49
'homework' assignments, 104, 196
hormonal influences, 37
horreur du vide, 3
Hostility and Direction of Hostility Questionnaire, 67
hypochondriasis, 8, 17
hypoglycaemia, 59, 180
'hysterical personality', 17, 38
Hysteroid/Obsessoid Questionnaire, 67

imaginal exposure, 49, 79, 82–106, 169, 193
  brief *vs*. protracted, 84–85, 186

imaginal exposure–*cont.*
compared with graded practice, 92–93
compared with *in vivo* exposure, 85–87
compared with systemic desensitization, 80, 92–95
in groups, 87–88
irrelevant-fear stimuli, 83–84
with Methohexitone, 100
with Thiopental, 100
Imipramine, 99, 102
and group *in vivo* exposure, 102
and supportive psychotheraphy, 102
and systematic desensitization, 102
implosion, 79
in vivo exposure, 40, 45, 48, 49, 63–65, 79, 82–106, 169, 193–194
brief *vs.* protracted, 84–85, 186
compared with cognitive restructuring, 96–97
in groups, 87–90
patient-controlled, 90–92
with Diazepam, 100–101
with Imipramine, 102
with Phenelzine, 102
with Propranolol, 101–102
'incubation' of conditioned responses, 175
indecisiveness, 29
independent clinician ratings, 48, 72
see also clinicians' assessments
informational model, of classical conditioning, 176
instrumental learning, 168–169, 170–172
integrated model, of agoraphobic aetiology, 183
intellectual status, 11
interpersonal relationships, 17, 21, 38, 41–47, 61, 180
interview, 65–66, 114
Iproniazid, 99–100
and systematic desensitization, 99
irrelevant-fear stimuli, 83–84, 185

jealousy, 43–46

law of initial values, 141
learned helplessness, 34, 55, 182
Leonard, autobiographical account, 3, 4
lie scale (L), 123, 127, 130, 134
life changes, 15, 23
light-headedness, 53
limitations of research findings, 195
locomotor anxiety, 3
locus of control, 40, 47, 184
internal–external control scale, 47
long-term treatment effects, *see* follow-up studies
loss of control, as central phobic element, 51, 61
low back pain, 45

male agoraphobics, 3, 9, 37, 45, 98
marital problems, 35, 38, 41–48, 54, 59, 61–63, 78, 105, 180, 188, 204–206
assessment of, 47
exposure treatment and, 47
treatment of, 47, 189
see also marital relationships
marital questionnaires, 66–67
marital relationships, 23, 26, 27, 135
marital status, 9, 20, 22, 30, 32, 135
massing of practice, 85, 95, 186
Maudsley Hospital Questionnaire, 67
Maudsley Marital Questionnaire, 66–67
menopause, 9
menstruation, 9
Meprobamate, 98
Methohexitone, 99, 100
and imaginal exposure, 100
and systematic desensitization, 99
Mill Hill vocabulary scale, 11, 111, 114, 122, 126, 134
minor tranquillizers, 100–102, 104–105, 194
miscarriage, 24, 50
Mitral Valve Prolapse syndrome, 36
modelling, 48, 82, 88
'negative modelling', 96
Monoamine Oxidase Inhibitor, 99
morbidity in children, 10
motivation, 12
multimodal behaviour therapy, 59, 63, 78, 166, 188
multiple schedule, 171

nail biting, 21
Napalkov phenomenon, 175
narrow band approaches, 107
National Survey of Agoraphobics, 68
negative reinforcement, 54, 169, 170
neurotic introverts, 176
neuroticism scale (N), 123, 127, 130, 133, 134, 136, 139, 140
new problem emergence after treatment, 49
night terrors/mares, 10, 21, 204

non-specific insecurity fears, 3
non-specific treatment effects, 141, 144, 167, 189–190
nosographic and nosologic terms, 62
nurse therapists, 145

obsessive compulsive behaviours, 8, 16, 17, 37, 47, 72
occupational adjustment, 49
occupational disablement, 11, 20, 21, 26, 27, 28, 30, 32, 135
occupations, 20
Open Door, The, 42
open spaces, 2, 3
orgasmic dysfunction, 43–44
overinclusion, 8

palpitations, 3, 36, 98, 101
panic attacks, 5, 13, 15, 16, 24, 25, 29, 58, 63, 80, 88–89, 98, 135, 166, 177, 180–185, 193, 194, 196–199
  and prognosis for agoraphobia treatment, 88, 194
paradoxical intention, 78, 91, 104, 198
paranoia, 43, 45, 188
parental attitudes, 21
pathogenic interaction, 42–43
personal psychological effect, 26–28
personality deviance, 17
personality variables, 11, 12, 38
peur des espaces, 3
pharmacological treatment, 44, 78, 88, 98–103, 194
  antidepressants, 44, 88, 102–103, 194
  barbiturates, 99–100
  minor tranquillizers, 100–102, 194
Phenelzine, 99, 102
  and *in vivo* exposure, 102
phobic-anxiety-depersonalization syndrome, 3, 15
phobic anxious states, 3
phobic society, 19
phobics among psychiatric patients, 7
phobos, 1
physical activity, 78
physical confinement, 167, 181–191
physiological correlates of agoraphobia, 35–36
placebo effects, 76, 94, 99–103
'Platzangst', 3
'Platzschwindel', xvii, 3
positive reinforcement, 182–183
precipitaing factors, 23, 24, 50–51
pregnancy, 23, 37, 50
preparedness, 170, 173–174
prevalence rates, 6, 7
prognosis, 45, 88, 202, 206
prognostic variables, 138
Propranolol, 101–102
  and group *in vivo* exposure, 101–102
psychoanalytic therapy, 107
psychological assessment of therapeutic outcome, 140–144
psychological gain; *see* secondary gain
psychophysiological assessment, 70–71, 77, 82, 87–92, 94
psychophysiological system, 1
psychotheraphy, 79, 93
  'associative psychotheraphy', 93
  're-educative psychotherapy', 93
psychotic reaction, 44
punishment, 177, 181

questionnaires, 66–69

Rathus Assertiveness Schedule, 67
rating scales of phobic severity, 47–49, 66, 72–73, 83–84
  standard fear-avoidance scales, 72–73
rational-emotive therapy, 96, 107, 201
reactive inhibition, 169, 179
reactivity of behavioural assessment, 76, 190
reciprocal inhibition, 179, 184
reinforced graded practice, 116, 117, 120, 144, 162
relapse, 44–46, 71, 98, 99, 103
relationships with parents, 21
relatives' assessments, 114, 115, 121, 122, 126, 131, 143, 155, 156
relaxation training, 80, 114, 120, 183, 198–199, 201–202
religious preferences, 20, 135
repressive response style, 17
retrospective studies, 79, 181
reversal design, *see* ABAB design

saline-injected control group, 99–100
satiation, 178
schedule of assessment/therapeutic sessions 157, 158, 159
school phobia/fears, 10, 21
secondary gain, 39–40, 61, 182
secondary phobias, 68
self-efficacy theory, 73–74, 82, 95, 97, 104, 166, 183, 186–188
  and imaginal exposure, 187

self-efficacy theory–*contd.*
  assessment of self-efficacy expectations, 67, 73–74
  predicted anxiety *in vivo*, 94
self-exposure homework, 90–91
self-help groups, 38–39, 203
self-instructional training, *see* cognitive restructuring
self-monitoring, 69–70, 81, 85, 201
self-observation, *see* self-monitoring
self-report measures, 142, 145
self-statements, 58, 60, 66, 89, 178
self-sufficiency, 17, 40, 58, 64, 66, 122, 180
semantic conditioning, 54
semantic differential ratings, 87–88, 94
semi-automated treatment, 80
separation anxiety, 54
separation during childhood, 21
sex differences, 8, 9, 20–24, 26, 28, 29, 35–37, 135
  prevalence of agoraphobia, 35
  reasons to account for, 9
sex-role stereotyping, 36–37
sexual dysfunction, 45, 46, 61–62, 188
'sick' families, 46
side-effects of treatment, 204
Sidman avoidance, 171–172
simple agoraphobia, 17, 18, 64, 65, 180
single-subject experiments, 81–82
situational confidence ratings, 74
situational specificity, 74–75
Sixteen Personality-Factor Questionnaire, 61, 67, 69, 86, 111, 114, 115, 122, 124, 126, 128, 130–132, 134–136, 138–140
skin conductance, *see* electrodermal response
sleep walking, 21
snake phobics, 183
Social Avoidance and Distress Scale, 69, 112–113, 115, 122, 123, 126, 127, 130, 133–136, 138–140
social cohesion, 88, 90
social contacts, lack of, 26–28
social learning theory, 51, 71, 183
social phobia, 35–36, 45, 72, 94, 99–100, 183, 189, 200
  behavioural *vs.* physiological reactors, 36
social reinforcement, 78, 81, 82
sociocultural factors, 9, 11
socioenvironmental treatment, 69
space phobia, 64
specific fears during childhood, 10, 11
specific phobias, 16, 80, 83, 94, 97, 189
speech anxiety, 95
spider phobics, 84, 95
spouse of the agoraphobic, 38, 41, 65, 90, 195–196, 200–201
stammering, 21
standard progressive matrices, 11, 111, 114, 122, 126, 134
standardization of outcome measures, 145
statistical definitions of treatment effectiveness, 146
strategems, 14, 15
street fear, 3
stress, 46, 50, 62, 184
  resulting from treatment, 46, 61–62
stress inoculation, 95–96, 117, 120, 162–164
structured groups, 88–94, 95
successive approximation, *see* graded practice
suicide attempts, 45
supportive psychotherapy, 40, 102
  with Imipramine, 102
symbolic instruction, 51
symbolic logic, 51
sympathy of others, 28
symptom sign inventory, 114–115, 120, 125, 131
'symptom substitution', 43
'symptom-symbol' hypothesis, 50
syndrome, 62–65
system-method-content confounds, 72
systematic desensitization, 36, 40, 49, 54, 59, 63–68, 69, 78–80, 103, 116, 161, 169, 192–193
  compared with graded practice, 92–93
  compared with imaginal exposure, 80, 92–95
  role of muscular relaxation, 80
  with Imipramine, 102
  with Iproniazid, 99
  with Methohexitone, 99
  with Thiopental, 100

Tavistock self assessment inventory, 136
temporal lobe dysfunction, 4, 15
temporal lobe epilepsy, 39
tension, 14
test anxiety, 95
therapist characteristics, 194–195
therapists effects, 126, 133

Thiopental, 100
  and imaginal exposure, 100
  and systematic desensitization, 100
thought-stopping, 78, 201, 202
thumb-sucking, 21
traumatic experiences, 23, 24
travel restrictions, 26–28
treatment helpfulness, 22
treatment manuals, 83, 161–164, 196
treatment plan, 199–200
tricyclic antidepressant, 99
triple-response-mode assessment, 70
twin studies, 35
two-factor theory, 71, 77, 167–177, 187, 197
types of agoraphobia, 17–18

unconditioned response, 167
underinclusion, 8
unhappy childhood, 10, 51

vaginismus, 43
validity
  of behavioural assessment, 76
  of self-report measures, 73
  see also psychological assessment of therapeutic outcome
'vertical' interaction pattern, 44
vicarious experiences, 24, 51
'Vincent', autobiographical account, 4, 5

waiting-list control groups, 48, 75
'well-adjusted' families, 46

'zoned' groups, 92